HOT RIGHT NOW

Rita Ora

THE DEFINITIVE BIOGRAPHY

DOUGLAS WIGHT & JENNIFER WILEY

22five
PUBLISHING

Also by Douglas Wight
Calvin Harris: The $100 Million DJ
Leonardo DiCaprio: The Biography

First published in Great Britain in 2015 by
22Five Publishing Ltd
Suite 3, Unit 8, Kingsdale Business Centre, Regina Road, Chelmsford CM1 1PE

www.22fivepublishing.com
www.facebook.com/Hot-Right-Now-The-Definitive-Biography-of-Rita-Ora
wwwtwitter.com/TheRitaOraBio
https://instagram.com/theritaorabio

HB ISBN 978 0 99343 050 3
EBOOK ISBN 978 0 99343 053 4

10 9 8 7 6 5 4 3 2 1

Typeset by Jill Sawyer Phypers

Printed and bound in the UK by Clays Ltd, St Ives, plc

Author's Note

LIKE many music fans, we first became aware of Rita Ora when she burst onto the pop scene in spectacular fashion in 2012 with 'Hot Right Now'. When she followed that success with three more number one singles in the UK and a chart-topping debut album we began to take notice. Soon she was such an irresistible force in popular culture that our curiosity got the better of us and we were determined to not only find out more about this remarkable woman but also to tell her story in as entertaining and informative a way possible.

This is an unauthorised biography and neither Rita, nor her family, has cooperated with its publication. However, many of her friends, former colleagues and teachers were happy to speak and share their knowledge and memories of this special talent.

Although Rita was not involved in the writing of this book, she has been so vocal and open in interviews and is such a presence on social media that there has been no shortage of opinion from her. Sources for the majority of comments from Rita and her family are listed at the back of this book. Tweets quoted in the book retain their original spelling and punctuation, and expletives have been asterisked as they were in the source material.

We hope you enjoy reading this book as much as we enjoyed researching and writing it.

Contents

Contents

Prologue

THE black and white princess dress, long black leather gloves, platinum hair slicked into a mean side parting. When Rita Ora took to the stage at the 2015 Academy Awards she oozed Hollywood glamour. A television audience of more than one billion was witnessing Rita take her place at celebrity's top table and she grasped the opportunity with both hands.

Dazzling like the silver Bvlgari jewels around her neck, Rita looked every inch the star.

The significance of her appearance was not lost on her. It was the pinnacle of her career to date – an opportunity that, according to friends, 'made her life complete'. Not only that, it was also the fulfilment of a prophecy from her grandfather back in her native Kosovo, himself a famous film director in his homeland, who predicted when she was just a baby she would be a star.

At the first sight of her, however, much of that global Oscars audience would have been forgiven for scratching their heads at the mention of her name. Who was Rita Ora? Here was a singer without a single solo chart hit in America and a movie career that extended to two cameo appearances.

What was it about this girl that prompted Hollywood giant Harvey Weinstein to gush that she was 'the discovery of the year'; persuaded powerful hip hop star and music producer Jay Z to take a punt on her when she was only eighteen; drove Calvin Harris, the world's most successful DJ and record-breaking hit-maker, to fly 8,000 miles just to be with her for a few days; inspired gossip guru Perez Hilton to say he is 'obsessed' with her and prompted two of the biggest shows on British television to scrap over her signature?

Fittingly performing on a pedestal – where it seemed the world's most powerful men had already put her – Rita went some way to answering. From within her diminutive frame, she unleashed her big voice and, displaying not a hint of nerves, powered her way through the appropriately titled 'Grateful', the song from the romantic drama *Beyond the Lights*. Her performance was awe inspiring, justifying the faith placed in her. Not only did she look at home amid Hollywood's biggest names, she stole the show at the after parties in a daring figure-hugging – and transparent – Donna Karan Atelier dress that showed off her slender curves and a sizeable amount of her pert posterior, not to mention a raft of tattoos.

The risqué look, complete with hair now coiffed up into party mode, was tailored for the exclusive *Vanity Fair* after-show bash that guaranteed headlines around the world. Rita – as she has done since she burst onto the British pop scene in 2013 – was playing the game. A modern celebrity in every sense of the word, her day job – her music – is only part of the story.

One of the hardest working people in showbiz, she clocked up 130,000 miles in the twelve months preceding the Oscars, travelling from red-carpet event to TV appearance to gig.

She survives on less than five hours' sleep a night and regards any more as a waste of time. This relentless work ethic can be traced back to her roots and her family's background in Kosovo when war threatened to tear their country apart. The story of how she emerged from refugee status to amass a personal fortune that certain sections of the media estimate could soon top £100 million and an account at the Queen's private bankers Coutts & Co. Ltd is like a fairytale.

Indeed, when Rita was still an aspiring teenage musician, her mother told her, in words that could have come straight from the Brothers Grimm: 'Not everyone will wish you well but those that do will have more power than those that don't.'

Amid her many tattoos – as many as twenty-five – Rita bears words of wisdom from her mother, but none could have served as a more apt motto for her career than those. Even aside from Jay

Z and Weinstein, Rita can boast an impressive list of powerhouse mentors, from Beyoncé, her 'sister from another mister', Madonna, who signed her as the face of her Material Girl fashion line, fashion designers Tom Ford and Karl Lagerfeld and Simon Cowell who snatched her from *The Voice* – where she had been credited with adding four million viewers – to become part of the new judging panel on *The X Factor*.

All this has been achieved in fewer than three years. With all the ad campaigns – Rimmel, Coca-Cola and Adidas – and the high-profile appearances (she sang for President Obama in Washington) it is easy to forget she has a day job. And she's not been too bad at that either. Her first three singles, either as a solo artist or collaborator, shot to number one in the UK – as did her debut album *Ora*.

Like a modern-day Midas, everything she touches turns to gold.

She breezes effortlessly between two personas – a street-smart hustler and a friendly – sometimes ditzy – blonde oozing with charisma.

She is an everywoman and she's everywhere. A day doesn't go by without her appearing in a tabloid newspaper or glossy magazine. Delighting the red tops by not only enjoying a love life that has at times bordered on car crash, she keeps them guessing with a delectably teasing relationship with model star and fellow tabloid darling Cara Delevingne.

She seems to bend both old media and new to her will. Prolific on Instagram, she is a queen of the selfie, frequently posing with famous friends at a freight-train load of parties. While on Twitter, where fiery posts have landed her in the kind of hot water that would scald a lesser mortal, she holds court, name checking her latest collaborators and sparring with rivals.

Such success suggests she's had it all her own way. Far from it.

'I've been told "no" so many times in my career, it doesn't mean it's over,' she says, displaying wisdom beyond her years. 'I can remember every single "no" I've been told in my life. They do not leave my brain but they build you up.'

For a long time it looked like Rita would be one of life's 'nearly' girls, as flirtations with fame proved fleeting. Yet, time and again she bounced back, dug deeper, worked harder, made brave choices and was ultimately rewarded.

Hers is the ultimate lesson in persistence. A student of role models like Madonna and Rihanna, she has blended their work ethic with that of her family. Famous for never calling in sick, never skipping an appointment and never slacking, she is now a role model herself – and an example for the youngsters hoping for their own chance of stardom on *The X Factor*.

To paraphrase one of Rita's comments, life must be lived forwards but it can only be understood backwards. As the world awaits her new album – delayed because of a high-profile breakup from Harris – it is the perfect time to look back and assess just how Rita Ora became *Hot Right Now*.

It is a story worth telling.

1

Flight to Freedom

Pristina, Kosovo, 1991
YOUNG parents Besnik and Vera Sahatçiu gathered their daughters, Elena, three, and one-year-old baby Rita, and clutched them close. Grabbing their last remaining belongings, they closed the door to their flat. The modest first-floor apartment in the Dardania neighbourhood had been their first family home but now it lay empty. As they walked out into the street Besnik and Vera were conscious they were stepping out into the unknown. A new life awaited but what form it would take they had no idea. Neither knew when they would next return to this part of the city – or if they would ever return to Kosovo at all.

Time was running out.

They were heading for the airport but as they held their precious cargo close to their chests they knew there were no guarantees. The city was creaking under the crackdown imposed by an oppressive regime. The former Yugoslavia was falling apart. People could sense war was coming. This might be their only chance. But if their flight were to take off luck would have to be on their side.

Their destination was London, their future anything but certain.

At the airport chaos reigned. Kosovo Albanians – those like the fleeing family – were being prevented from leaving. The Serbian-led government, fearful of a mass exodus, had to resort to extreme measures. The airport was shutting. Only one more flight would take off. Thankfully for the Sahatçius it was the one carrying Besnik, Vera and their young family.

1

'We were lucky to get out,' Rita said years later. 'The airport was closing down and they weren't letting anyone leave by that stage. We were on the last flight out. It was really scary for them.'

For Besnik, then thirty, and Vera, his twenty-seven-year-old wife, the writing had been on the wall. Besnik, the son of the famous Kosovan film director Besim Sahatçiu, had worked as a teacher and had experience running restaurants, while his wife worked as a GP in Pristina, the capital city of Kosovo, an autonomous district within Serbia, in the Federal Republic of Yugoslavia. For a while life for the Sahatçius was comfortable. Besnik and his family might not have known it then but, like all Kosovan Albanians, they were living on borrowed time.

After the death of Yugoslavian president-for-life Josip Broz Tito in 1980 the federal state, which had been in place since the end of the Second World War, began slowly to split apart.

At first there were few repercussions. Life continued as normal.

The Sahatçius – the word means 'watchmaker' in Albanian – were an old family, hailing from Peja, a city fifty miles due west of Pristina in the picturesque setting of the Rugova mountains. Being an established family meant they were comparatively wealthy with properties and good educations and they enjoyed a favourable reputation.

Rita's grandfather Besim would go on to become a renowned film and television director but he experienced discrimination first hand when he was prevented from studying in his home country and had to go to Zagreb, Croatia, instead. Besim then had to move from his native Peja to Pristina, with his wife Besa, a teacher, when he worked for a television station.

The couple had two sons, but it was the eldest Besnik who was keen to spread his wings. Realising the importance of learning a universally spoken international language, he studied English and during his degree travelled to London in 1986 to experience life in Britain. He could scarcely believe his eyes. Paved with gold the streets were not but in London he discovered a multicultural melting pot where opportunities existed for all.

While he was having the time of his life in London, his future wife Vera Bajraktari was broadening her horizons too. The daughter of Osman Bajraktari, an ex-Yugoslavian ambassador in Russia, Vera studied for a degree in medicine in Moscow. As a young student Vera turned heads with her striking looks and when she met Besnik it was impossible for him not to be beguiled by her beauty.

Shaqir Foniqi, a journalist and writer who worked alongside Besim for twelve years, recalls Rita's family with fondness.

'I remember they found each other as students,' Shaqir said of Besnik and Vera's romance. 'If they went walking everybody would look at them because they were a beautiful couple. It was impossible for a guy not to notice a girl as beautiful as Vera.'

As Besnik and Vera's love blossomed events were happening that would have a profound impact on their lives. Since Tito's death in 1980 Kosovo Albanians had been campaigning for their region to be declared an autonomous republic. During the decade tensions grew between Albanians and Serbs living in Kosovo. Just a year after Besnik returned from London Slobodan Milošević seized power in Serbia on a wave of hatred in 1987 and it signalled the beginning of years of unrest. Almost immediately Milošević assumed control over Kosovo, independent province Vojvodina, and the republic of Montenegro. He won support from Serbs for his centralist policies. He also sacked 100,000 ethnic Albanian workers in Kosovo and his actions unleashed waves of violence that would eventually lead to the Yugoslav Wars.

Even against this backdrop Rita's parents Besnik and Vera managed to carve out a successful life. They were smart and well educated, in possession of university degrees and led an enviable social life. Vera became a doctor, while Besnik launched his own import/export business, which quickly thrived. The couple became well known in society and hung out with intellectuals, businessmen and professional people from all backgrounds. They married in a quiet ceremony in Peja and soon afterwards welcomed to the world their first child Elena in 1988.

Family friend Shaqir recalls how excited Besim was when Elena was born – a trait not shared by all Kosovan men, who traditionally only viewed boys as direct descendants. She was beautiful, with piercing green eyes like her father. And Besim was even more excited when he learned Besnik and Vera would soon provide him with another granddaughter.

'He was very excited that she was coming,' Shaqir said. 'I remember when Rita was born and we were working in television, he [Besim] came in to the small cafeteria that was there and said to us: "Come and let's have a drink because my granddaughter is born."

'You know our mentality and a guy that was drinking with us asked Besim: "Ah, you have a granddaughter and we are celebrating?" And Besim quoted a fragment from an Albanian song: "Who has girls has the world."'

Besnik and Vera named their second daughter Rita – after Besim's favourite actress, Hollywood legend Rita Hayworth.

It was not long before Shaqir cast his eyes on the new baby and even from those early days it was clear she had inherited her mother's stunning looks – deep brown eyes and the first signs of chocolate-coloured curls. In addition it seemed she had already developed a healthy set of lungs.

'She was as beautiful as she is today,' he recalled. 'I don't remember her crying just shouting-like singing.'

Besim was smitten with baby Rita, and immediately nicknamed her 'Rita Pita'.

'Besim was always talking about her,' Shaqir said. 'Besim was a very lovely parent and grandfather also. He called Rita "Rita Pita" and he was very lovely with Elena also. Whenever I saw him after and he had his granddaughters he was always holding their hands and walking with them.'

Shaqir would meet Besim with the girls for coffee and even though Rita was then just a few months old her grandfather could tell she had potential to be a huge star.

'Besim said: "Remember, my Rita Pita is going to be famous and the entire world will listen to her voice." I asked him, "What do you mean?" He told me she had a special talent in music. He asked Rita to sing something and she started to sing in her way in that time.'

Not long after he was privy to one of Rita's first public vocal performances, Shaqir learned the devastating news that things had got so desperate for Besnik and Vera they were considering taking their family out of Kosovo – for good.

It has since been written and almost accepted into Rita Ora folklore that her family 'fled war-torn Kosovo' but this is not strictly true. The full-scale war between Yugoslav forces and ethnic Albanian independence fighters backed by NATO that left 10,000 people dead did not break out in the region until 1998 – but life was growing unbearable for people of their ethnic origin.

While Rita's family weren't overly religious, (Besnik comes from a Muslim background and Vera from a Catholic one) ninety-five per cent of Kosovans identify as Muslims. Yet discrimination at the hands of Orthodox Christian Serbians was rife on religious as well as ethnic grounds.

'Because of the situation here [in Kosovo] in the late Eighties it got to be dangerous,' Rita's grandmother Besa, who still has a home in Pristina, said in one interview. 'There were riots, uprisings and suppression by the government of the former Yugoslavia. Kosovars wanted rights, like other Yugoslav republics.'

With an autocratic regime in power, the chances of autonomy for Kosovo seemed as remote as ever. Kosovan journalist Selvije Bajrami explains: 'In 1990, it was a very hard situation especially for Albanians. I know from my father's experience, just because he was Albanian, he was faced with the typecast of choosing between two options, either to work with the Serbian system or to quit his job. Ninety per cent of Albanians had to quit their jobs. People started to work different jobs just to live.'

Prospects also looked bleak for children born into this system.

'All Albanian schools were closed and for Albanian students just to continue education, they were obliged to study in private houses,' Selvije explained. 'Some Albanians opened their house doors just to let the younger generations be educated. Those people were also under pressure because the regime [would rather people were] not educated.'

Besnik, it seems, fell foul of this system. As a young man he made a conscious decision not to join the army – something many men felt pressurised to do. It was a decision that might just have saved his life as, terrifyingly, there were indications that ethnic cleansing was clearly being practised by the regime.

'In that time some Albanians that were part of the Yugoslavian army were killed – just because they were Albanian,' family friend Shaqir said.

5

Stories started to circulate that women were being raped by Serbian soldiers.

'It was a very hard situation, and all the people were thinking to stay or to go?'

Rita has since spoken of her gratitude for her father's decision not to enlist. 'My father didn't want to attend the army,' she said. 'He chose to bring up his children instead. It was something that my mother and father chose for us. As parents, I am not one, but I can imagine you would do anything for your children. So they did just that, and I'm very, very grateful.'

Yet, although Besnik managed to avoid the potential misery of life in the armed forces, his ambitions to create the best life for Elena and Rita were continually thwarted. Although highly educated he had been working in restaurants to make ends meet.

Besnik has told how the family's lives had become 'intolerable', adding: 'Financially, we were okay. But we were not free.' Growing increasingly uneasy, Besnik began to think about London and whether their future might be better in Britain.

'Besnik was in love with London and had often spoken to me about this magical city,' Vera recalled in an interview years later. Despite not being able to speak a word of English she was willing to sacrifice everything to take a chance on a new life. 'I was eager, just as much as Besnik,' she said, 'to pack my suitcases and visit this city and its streets where my husband had spent some of his youth.'

Besnik sought advice from his father. With a heavy heart Besim knew there was only one answer he could give. His son had to leave – to be safe and to give his family any real prospects of making something of their lives.

Shaqir remembers Besim's reaction: 'He made a big groan and in a way it was very hard for him. And he said to me, "Shaqo, this is life." He knew it [was] better to live in London or Paris.'

Shaqir added: '[Everyone had] an idea that war was coming. Besim could also [have gone] but he helped [his] son to go and he stayed in Kosovo. For Besim [it] was important to have [his] kids in a safe place. Besim helped them to move.'

Another factor played at the back of Besim's mind. If the baby Rita had potential to be a star there would surely be more chance of that happening in Britain than in Kosovo.

'If they were living in Kosovo, I am sure that Rita would not be the same as [she] is now,' Shaqir said. 'Kosovo is a small country and you have nowhere to show your talent. Here is a country with not many opportunities for young talented people. Rita had a talent and if she was here her talent would not have been revealed.'

Eventually Besnik could wait no longer. With a real danger of flights out of the country being blocked for Albanians they fled.

'So our adventure with London began with this desire,' Vera said.

Vera and Besnik must have hoped their prayers would be answered the moment they touched down in the UK. But in those first moments in their new country they must have feared they'd made a terrifyingly wrong decision. On arriving in London the family declared themselves refugees. Whether they were aware of what happened to people claiming asylum in the UK or whether they arrived assuming they'd be welcomed with open arms is unclear. But quickly they were to discover that the hospitality and sense of fairness for which Britain is famous for around the world only applied in certain situations.

Rita's version of the events that took place when her family arrived in London usually misses out what happened immediately after they got off the plane. It is generally accepted they were housed in modest accommodation. But speaking in 2013 in a television interview, Rita revealed shocking new detail.

As refugees, the Sahatçius had to be assessed and their stories checked out before they were allowed to remain in the UK. In order to do this, people are usually held in detention centres. In Rita's case, her parents were horrified to be told their daughters would be taken and placed in a care home while the assessment took place. To make matters worse it seems Vera was not allowed to remain in the country until a decision had been reached.

One can scarcely imagine how Vera and Besnik must have felt as their children were taken from them.

'When I first moved to London, when me, my sister, my mum and my dad stepped foot in London we were sent straight to the children's home, me and my sister, because my mum and dad were refugees,'

Rita revealed. 'And so were we. So my mother couldn't legally live in the UK. They separate [parents and children], yes, they do.'

Such shocking detail is a reminder that immigration was as big an issue back in 1991 as it is today, and the system dealing with it was as flawed.

And so began a fight for Besnik and Vera to convince the authorities the family should be together. It took several months, but finally they won their battle and the Sahatçius were allowed to stay.

'I was only in there literally for a few months because my mum and dad were, like, fighting hard,' Rita said. 'They got it.'

Rita, then still a babe-in-arms, had no idea of the gamble her parents were taking with all their lives. 'I was really young so I never understood it exactly,' she said. 'I never realised how much they had to sacrifice. I think my parents are the strongest people I've ever known. They made a life all over again, from scratch.'

Rita's parents' first months in the UK might have been frightening but their decision to leave Kosovo ultimately proved to be the correct one for many reasons. A few days following the family's departure Rita's grandparents were persecuted. 'They were evacuated,' she said, 'and had to walk to the next city.'

At least, once the family was reunited, Besnik and Vera knew they were safe. They were eventually housed in a tiny flat as they started again with nothing. The next task facing them was to find work, anything to bring in some income to improve their situation. Rita has few memories about this time but what she does recall is the chaos of those early days in a strange city.

'I can't say I remember anything when I was one,' she said. 'I do remember having a hectic kind of life because we weren't really set into one house. I can't really remember having a place to call home growing up.

'My mother and father were trying to find their feet. They came from a fresh country and having two kids and not speaking the language there's only so much work you can do. My dad ended up working in a pizzeria to find a flat that we could at least live in. My mum was just looking after us. Her doctor's degrees did not pass through to London so it wasn't equal at all ... so she basically started from scratch. It was such a crazy world for her because we were

8

moving house literally like every month.'

When the Sahatçius did finally find a place it was a single room on the Old Brompton Road in Earls Court, West London, near Brompton Cemetery. If you're a refugee looking to start a new life abroad you could do far worse than landing there. Located in the Royal Borough of Kensington and Chelsea – the most expensive neighbourhood in the UK – it is a road where the average price of a home in 2015 was around £1.5 million.

Curiously, one-year-old Rita found herself living just two blocks away from the former home of another young woman who would go on to find fame in the UK – Princess Diana. Then Lady Diana Spencer, Prince Charles's future wife, lived with three friends at 60 Coleherne Court, Old Brompton Road, in an elegant building made from red brick and Portland stone from 1979 to 1981. She left the flat on 23 February 1981, the night before her engagement was announced.

Ten years later, the Sahatçius moved to London and eventually into their apartment just down the road in a block of flats, a somewhat less elegant brick building, run by Kensington and Chelsea Housing Association. Nevertheless, privately owned flats there now change hands for around £500,000 on average.

Their flat overlooked Brompton Cemetery, something Rita never got over. 'Scary', was how she described the view from her window of the graveyard, which although well tended gives off an eerie atmosphere with its cracked stones and elaborate memorials. Little did she know that inspiration for some of the nation's best-loved children's books came from within that thirty-nine acre nineteenth-century resting place. World-famous author Beatrix Potter, who was born and lived little more than a stone's throw from Rita's flat, was said to have got the names for her characters – Mr Nutkins, Mr McGregor, Mr Brock, Mr Tod, Jeremiah Fisher and even a Peter Rabbett – from the etchings on those very same headstones.

One of Rita's earliest memories is when she used to play hide-and-seek with her sister and friends among those same gravestones. 'No one found me and I thought I was going to get stolen by ghosts,' she said.

Rita might also have been interested to learn that among the 200,000 people buried there is the suffragette Emmeline Pankhurst, a trailblazer whose ferocious campaign for equality for women helped create the society that has allowed girls like her to carve out a career.

Although Kensington and Chelsea has a higher-than-average number of people in social housing, the contrasts between those at opposite ends of the pay scale are not hard to find. Head east from Rita's old flat and you arrive at South Kensington Underground station, always mobbed with tourists heading to the Natural History, Science, and Victoria and Albert museums. And just yards from the station you can find Lamborghini and Ferrari dealerships as well as a number of top restaurants and shops.

'One room for all four of us,' Rita said of their flat at the distinctly less opulent end of the road. 'My sister Elena annoying me by doing her times tables when I was trying to sleep.'

One of the first things Besnik did in their new home was hang a clock on the wall. It would be the first of many. They were watchmakers after all. Their flat was damp, with cracks in the ceiling. Those first weeks and months would test their resolve to the limit. For a young family, a long way from home, struggling to understand the language and culture of their new country it was a tough existence.

Yet Besnik refused to be downbeat. 'Despite the difficulties,' he said, 'we were young and we were free.'

They had no option. They had to make their lives in London work. Their children might still have been small but already two very different personalities were emerging. Elena was calm, good-natured and little hassle to her parents. Rita on the other hand was full of life and demanded attention.

'Rita was a child that was writing her story every day,' her mum said. Being the little one, as she was born after Elena, Rita knew the family was under her orders.

'When Rita was little she was a vivid child and different from other children her age because she always wanted to be in the centre of attention. Either with her voice, acting like movie characters, or with her outfit, she was always attracting attention to herself. She was unpredictable and always able to attract people and receive what she wanted.'

The family had to deal with another issue – being viewed as refugees, outsiders in a foreign land.

Rita has memories of those years living with the label 'refugee'. 'That word carries a lot of prejudice. But it also made us determined to survive,' she said. 'When you put anyone into an alien environment, where other people aren't completely comfortable with them being there, they are automatically going to be defensive. It's the rule of the jungle, right?'

Once again, for refugees, Rita's family enjoyed freedoms not normally associated with the tag.

For several years after they fled to the UK war had not yet broken out. Life continued to be tough for Albanians but the situation allowed the family to return to Pristina to visit relatives. Being able to spend summers in Kosovo and then return to their new life in Britain was something of a luxury.

Regardless of their status and of the growing tensions back home, Rita's family faced terror of a different nature – and it was something that did not discriminate when it came to wealth or social status. Not long after the family moved to London, Vera received devastating news – she had breast cancer.

Fortunately, she had access to treatment through Britain's National Health Service, but it was a desperately worrying time for Besnik – and a deeply confusing time for young Rita. 'We were young, we didn't realise what was actually happening,' she said.

Mercifully, Vera survived and came through her ordeal stronger than ever.

'She was cured,' Rita said. 'She is literally one of the most inspirational, funnest [sic] [people]. I don't think she's human.'

Once her health was restored a more determined Vera set about remedying her qualification dilemma. If her degree would not be accepted in the UK then she would get one that was.

'He [Besnik] encouraged me to make every effort to pass the required medical exams in order to practise as a doctor in England,' Vera said. 'The biggest challenge for me was to learn the language that I could not speak at all.'

So began six years of hard graft for Vera, retraining in medicine by day while working as a waitress at night. Throughout this time, however, she refused to neglect her family.

'Rita was being brought up in an environment of peace, love, well-being and encouragement to move forward,' Vera said. 'In this reality, Rita was showing all her potential and her abilities were always improving.'

In order to nurture this potential Vera and Besnik had to find their daughters a school, ideally one that would be sympathetic to their immigrant status. Luckily, a Church of England school just streets away from Rita's flat fitted the bill perfectly. St Cuthbert with St Matthias primary school was a popular place of learning for immigrant families, particularly Albanians.

Rita thrived in her new environment. Teaching assistant and caretaker Jill Biggs remembers her fondly.

'Although it was a Church of England school we would take anyone from any background or nationality,' Jill said. 'Because we were right in the middle of Earls Court it was very diverse. It was a close-knit school. We had a big influx of refugees at the time Rita and Elena came.

'Lots of kids were from poor families. We've always had a lot of Moroccans, Egyptians, Arabic-speaking children. So we had a lot of TAs [teaching assistants] to support children with English as a second language. I think Rita and Elena needed a bit of help with their English but not a lot.'

Rita loved going to school but little did she know it would be the place where her musical dreams would first be realised.

The youngster had been introduced to music through her dad and his extensive record collection. His favourites included James Brown, BB King, The Supremes and Eric Clapton. Rita's earliest memory is a tender moment dancing with her dad to Celine Dion.

'Every morning when I woke up, my dad believed in music to make the energy in the house higher. [He] believes that playing music loud and having the windows open brings good energy in, and there was always a great vibe in the house. I'd literally wake up and start singing along to whatever he was playing.

'Tina Turner's *Private Dancer* was one of my mum's theme albums to cook to. Everyday she'd say, "Just think of yourself performing in front of a sea of people and it will come true". She was a great believer in putting positive thought into your energy. That's how I grew up believing in music – feeling freedom.'

The family needed something to lift their spirits. For by the time Rita was seven the inevitable happened – war finally broke out in Kosovo.

For the Sahatçius it was a nightmarish situation. Grateful for their own freedom, they felt anguish at being unable to help loved ones back home, and frustration they didn't truly know what was happening.

What they did hear horrified them. Milošević would go on to be responsible for the deportation of almost 750,000 Kosovo Albanians, as well as the murders of hundreds as part of a campaign of genocide. It would emerge years later that thousands of women were raped and sexually assaulted by Serbian forces and paramilitaries.

In those early years in London, thoughts of returning to Pristina were never far from Besnik and Vera's minds. Previously they were able to return home once a year to visit relatives. The outbreak of war – and hearing of such atrocities – changed that.

Vera recalled: 'The option of returning to Kosovo was always open and we considered it until the Kosovo war in 1999 when we finally realised that the dream of living again in Pristina had gone.'

Rita also recalls tension rising at home because of the war back in Kosovo, with her own relatives in real danger. 'I couldn't figure it out,' she said. 'All the arguments, all the tension – I knew it was coming from something. Like, something wasn't quite right.'

But as her family got to know other Kosovans who had fled the conflict they realised other children had begun their lives in Britain in the same home as Rita and Elena. 'I know some kids I'm still friends with that were in the children's home when I was in there,' she said.

The war lasted sixteen months and ended following controversial NATO air strikes. Thankfully Rita's relatives survived unhurt and peace was finally restored.

After such a turbulent start to life, Rita could concentrate on enjoying life in her new home. It was time for her to find her voice.

2

A Star is Born

HANA Hajaj wasn't relishing the Year Five end-of-school play. Short of catching her younger brother Omar's performance there wasn't much else about the Church of England school show to get excited about.

That was until she set eyes on Omar's tomboy friend. The little girl, all in black with her long dark hair scraped back into neat bunches, stood head and shoulders above the rest in terms of her performance. Her voice, deep and textured, could surely not have come from such a small frame. And when it came to dancing the little ten-year-old moved around the stage like a gymnast. Such energy, such style, what confidence!

Afterwards she pulled her brother aside and whispered: 'Who. Is. That? You HAVE to introduce me!'

A bit embarrassed and not really understanding why his fifteen-year-old sister was suddenly more interested in his tiny pal than him, Omar introduced them.

'Hana, this is Rita.'

Some little girls might have found it a little bit weird to have a stranger approach them for a photo, but Rita Sahatçiu didn't mind. In fact, she revelled in it – proudly posing amongst the stacks of chairs backstage.

Hana said: 'I don't remember much about the performance but I do remember Rita standing out. She was the star of the show. She was a really cute little girl. I asked to take her picture and joked, "You never know, you could be rich and famous one day." I remember she

14

was flipping around on stage and doing some impressive moves. After the performance I wanted to take a picture of her on her own as a memento. She was really sweet and very willing. She wasn't one of those shy girls who would freeze when you asked them to perform. She was brave.'

Although Omar was a little embarrassed by his sister's attention he too knew Rita was special. He'd met her for the first time in Year Four when he had enrolled at St Cuthbert with St Matthius Church of England School after spending some time with his family in Jordan. And Rita immediately made him feel at home.

'I was nervous and shy about starting at a new school,' Omar said. 'Rita was in my year and sat at my table. She was so nice and friendly and would make sure to always include me. She would smile a lot. She had a good heart. I had a crush on her – but I never told anybody. I remember her always singing – it was always Mariah Carey. Even though she was young she really sounded like her.

'It was a Christian school so we would have to sing church songs all the time – we did it because we had to do it but Rita really loved it. She'd be right up at the front. She would sing in the assemblies and was always the star of the school performances. Rita was really ambitious from a young age. She knew she wanted to be a singer.'

Rita's passion for singing and performing came almost from nowhere. Sure, she loved the music her dad blared out of his stereo early in the morning. But when a chance arose to sing in a choir something magical happened.

Rita was six when she met Suzi Digby, founder of the Voices Foundation, a music education charity that works with schools to improve kids' learning and confidence through song. Suzi asked Rita to sing for her Kodály class, using a method that encourages children to sing unaccompanied. Given an audience and a chance to showcase her extraordinary talent, Rita didn't need any prodding and snatched it with both hands.

Her school music teacher Mary O'Connell was also immediately blown away when she heard Rita's voice. Sadly she died two years ago. But her colleague and Rita's old teaching assistant Jill Biggs remembered the impact she left. 'From the beginning Mary said Rita would make something of herself in years to come,' Jill said. 'Rita was just cute. She was petite with curly hair and a big smile. She stood out. She had star quality even then. We knew if Rita didn't do something with herself it would be a loss. We all knew that. We'd discuss it in the staff room. Her voice was quite strong for someone so small.'

Rita loved the reaction her singing produced. 'Even at the age of six, I'm not saying I understood it completely, but I saw people were reacting, and it made me feel nice,' she said. 'It made me feel like I was touching something. I just liked the feeling of it.

'It made me feel like I was doing something right.'

To an impressionable young girl Suzi seemed impossibly glamorous. With her striking blonde hair and razor-sharp style she was nothing like your archetypal singing teacher. She'd travelled the world, set up the charity and would later find television fame in 2008 as a judge on the BBC One series *Last Choir Standing*. One former pupil said the effect of singing in Suzi's choir was like 'walking into a dark room inside your mind and having all the lights switch on'.

'The transformative effects and benefits can be phenomenal,' Suzi declared.

'She was cool,' Rita said. 'She wasn't a proper teacher. She just used to come into school and teach the choir. She was so hot. She had hair like Marilyn Monroe and she would always wear suits and a waist belt. She was a little gangster.'

Rita was desperate to join the Voices Foundation choir, which met after school. But when she floated the idea at home her parents were baffled.

'When I told my parents, "Okay, I want to sing", they were like, "Huh?" My mum wasn't sure I even COULD sing so she came to my choir to check and once she heard me, she got it.'

Rita's development was swift. A year after that first audition she was starring as Cinderella in the school play.

'She was a good little actress,' said Jill, who worked at the school for thirty-three years before departing in 2009. 'As good as she was a singer – she was a natural performer too. She had a twinkle in her eye. If there was a school play you knew she would have the leading role. And she could support others.'

Performing brought Rita and her friends closer together.

'They'd sit on the benches in the playground going through their lines,' Jill said. 'Rita was always a bit of a star. She was quite a bright child as well. She was eager to learn and wanted to know stuff.'

One of Rita's closest friends was another little girl from Pristina, whose experience of life in Britain closely mirrored hers.

'They were so close,' Jill said of the girls. 'They were like Siamese twins, they were joined at the hip. They were very close all the way through.

'Rita was close to Elena too,' Jill went on. 'Rita and her friend would always find Elena in the playground. Elena was very quiet and bright. I got the sense she was looking after her sister even then. She looked out for her always.'

It must have been a confusing time for Elena as early on she had to accept she was going to play second fiddle to her younger sibling.

'Elena is our older daughter, and she always tried to please Rita, as she was crying until she had achieved what she wanted,' Vera reveals. 'For Rita, there was no turning back. We as parents were always saying to Elena, "Elena, leave Rita alone as you are older than her, try to please her, please." Now we sometimes do feel a bit guilty that we always asked Elena to tolerate Rita, because Elena was little herself. I remember Elena saying, "Why is it always me to let her have her way?"'

Singing gave Rita confidence and a sense of freedom like never before. She started experimenting with it in different ways – even punking up her school uniform to make her stand out amongst the other kids in their royal blue.

'Rita wasn't at all naughty but she would always have a little something to stand out,' Jill said. 'She liked to be different. She wouldn't just wear the uniform ordinarily, she'd have to add something to it – a piece of jewellery or put her hair to one side.'

At school Rita was having fun. And at home the family had found cause to celebrate once more following the dark days of Vera's cancer battle and their fears for the family back in Kosovo. Vera was expecting her third child. Things were looking up.

'There was something about her too,' Jill said of Rita's mum. 'She was always stunning looking. She has an amazing smile. Very beautiful lady. She wasn't the type to throw something on and bring the girls to school. She would have got up that little bit early to make sure her hair was right. Their dad is very nice too.

'I always had a conversation with mum. It was usually mum dropping them off for school and picking them up. Rita and Elena stayed for lunch. Rita had a cousin and an aunty who lived nearby too so there was always someone to pick them up. Some kids came to school a bit untidy, but Rita and Elena were always immaculate.'

Rita's best friend from Pristina, who remains part of Rita's tight clique even now, moved to another school in Year Four. It meant Rita grew close to Yemi Akintoye Dedier, who she had known since the age of seven. Yemi was shy but Rita spotted her talent for singing and encouraged her to join her in the choir.

Yemi said: 'We did a little production in school and she told me, "Come to the choir with me," and I thought, "Why not?"

'We performed in the Guildhall with the famous opera singer Willard White when we were about eight years old,' Yemi said. 'Rita was always doing solos. We always knew she would be famous. I could sing too but I don't like the limelight – I get stage fright.

'We'd go to choir twice a week. We used to sing a range of songs,' Yemi went on. 'We did an Italian song, a few hymns. A few contemporary songs. We did a gospel song. Rita had a really soulful voice. We used to always say, "Rita has the huskiest voice going." It was so raspy and different. It was amazing to hear it come out of a little girl. It was like, whoa, where did that come from? Her voice is made for soulful, gospelly music.'

Rita was seven when Vera gave birth to a baby boy – their first son. They named him Doni and Rita was ecstatic.

'Rita's mum would bring her little brother to pick her up at school when he was first born,' Yemi recalled. 'Rita was obsessed with him. He was the cutest curly-haired little boy ever. Rita would walk him around – the proudest big sister ever and tell everybody, "This is my little brother, Doni."

'He was so cute. He had beautiful curly hair. He was the spitting image of Rita – it was quite scary.

'I saw Rita's mum a lot. When we were in school she was still doing her medical training. I knew she had had breast cancer but I didn't know much about it. We were children and didn't understand the impact of such a thing.

'There were times where you could see Rita was a bit upset but on the whole she's such a strong person. Unless you know her really well it would be hard to tell that something was wrong. She just put on a brave face and got on with things. She wouldn't let things get to her. She was always a head-strong determined person who knows what she wants to do and she's going to go for it.'

Yemi remembered Rita talking about those dark days when she and Elena were in the care home. 'She mentioned that she and her sister were separated for a while when she first came to England and that it was a scary and stressful time for the whole family.'

The arrival of Doni meant the already snug one-room flat was now at bursting point. The family found a bigger apartment but it meant moving to a new location. Ladbroke Grove, near Notting Hill, might only have been three miles away but in terms of culture and influence it might as well have been on another planet.

Flat 22, a second-floor two-storey apartment in Foreland House would be the Sahatçius' home for the next fifteen years. Outside, the flat is remarkable for the lack of graffiti around the door – a feature not shared by the homes around it. Inside, the apartment would have looked massive to Rita and her family compared to their previous cosy arrangement. On the lower level a compact kitchen to the right of the doorway looked out onto a walkway access to other flats and then out onto Walmer Road. At the back the windows of a generous lounge overlooked the gardens of the flats below. To the left of the entrance a staircase led to the three bedrooms, one of which Rita shared with Elena, and where she can remember having to stay silent whenever her sister was sleeping.

Owned by Kensington and Chelsea Housing Association, the building is typical of council built properties of its period in West London. Part of a small estate, it is surrounded by beautiful – and much more expensive – properties. But its location would have a significant bearing on Rita's future style and attitude. Such is the clash of cultures in Ladbroke Grove, where the well-heeled rub shoulders with the impoverished and the huge influx of immigrant populations creates a unique atmosphere. Take a walk off the estate and you enter Blenheim Crescent. Less than a five-minute stroll from there, past the secure-entry villas and elegant shops of Kensington Park Road, and you end up straight in the middle of Portobello Road with its world-famous shops and über-trendy market. There, posh girls with trust funds on the hunt for some bohemian-chic clothing fight for tables in cafés with street kids in crop tops and over-sized jewellery.

There, you'll find Coffee Plant, the café that would soon become one of Rita's favourite spots, and Size? – a shoe shop where Rita used her staff discount to keep her street cred on point while earning some much-needed dough on the side. Close by is the Mau Mau live music bar where Rita played pool with friends before she was famous, and a fruit and veg stall where seller Bella Devlin remembers Rita's smiling face and unique sense of style that made her stand out from the crowd.

When they first sampled the delights of shopping on Portobello Road, with its rainbow-coloured store fronts, they would have been amazed at their luck at landing in such a place. Head south towards Notting Hill Gate Tube station and you're in the streets that provided the location for the movie *Notting Hill*, starring Hugh Grant and Julia Roberts and showcasing the world-village charm that had tourists flocking from all over the globe.

Before then the district had been famous for the Notting Hill Carnival – a three-day celebration of Caribbean culture over the August bank holiday weekend – where once a young Beyoncé would bring the first incarnation of her band Destiny's Child in a bid to win new fans.

The Sahatçius found their new home quintessentially British, but with the best the world can offer on their doorstep: French cheese stalls, Jamaicans selling jelly coconuts, eastern Europeans touting olives, Italians serving up bruschetta, while Cockneys belted out the best fruit and veg bargains of the day at the top of their lungs. And all of this played out against a musical mash-up of reggae, folk, hip hop and jazz. What better way for a star in the making to become inspired?

Rita might have been destined for the top regardless of where her family settled but – as anyone who spends any time in Ladbroke Grove will testify – there are few places like it.

At the same time as finding his family a home, Besnik found a fresh challenge for himself – taking over the Queen's Arms pub in Kilburn. It was a demanding job, requiring much hard graft in the early days, but after years of working for other people Rita's father was delighted he could be his own boss. His experience of working in restaurants in Kosovo left him in good stead. The curious thing about his move, though, was that he never touches alcohol himself – perhaps the best trait for someone owning a pub. 'I learned to pull a pint at a very young age,' he said, 'but I didn't drink it.'

Living more than two miles away from school meant a Tube ride there and back. But Rita was delighted when she discovered she now only lived a street away from Yemi.

'We did a performance and her mum dropped me home one day – it was only then that we realised we lived literally one road apart,' Yemi said.

Another person who tagged along with Rita on the Underground commute was Omar Hajaj, who reintroduced Rita to some Muslim customs that would have been well-practised in her homeland.

'In Year Five or Six we started taking the Tube home from school with a group,' Omar said. 'I remember one time, during Ramadan, Rita fasted with us for a day. We were on the train together when the sun set at four p.m. and we broke our fast together – had some chocolate and a drink. That was special.

'There were three or four Muslims in our class at that time. She wanted to take part in what we were doing and to experience the feeling with us and be respectful.'

Aside from her singing, Rita was discovering passion for all sorts of things, from football – 'I was really good, I was a goalie in the girls' team at school' – to fashion. Interestingly, however, her first love when it came to trainers and sporty gear was Nike – years before she became the face of Adidas!

'Rita was always trendy,' Yemi recalled. 'She's always loved fashion and liked to wear Nike. We both had the same trainers – they were baby blue Nike Air Prestos. It was the most amazing thing when it happened – we both came to school and we both had the same trainers on. It was like, "Oh my gosh, we've got the same trainers, we're the best". It was the coolest thing.'

Like many close girlfriends, however, the two best pals enjoyed competing with each other for the lead roles, and in class tests and at sport.

'Rita was always sporty like me,' Yemi said. 'She always used to be faster than me. But one year at school sports day I finally beat her.

'Rita was a smart cookie – I wouldn't say she was as smart as me though,' Yemi joked. 'We were always competitive together – usually in a fun way. I excelled at maths and she excelled in English. We were always competing for the lead and solo in music.'

Although the two friends seemed joined at the hip, Yemi revealed there were times when they fell out.

'We had a close friendship but we always had our ups and downs,' she said. 'I remember one time I threw a basketball at her head. She was rude to one of my other friends and I was like, "Ugh, you're such an arse." I didn't actually mean to but it hit her on the head. We had a big argument on the train one day too – we used to get either the Piccadilly Line or the District Line to Holland Park or Notting Hill Gate station and walk down. I can't remember what it was about but I think it was the same week that I threw the basketball at her head. We were always getting into little arguments then we were best friends the next week.'

And it was inevitable that as she grew older, Rita, with her stunning looks, would start developing an interest in boys. Rita enjoyed the attention, and she liked flirting and the teasing games kids play. One boy, in particular – a handsome Kosovan – caught her eye.

'Lots of the boys had crushes on her,' Omar said. 'There was another Kosovan boy in our class. There was always a rumour that they liked each other. He was a good-looking, popular boy. Very funny.'

Yemi too confirmed Rita had taken a shine to the boy and revealed he might have been the recipient of Rita's first ever kiss.

'All the girls fancied him,' said Yemi. 'He was such a handsome young boy. He was really well mannered. I think he liked her too – I'm pretty sure they kissed once. It was a Chinese whisper kind of thing where I'd say, "I'm going to tell him you fancy him" and she'd be like, "No, don't do that!" chasing me in the playground.

'When we were in Year Six we went to the Isle of Wight with our class,' Yemi recalled. 'We stayed there for about four days. It was like an activity place, we did rock climbing and stuff like that. Me and Rita used to get into so much trouble together – the boys and everything like that. All the boys fancied her. She was lovely. It would just be like pushing and everyday play fighting with the boys. Joking about who fancies who in the class. Childish banter between friends.'

Rita thought nothing of teasing her teachers, using her natural charm to get away with the kind of comments other children might get pulled up for.

'We had these two teachers. Me and Rita always used to joke that they fancied the pants off each other. We would tease them about it. Well, they got together – we were right. It came true – they got married!'

Life wasn't all just one big game to Rita, though. She showed maturity beyond her years by helping out in the school's nursery, with Yemi.

'We were obsessed with this one little girl. She was the dinkiest, tiniest little thing,' Yemi said. 'Me and Rita would want to go down to nursery just to play with her. She was like our little dolly. Every chance we'd get we'd be in that nursery playing with her.'

That compassion, which Rita has clearly taken from her parents and grandparents, convinces Yemi that she would make a wonderful mother herself one day.

'I think Rita will be a brilliant mum,' she said. 'I've seen her with children, her little brother, my little cousin. She's always been really good with children and when the time comes she will put just as much hard work into being a mum as she put into her music career. Because of what she's been through I think she'll be what every child wants in a mother – one of those parents you can relate to and be open with without fear of judgement. That's the type of person she is.'

In 2001, as Rita was turning eleven, she entered her last year of primary school. It was to be a year of mixed emotions. Rita was sad about saying goodbye to the school that had nurtured her talent and given her so many happy memories. She had fulfilled her early promise and continued to impress with her singing. But at the same time she was excited about what the future would hold.

After performing one big solo for her beloved Suzi aged ten, Rita convinced the choir teacher she had the talent to go far. She told Rita stage school might be the best option for her. The one she recommended was Sylvia Young Theatre School, then in Marylebone, where singers like Amy Winehouse and Spice Girl Emma Bunton had studied, as well as Jade Ewen, whose path would one day cross Rita's in the search for a UK Eurovision Song Contest entrant in 2009.

At the same time music teacher Mary said to Vera that stage school was something seriously worth considering.

Rita's Year Six teacher and Mary's friend Ilona confirmed: 'Mary recognised her talent and said to her mother that Rita had talent and she should encourage her. Her mother took this on board and helped Rita to develop this career she now has. Mary encouraged Rita's mother to apply to Sylvia Young. She knew it was a big financial undertaking for her family but she believed in Rita's talent. Mothers always think their children have talent but if Mary said, "Your daughter's got talent you should encourage it," she probably thought, "I know she does and I'll encourage and support her."'

Ilona added: 'I've known Mary for many years and she was my best friend at the time of her death. I don't remember her talking about anybody the way she spoke of Rita. She would say she was special and she had a talent that should be encouraged. I think Rita was okay academically but she was not exceptional. I'm not sure if you'd say she had an athletic talent. She was athletic and she enjoyed sports, and again always put every effort into everything she did.

'She was one of these people who enjoyed life and would always give one hundred per cent.'

Vera did take on board Mary's comments. But Besnik was harder to convince. He believed in pursuing a traditional path. To him, trying to carve out a career in a music industry that was notoriously hard to break into seemed too much of a risk. 'My dad wanted me to go down a more academic route,' Rita explained. 'He is very much about sticking to the rule book and sticking to the blueprint of a successful career.'

Eventually though Rita and Vera convinced him she should at least audition.

'The audition was massively exciting,' Rita said. 'I really didn't think I'd be good enough, but then the only thing I was ever interested in was singing. Ever since I was really little, like six or something, it's all I've wanted to do.'

As she waited on the results of her audition, Rita was determined to end the year on a high. With an end-of-year show to look forward to she wanted to go out with a bang. That she did – but not quite in the way she had hoped.

Just two days before the big performance – a show featuring a medley of songs and dances through the ages – Rita fell off a swing in Avondale Park and cracked her head off a pole. It was so serious she needed the wound on her scalp glued together.

Devastatingly for the young Rita she was told she would have to miss the first performance in front of the school. Yemi was asked to stand in for her.

'She was so upset,' Yemi said. 'There were two performances, the first she couldn't do because she'd cut her head and had to have it glued together on her scalp. I was excited because it was a great part and Rita was all glum. She was really gutted about that. We recorded the first performance for Rita and the next day we showed it to her. It was amazing – that was the best performance we'd ever done.'

Rita's teacher Ilona recalled how devastated her star pupil was.

'It's a shame really that happened,' she said. 'It wasn't Rita's fault. She did her best. She always had that kind of do-her-best attitude.'

Rita was able to perform on the second show for the parents at least.

'On the second day she got her role back and she was happy,' Yemi said. 'We did the Charleston together in our frilly little outfits with bows in our hair.'

Despite Rita's mishap, her teacher knew the future was going to be a bright one.

'I just remember her as being a really lovely girl. Sometimes you've got kids in your class and you don't like them, or they're annoying or they're naughty or rude or difficult,' Ilona said. 'But Rita was always charming and delightful. She was very popular. You can see that in her now. She's the same kind of person she was as a child.'

It is testament to the school that someone like Rita could arrive there with limited English and blossom into such a success story.

Ilona explains: 'In our school that was a common story – a common history of the children – it was a school full of refugees. Children from all over the place with terrible stories. I would say Rita and her family were making the most of their new life in the UK.'

That faith in Rita's ability was confirmed when she got the news she had been waiting for. She was accepted into Sylvia Young. No mean feat considering only one in twenty-five applicants gets accepted. Not only that but she had secured a scholarship, meaning her family would be spared having to fund the £4,000-a-term fees, for the first year at least.

Yemi recalled the day when Rita found out. 'I remember one day at school we were standing around talking and Rita came in and said, "I got the scholarship, I'm going to Sylvia Young," and we were so excited we were jumping around like, "Oh my God, you lucky cow!"' Yemi revealed. 'I was like, "You're gonna be famous." All she kept saying was, "I'm gonna be famous, I'm gonna be famous." Her whole face was full of excitement.'

'When Rita found out she had been accepted into Sylvia Young she was very excited. It was a wonderful opportunity – she knew that,' her teacher Ilona said. 'It obviously makes me really proud to see someone be a great success. But in particular what I'm proud of is she's not spoilt. She's retained that loveliness she had as a child. We tend to think of it as the St Cuthbert's way. She's a St Cuthbert's child and we're based on being fair and kind and sharing. All those kinds of things. That was our philosophy. And she was a child that fitted in well to that.'

The last day of school was an emotional one. Rita was leaving her best friends to pursue her dream.

'I remember Rita crying in the toilets on the last day,' Yemi said. 'We were all getting ready to leave primary school. We were strong all day and finally we were getting ready to leave and she just broke down in tears in the locker room. She set us all off and we were all crying.'

As Rita Sahatçiu prepared to begin the next chapter in her remarkable life her father decided a different kind of change was necessary. Sahatçiu was too difficult to pronounce and spell. If Rita was to become a star he wanted people to be able to say her name.

He added the name 'Ora' to the family surname. Fittingly, for watchmakers, it means 'hour' in Albanian.

Rita Ora was born. Soon the world would know her name.

3

Fall in Love

SHE caught the eye of nearly every guy – except the one she wanted.

Rita burst into stage school with all the confidence of a future star. But soon that excitement would turn to turmoil.

The boy of her dreams was so close she could touch him – and she did. Yet the more they flirted, the more they laughed together – even when they kissed – it seemed only to tantalisingly push him further away.

Rita has only ever made one public comment about her teenage torment.

'I was really in love with this boy in high school. Jamie. But I'm not going to tell you his second name,' she said.

But friends now say the object of her affection back then was likely to be Jamie Blackley, an impossibly handsome young man, eight months younger than Rita, but someone who kept her at arm's length – sometimes.

On other occasions, if their friends are to be believed, they only had eyes for each other.

Rita met Jamie at the Sylvia Young Theatre School. He had been there since the age of ten and was well versed with the ways of stage school by the time Rita burst through its doors. This must have made him appear even more worldly, wise and appealing.

Born in Douglas, on the Isle of Man in 1991, Jamie grew up in Kent and was learning guitar by the time Rita crossed his path. Despite his flirtation with music, however, acting was his real passion and he had his sights set on big things when he left school.

With his wavy dark locks and deep brown eyes, he already ticked all the Hot and Mysterious boxes on impressionable teenage Rita's checklist. Into football (Crystal Palace is his team) and pop music, she would have felt they had a lot in common. And what's more he had a rebellious streak.

'Rita had a huge crush on Jamie,' one of their friends from Sylvia Young said.

'She and Jamie Blackley were very good friends,' said another friend. 'It didn't get further than friends to my knowledge. At parties I think they had a kiss from time to time. They were both quite rebellious.'

By Rita's own admission it was clear that, as adolescence kicked in, it hadn't taken her long to start shaking off the 'St Cuthbert's way' nice-girl image she'd cultivated at her last school.

'I loved it there,' Rita said of her time at Sylvia Young, 'but I wouldn't say I was a star pupil, or stood out, because they were focused on singing musical theatre and I've never been that kind of singer. I've always had a husky voice. To tell you the truth I couldn't sing like that at all. Going there was an amazing experience but I was naughty growing up. I liked to have fun and I'd mess around like kids do.'

The Sylvia Young Theatre School had been teaching kids performing arts since 1972 and for eleven years expanded until it moved to Marylebone in 1983, which is where Rita attended. Since 2010 its premises have been a converted church in Westminster.

Although its speciality is the arts, the emphasis is on the curriculum. Children are expected to wear uniforms – red sweaters, black blazers and black, red and white ties – but alongside maths and English sit the type of subjects you wouldn't find in regular schools, like tap dancing, vocal technique, dramatic improvisation and audition, recording and microphone technique.

Stalking the corridors constantly was the school's founder, Sylvia Young. An indomitable woman now in her sixties, she was not afraid to pull up even the most talented of youngsters for their behaviour. She was a tough disciplinarian, even towards her own daughter.

If anything Rita should have towed the line, just like she'd done before. However, instead of cosying up to teachers here, she was sparring with them.

'I was mouthy, cheeky, messing round a lot,' she said. 'I hated wearing a hairnet. Sylvia would come into ballet class and catch me. "Rita, there are some rules. This is a serious matter." She always had a soft spot for me, though. I was never rude, I just wasn't great at listening.'

At choir practice she loved stretching her alto/mezzo soprano vocal talents – but it didn't always go down well. 'I was always getting told off by my choir teacher for, you know, riffing when I shouldn't,' she said.

Rita's old classmate, who asked not to be named, confirmed she liked to play the role of the rebel.

'She did skip school a lot,' he said. 'But when it came to music she was so committed. She got told off a lot and sent out of class – she'd answer back to teachers, skip homework and talk during class – normal kid stuff.'

That attitude would not have been music to her parents' ears. They sacrificed much to put her through theatre school. '(Our parents) had to save up money and pay every month to send her,' Elena said.

Life at stage schools can be tough, however – and there's always the misconception that they are all like the TV series *Glee*, with kids breaking out into song every two minutes, waving their jazz hands.

But Rita said, 'No, it's not like that. Sure, there was the musical-theatre lot and you have to do every class – tap, ballet – but it was cool. It wasn't just jazz hands. Sylvia knows everyone's name. She was, like [she puts on a prim upper class English accent], "Miss Ora, collar down, thank you."'

Aside from Jamie Blackley, Rita also grew close to Monet Edgson, the daughter of soul singer Mica Paris, Sasha Russell and, from the year above her, Vanessa White, who would later find fame in the girl band The Saturdays. Also in her class for a short time was Jesy Nelson, who made it big as one member of Little Mix, the only group to win *The X Factor* when they triumphed in 2011, and Charlotte Finlay Tribe, who would also one day meet Rita and Jade in the battle for Eurovision glory in 2009. As further evidence that Rita was in talented company, Nathan Sykes – who would later join The Wanted – was in the year below.

'We were a close class during those years,' one of her friends confessed. 'I would agree [that she didn't fit in]. It was a musical theatre
school. Perfect for the likes of myself whose passion is that, but Rita
was so much more. There wasn't a great deal of opportunity for her
to showcase what she is really capable of. She never showed a passion for musical theatre. She loved music but the dancing and acting
wasn't really her thing.'

But he added: 'Rita was always amazing. She was always a star
but she would rarely be picked to do lead roles in stuff. It didn't
bother her. When she did sing solo parts it stood out. Vanessa was
in the year above. In terms of talent, they were pretty much on par.

'Rita was very popular. It's easy to feel that way [like you don't fit in
because you're poor] in a school full of rich kids. I felt the same. But they
didn't treat her differently. And Rita never had any airs or graces.'

Kai Taylor, who attended Sylvia Young for a year with Rita in
2004, was part of her close-knit group of friends.

'We were in the same year so she was in my form,' said Kai, who'd
already had a taste of stardom by reaching the final of *Stars in Their
Eyes* in 2003 while just eleven. 'We were good friends. We got told
off a lot for being mischievous in class. We just used to be silly and
giggle – it was either me, her or Monet that got sent out of the class.
It wasn't anything bad, it was just for being daft and laughing.

'Rita loved to sing,' Kai, who auditioned for *The X Factor* in 2007,
went on. 'We used to sing Mariah Carey together in maths and got
told to shut up. She loved Alicia Keys, Beyoncé, all the R'n'B stuff.'

Offering an insight that can only come from someone who knew
her well, Kai revealed that, despite her outward confidence, Rita
was actually insecure about her abilities, and seemed self-conscious
about the wealthy backgrounds of some of the other pupils.

'Rita was amazing but didn't really believe in herself,' he said. 'She
was a bit shy, like me. I connected with her straight away because
she was down to earth. A lot of people go there because their families are rich. I just got on with her because she was real and didn't
pretend to be anything she wasn't.'

With Jamie coming from a distinctly middle-class background,
could Rita have been self-conscious about her relatively poor
upbringing? Perhaps, but Kai said she refused to let it get to her.

'She got on with everyone,' Kai said. 'She had a sense of humour like she has today. She was bubbly and friendly all the time. I knew she would be a star. She could sing and she was feisty and she just had it.'

Surrounded by kids who could afford designer brands, Rita started to develop her own style on a budget. After class she and her friends would head to Portobello Road and look for bargains. She grew adept at transforming the clothes she had and it was at this time that she really started experimenting with different looks and styles.

'When I was a kid, I'd spray-paint my hair, cut clothes up,' she said. 'I've always been into looking different. I used to cut up and make things myself using vintage shirts I'd bought for a pound on the market.'

Some of her earliest memories are of rummaging around her mum's dressing table and cosmetics bag – and it was through her mum she adopted a lip colour that would become one of her trademark style statements.

'I'd steal mum's YSL [Yves Saint Laurent] red lipstick and wear it with my school uniform. It must have looked ridiculous but I thought it was the most glamorous thing ever,' she said. 'I'm not saying girls need make-up to feel pretty but I love it – the colours, the vibrancy – and it makes me feel like me. I'm also inspired by old pictures of my mum – particularly when she was pregnant with me. She looked hot.'

Another huge influence was No Doubt singer Gwen Stefani who released her acclaimed debut solo album *Love. Angel. Music. Baby.* – which spawned one of the singles of the year in 'What You Waiting For?' and the American number one hit 'Hollaback Girl' – just as Rita was turning fourteen. Rita's future blonde look was based on Stefani and she loved Gwen's fearlessness and her approach to music. 'I really, really, really admire Gwen Stefani,' Rita said. 'I loved red lipstick after I saw it on her. Gwen was like my Marilyn [Monroe]. She made me want to dye my hair and do my lips red. I've been stuck on it since I was fourteen. She inspires me fashion-wise and she inspires me musically because she always knew what she was doing.'

Although outwardly Rita was displaying newfound confidence, inwardly she was being eaten away by insecurity.

She felt self-conscious about her status. Stage schools are a popular choice for kids with bottomless trust funds. Compared to people from wealthy backgrounds, Rita was acutely aware of how different she was. Once her scholarship had ended her parents had to find a way of funding her course. There wasn't much money sloshing around. Rita had to make do with what she had.

'I had so many embarrassing moments in high school,' she said. 'It was a private school and I grew up in a middle-class neighbourhood. I lived in an estate, which is council housing or government housing. Going to a private school, there was a lot of wealthy children around me.

'I would have the same red Nike backpack and they would have Louis Vuitton bags and I used to get upset about it. One day, I cut my bag up and made it into a handbag. It's so embarrassing but everyone wanted one! I cut it up, I made a handle and I would go to school with it. Everyone would be like, "That's such a nice bag."'

Rita compared herself to girls in other ways. Already at an awkward age, she felt she was maturing quicker and was self-conscious about the curves she was developing.

'There was a point in school when I didn't feel comfortable at all,' she said. 'I had bigger breasts and a bigger bum – and hated it. Every Thursday, we had to wear tight clothing for ballet. I'd get extra-tight leotards for dance classes to flatten me because I was ashamed of my body. You could see every bump and curve. And me and this other girl were the only ones who had breasts early on, and I'd try to cover them, hunching my shoulders. That is why my posture is still shit.'

Even today she says she still has problems with her body image. 'I dyed my hair when I was fourteen because it made me feel sexy. But I'm a female, and females will never be comfortable in their skin: I feel I've got a muffin top, that I can work on my butt.'

To combat what she saw as her imperfect body she wore baggy clothes to hide her boobs – something that still influences her style today.

Later in life she would joke that her bum had 'finally come in', suggesting she had worked it to a shape she was happy with. And she was certainly not afraid to show it off at the Oscars after-show party but her early insecurity is something she has battled hard to overcome.

Today she says, 'In the dress world for Rita Ora there's two things you've gotta do – what hasn't been done and what can I do to make myself feel as sexy as possible.'

Rita was also going to have to quickly get used to presenting her body for the camera. Kids at Sylvia Young are encouraged to audition for acting roles practically from the moment they arrive. Rita's first part was a small role in the ITV1 drama *The Brief*, a series featuring Alan Davies as a barrister with a messy private life. At fourteen Rita went for and landed a part that seemed made for her – that of a teenage Albanian girl in the 2004 British comedy crime drama *Spivs*, starring Ken Stott, Nick Moran and Jack Dee and directed by Colin Teague. She played Rosanna, a girl smuggled into the UK with her brother, who falls into the hands of some black marketeers – the 'spivs' of the title – who have taken on more than she bargained for. Rita featured heavily in the movie, speaking mostly Albanian. Watching her on screen it's hard to make the connection from the dark-haired, fresh-faced girl and her peroxide blonde, heavily stylised image now. 'Ha ha, before bleach!' is how she jokes about it. But the teenage Rita displays the same charm and feistiness that's won her an army of fans.

The film failed to set the box office alight but Rita had put down a marker. Her acting career was off the ground.

Jamie, by contrast, had to wait until he was seventeen before landing his first part, a small role in the BBC drama *Apparitions*.

For Rita, acting was a fun diversion, but it was singing she still wanted to concentrate on. In her spare time she made her first attempts at songwriting and tried out her compositions whenever she could.

One neighbour at Foreland House, who lived below Rita's family, said she used to hear Rita singing in her living room, which faces the back of the building and overlooks the gardens of the ground-floor flats. The woman would go out into her garden to hear the beautiful little girl sing. Rita had begun writing her own songs and it was these homespun compositions she tried out in her lounge.

Another neighbour who appreciated Rita's singing was Martin Dykes, who is the same age as Rita and still lives in a bottom-floor flat in Foreland House. He remembers when her family moved in.

They first met as Martin ran past Rita's front door and a little dog she used to have then, Coco, ran out and started chasing him. Rita came out to catch her pet and apologise to Martin, who quickly recruited the new girl in the block to join their gang of playmates.

'She used to love singing all the time,' Martin said. 'It was always Mariah Carey. The song "Hero" was one of her favourites. She liked the ballads. We all thought it was so cool she went to Sylvia Young because we were all at state schools. She was a good singer obviously and she'd tell us about the singing and the dancing she got to do there. Her voice was always so nice and pretty. We'd always be like, "Really, wow, did you just do that?"'

Martin remembers Elena as the more intelligent sibling, and other neighbours thought the elder sister was just as pretty as Rita. But Rita was always sparkier.

'I remember Rita was told she had to focus more on maths and English,' Martin said. 'I remember her sister Elena being very bright. Rita used to say, "Oh God, I've got more homework to do". She just wanted to sing. At the park we'd do the normal stuff kids do – play, play some games. There would always be a big group of us. Rita was always very outgoing and fun, easy to speak to. Anyone could speak to her and she'd approach anyone.'

As Rita got older she started leading two distinctly separate lives. There were her friends at Sylvia Young and her friends near Portobello Road and rarely did she mix the two groups.

One of her best friends was Mishka Stalham who lived on the same estate as she did. They liked the same clothes, liked the same music and liked to hang out in Portobello Road. They might have attended different schools but they formed a lasting friendship that survives to this day.

'After school, or when I bunked school … when I did naughty stuff, we used to come to Portobello and go to the cafés, and me and my friends had a lot of fun here. We always used to just chill out.'

She started rebelling outside school as well as inside. She started smoking at thirteen and began hanging around with a harder crew.

Her old school pal from St Cuthbert's, Yemi Akintoye Dedier, remembers being surprised when she saw how Rita was behaving.

'She started smoking at one point – she was about thirteen,' Yemi said. 'I saw her one time and I couldn't believe she was smoking. She had a phase of hanging out with boys – not good boys, bad boys. There were these brothers – two mixed-race boys. They were terrible. They were the worst kind. I think one of them went to prison for a bit. Rita liked her bad boys.

'I think that was her rebellious streak. I remember I saw her just off of Ladbroke Grove – she was wearing a tight little top and a pair of jeans. The boys she was hanging around with – I know them because my older brother knew them – they were quite a bit older than Rita. I knew the kind of stuff they used to do.

'She did hang around a few guys who were from gangs. I wouldn't say she participated in any gang activity because she had more sense than that. She would never do anything criminal. Rita always liked attention. She liked to be in the limelight and she liked to be in the mix of things and be in the know of what's going on around town. Quite a lot of the guys she hung around were into gangsta rap and things like that. So part of why she hung around them was probably for the music side.'

Rita was putting her body issues to one side by dressing provocatively, and other people noticed a difference in her too.

'As Rita grew up she became more aware of her fashion,' her former friend Martin said. 'She was always very risqué. She would always have to do her own thing, like have a little crop top on her with something hanging over it. She was always ahead of the game. She always had to show her own personality and her own style.'

When Rita wasn't hanging out near her home, she could often be found at the Rugby Portobello Trust clubhouse across the road from her flat. The trust provides help for 1,150 local children from deprived areas by giving them access to sporting activities, advice and providing a whole range of learning facilities. Rita took advantage of the recording studio there to lay down vocals or sing at the clubhouse.

Rupert Taylor, a youth worker at the trust who used to let Rita use their studio, said: 'Eleven years old, she used to sing "Killing Me Softly". I recorded it on my phone. I've actually got the footage saying, "You're going to be a star." She's that special, she's done good things – she's done great things.'

Since hitting the big time Rita has revisited her old stomping ground, where she has fond memories.

'Every summer we used to be out on the fences,' she revealed in one of her many YouTube video diaries. 'We just used to have a good time. I can say it wasn't the worst neighbourhood in the world, but it also wasn't the best neighbourhood in the world. The good thing about this area is that everyone knew each other. Everyone knew the family histories of everyone so everyone kind of knew what you had to do.

'When I was growing up my family used to sit around the sofa [in the living room] and I would always just sing. My dad used to make me sing – a lot – which was really frustrating because I never wanted to – but deep down I did.'

Rita might have been at stage school but that didn't make her above household chores. 'I used to hate hoovering [our] stairs,' she said. 'I always had to get that chore. It was either ironing, hoovering or dishes. I always chose the dishes because that means you don't move from one spot. But then my hands turned pruney and I just couldn't do it any more.'

The tiny room she shared with her sister contained two single beds with pink quilts and a print of another of Rita's favourite blondes – Marilyn Monroe – on the wall above Rita's bed.

'My sister used to get annoyed with me when I used to write and listen to music late because she wanted to sleep and she had to wake up early for school,' Rita said. 'My headphones were not that good – I used to always get annoyed and go to the bathroom and do it.'

The girls began a memory wall on the back of the door and a closet door – a collage of photos of them growing up with their friends.

She may have bickered with Elena at home, as sisters do, but outside the pair would invariably hang out together. And the presence of two stunning girls rarely went unnoticed by the local boys.

'Rita always used to hang out with her sister,' their neighbour Martin said. 'I'd see them going out. As they got older a few of the guys around here were definitely interested in them.'

Rita, it seemed, was never short of attention from boys. But the one she craved remained out of reach.

Jamie Blackley left Sylvia Young possibly without a clue that Rita had such deep feelings for him. Since leaving Jamie has kept in touch with his old classmates – and tweets Rita on Twitter, but his life has followed a different path.

Until the age of twenty-two he had to be content with minor roles in UK TV programmes *Casualty*, *Misfits*, *Midsomer Murders* and *Doctors*. He appeared in 2012's *Snow White and the Huntsman* alongside superstars Charlize Theron and Kristen Stewart but in 2013 he finally landed his first lead role in *uwantme2killhim?* – the true story of two teenage boys who are drawn into the murky world of online chatrooms and eventually turn on each other.

While Rita now jets around the world, Jamie lives in quiet Whitstable, Kent, dividing his time between there and the house he shares in London with actress girlfriend Amy Wren who he worked with on *uwantme2killhim?*.

Big things are on the horizon for Jamie, however, as he starred opposite American teenage starlet Chloe Moretz in 2014's *If I Stay* and in 2015 he appeared in the Woody Allen film *Irrational Man* alongside red-carpet heavyweights Joaquin Phoenix and Emma Stone. With greater exposure it's only a matter of time before more girls appreciate just what Rita saw in him.

There is one further slight for Rita, however. Jamie has made no secret of his adoration of Rita's pop star rival Katy Perry. 'I love Katy Perry. She's so good. She's like the ultimate pop star.'

He also admits he's a huge fan of Rita's boss Jay Z, but so far hasn't name-checked his former classmate.

And on the subject of love, he's fairly pragmatic. 'If you want something to work then it will work,' he said.

Rita always knew she had to carve out her own destiny.

But there was sadness in her household when tragic news came from Kosovo. Besim, Rita's beloved grandfather, had died, aged seventy. Sadly he would not live to see whether his prediction for his special granddaughter would come true. A book written about Besim, however, told how his 'last wish' was for his talented granddaughter to reach the top.

Rita did not travel to her homeland for the funeral, but she was devastated by his loss. In a tribute to Besim eight years on from his death she was grateful for the faith he had shown in her. Describing him as her 'idol', she thanked him for making her the person who was to become a pop star and a television personality.

Posting a black and white snap of the director on Instagram, she wrote: 'I miss you grandad. I love you. You made me believe this was possible. You believed in me before I even did. Dam (sic) you were such a gangsta. Don't get into any trouble up there. Love Rita Pita.'

Family friend Shaqir Foniqi said: 'I can imagine Rita, how sad she was. I know how he loved his granddaughter.'

It was October 2005 when her grandfather died. Rita might not have hit the big time by then but that year it looked like she had found a launch pad for her ambitions sooner than even she envisioned. She was fourteen and visiting a funfair with her mum. They noticed local talent was being given a chance to perform on a stage. Unbeknown to Rita, Vera spoke to the organisers and secured her daughter a slot.

'Out of the blue she put my name forward to sing onstage!' blurted Rita. 'I was like, "Oh my God, Mum, this is so embarrassing!"'

Despite her red face, Rita belted out her favourite Mariah Carey song. When she stepped off the stage a man approached her. It was a music producer and songwriter. 'You should come to the studio and write and sing some songs,' he said.

The man was Martin Terefe, a Swede who had worked with a host of top talent and had recently made a household name of Scottish singer KT Tunstall, with her acclaimed album *Eye To The Telescope*. By chance he had been in the audience with his children and instantly recognised Rita's potential. He invited her to his Kensaltown Studios, named after the area of London where it was based.

'I was only fourteen and still in my school uniform when we got there!' Rita said.

Something clicked between them, and Martin offered her a deal for them to work together. She was being offered £5,000 over two years to work on producing music. On the face of it the deal sounded promising, but Rita hadn't a clue whether it was worth the paper it was written on so her family enlisted the help of a lawyer. It's unclear how much advice he could give. The offer was there – it was up to her if she took it. He could only advise on what the fine print meant. But the meeting would prove significant later in Rita's life.

'I signed a deal for two years which was stupid money. I would say like five grand for two years – which is not a good deal,' she said.

Rita might have come to realise that £5,000 was not a lot of money. But she was an untried quantity. And, more importantly it was Rita's first production deal. She was going to be making music. Her dreams were about to become a reality. But as she looked forward to a bright future she had no idea the darkest clouds were looming on the horizon.

4

Losing It

IT was the best – and worst – thing to have happened.

Rita, buzzing from the interest in her talent, started to think she'd made it. What use was school when she had natural talent? Her chance meeting with Martin Terefe only seemed to confirm to what she knew all along – it was her destiny to become a famous singer.

It didn't matter that she was the unlikeliest new recruit to the music industry. This young teenager, working in a studio in her school uniform, trying to craft the hits of tomorrow. She and Terefe certainly made an odd double act.

By the time Terefe gave Rita her production deal he had been in the UK for eight years and his studio was still building a reputation. Aside from Tunstall his most notable collaborator was Canadian singer Ron Sexsmith. But his hiring of Rita coincided with a purple patch for the producer. He began working with up-and-coming stars like James Morrison and Jason Mraz and involved Rita in the process. She could walk to Kensaltown Studios, and to the young hopeful it must have been cool to hang out in the converted warehouse filled with hipsters with a balcony overlooking a courtyard.

'I would sit there, take it all in and learn,' she recalled. 'All my friends would be telling me to come out and I'd be in the studio. But it was fun for me. It didn't feel like work. I loved it.'

Rita worked with Terefe for two years, from 2005 until 2007, and it was an education of sorts into the way of the industry. Collaborations led to contacts, which led to further openings in the hope one day it would lead to her breakthrough moment.

And her belief that the planets were starting to align for her was confirmed when one day she walked into the studio and bumped into someone she recognised heading out.

It was Craig David – at one time the hottest property in British music. They got talking, hit it off and on the spot he asked her to demo on a track for him.

These days Craig is known as much for comedian Leigh Francis's mock characterisation of him on the Channel 4 series *Bo Selecta!* as for his own music. However, it's worth remembering that for a time at the start of the decade Craig had the music world at his feet. His *Born To Do It* album remains the fastest selling debut of any British male solo singer and the number ones it spawned – 'Fill Me In' and '7 Days' – were monster hits.

By the time he met Rita, however, the shine was starting to fade from his star status. He was nearly ten years older than Rita and would have been twenty-six to her sixteen. Like her he was raised on a council estate and he was living proof someone with talent could make it.

Craig asked Rita to sing on a demo for one of his tracks, 'Awkward'. It was a small opportunity, but if Rita put in a good performance, who knew where it would lead?

Life was looking good for Rita. She was just waiting for her big break.

Back at Sylvia Young, however, she was losing focus. Her partying increased. And she continued to keep her school friends separate from her home life.

'We had a lot of parties – house parties,' one of her classmates revealed. 'We had them in lots of different houses – but I don't remember ever going to Rita's. We'd dance and drink. We'd sneak alcohol. This was Year Eleven so we were approaching sixteen. Rita would drink with everyone. She loves to party. We were that kind of a year group. We had a lot of fun both in and out of school. I remember Rita was always dancing. Afterwards we would all crash out on the living room floor. It was a bit of a squeeze as there were so many of us.'

Rita felt she wasn't getting all she hoped out of the theatre school. Her production deal hadn't borne fruit yet but Rita was convinced if she left school after her GCSEs in the summer of 2007 she could concentrate fully on her singing. She'd continued to write her own songs and poetry. One called 'I'll Be Waiting', which she wrote at fifteen, seemed to sum up her mood at that time. With honest lyrics about having nowhere to run and feeling like she was hiding from the sun, she was describing her situation. Everyone was telling her to take her time, she sang, but she had no time to take.

Her mind was made up. She decided she would leave when the term ended in the summer.

The move came as a shock to her mum, who had continued to scrimp and save to fund the fees and to her dad who had reservations about going down the theatre school route in the first place. Elena was at the stage where she was choosing which university to go to and they hoped Rita would continue her education and go to college.

Stress was the last thing Vera needed. Her health was deteriorating once more. She had tests and doctors confirmed her worst fears – her breast cancer had returned. At the time when Vera was summoning reserves of strength to fight the killer disease, while continuing with her own studies, her youngest daughter was making a decision that could affect her whole life. Despite this, Rita's mind was made up. 'I understood what was happening with the cancer and I didn't want to go to school, although I had a great music teacher, Ray, who forced me to work hard,' she said. 'But I was not focused on anything, I just wanted to get out.'

Rita now acknowledges at the time she could and should have been a better daughter and has since realised just what trauma her mum was silently enduring.

'I just feel like the worst kid. I was, like, so bad in school and not knowing that she had all that shit to deal with when we were young. To have to do it again and then she's paying for my school and I was being so ungrateful about it because I didn't understand that she was physically unwell.'

It was agony for Rita to watch her mother go through the punishing treatment.

'All I remember caring about was whether my mum was alright,' she said. 'It was very strange. I really didn't care about myself.'

43

Vera underwent chemotherapy and radiotherapy but the invasive treatment took its toll.

'It's the worst thing in the world to see your mother kind of crumble in front of you,' Rita said. 'She got chemotherapy, radiotherapy, she lost all her hair.'

But Vera amazed her family with her positive attitude.

'There was not one day when you wouldn't see her smile,' Rita recalled. 'To us, she was a superhero. She just didn't have hair. I got her wigs and we made her feel really pretty and she felt gorgeous regardless because she's so confident in herself. Having it again she said, "You know what, this is the final straw," so she removed her breasts and she got a whole new one [pair of breasts with reconstructive surgery] and now she looks hotter than Pamela Anderson!'

Yet the thoughtful daughter still harbours guilt over how she behaved as a teenager to this day. 'That's why I get her a house, and I get her a car and I know it never ever compares to, like, a kid's love for their mum and the connection they have. It's just so annoying when you're like, "I wish I could have been a good kid." My sister was a good kid. I was always independent, I can say that much. My mum was really keen on me going to school and wearing my uniform the right way and not putting red lipstick on with your uniform, which is what I always did.

'I just felt like I never knew what was about to happen. You just don't know what's going to happen around the corner. I was kind of like, "If I lose my mum then who's going to be proud of me?" Who would I have done it for? I don't do anything for me, I do it for her. Everything is for her.'

Graciously, Vera won her cancer battle for the second time – and since then has been all clear. 'I can officially say now she is past the five-year mark,' Rita said in 2013, 'and she is one hundred per cent clear and it has not come back, so thank God.'

But that period when Rita pressed ahead with her decision to quit school put enormous strain on her relationship with her parents. It seemed to make sense for Rita. Quitting meant she could concentrate everything on her career, which at the time extended to a paltry production deal, which was starting to show signs of not going anywhere.

Rita decided to get a job, something that would give her some cash of her own. Her options were limited. She had worked a few shifts in her dad's pub but that wasn't compatible with school work. One of the few things she was passionate about was fashion and trainers. So was her friend Mishka. Luckily for her one of the trendiest chains of shoe shops was right on her doorstep – Size?. She had just turned sixteen and it was nearing Christmas in 2006. The store was looking for extra weekend staff to help them through the busy festive period.

Although their passion for fashion was undeniable, it seems the girls felt that wouldn't be enough to beat off the competition. So they enhanced their CVs with a few fibs about their previous experience.

Former Size? assistant manager Antonio Fumarola remembers how Rita immediately impressed him and then-boss David Roddie – despite her being economical with the truth.

'We hired her just prior to Christmas 2006 – together with my manager at the time,' he recalled. 'We were looking for extra staff for the weekend because it was the busy time of year. She came in the store with her CV with her friend Mishka.

'My manager was like, "Wow, she's young, but she's a beautiful girl and she knows all the local people."

'One day they came in and dropped off their CV. My manager was like, "You remember those girls? We should give them an interview, I think they're gonna be good, they're nice girls, young, but they're nice girls."

'We did an interview with Rita. I think she fibbed on her CV and in the interview. She said she had experience working in a few stores. But you could see because she was young she couldn't have had that much experience,' Antonio said. 'But we really needed help on the weekend and we liked that she was local and had connections with the local kids. I remember she had a couple of shop names on her CV and again in the interview she said she had experience, but I don't think that was true. But again, my manager said, "I think she's nice," so I was like, "Let's go for it." We decided to give her a chance.'

Rita couldn't believe her luck. She was going to be working in her favourite shop on Portobello Road, where all the cool kids liked to hang out. Plus she'd be earning her own cash from now on.

Rita was hired as a sales assistant and her first role was as a runner to get the stock. Antonio remembers she was a bit untidy but when it came to dealing with customers she was an immediate hit.

'She was a phenomenal sales assistant,' he said. 'I want to be honest with you – lots of guys came into the store just to impress her. She was very nice looking. All the Jamaicans around there would come in and try to impress her and buy sneakers all the time. It was good money. I was like, "Rita, stay downstairs, don't worry about anything else, go, smile, sell shoes – that's all you need to do." We did a bit of training, learning all the basic rules. She was very good. She wasn't so good at things like keeping the stock room tidy.

'She was a big character and always singing. She was really into R'n'B. I was into electronic music and we'd compete over who got to play the music they wanted in the store.

'She'd be singing on the stairs, in the stock room or when she was on the floor. She was always with Mishka, who was one of her best friends. On the weekends she was making the store a lot of money because she was very friendly with the customers.'

Rita loved having some disposable income at last.

'I used to work on the weekends and I would get sixty pounds a week and I would spend it on trainers,' she said. 'My oldest pair are Stan Smiths and Reebok Pumps too. I didn't even feel the pump. Do they even pump? They just looked cool.'

Rita had adapted to the job well but she hoped it wouldn't be needed long term. As summer approached she would soon be graduating and could focus solely on her career.

Before then, however, she had the small matter of her prom to attend.

She did manage to land a date with a boy called Jamie for the night – but it wasn't Jamie Blackley. Friends said it was another Jamie and they say she was never going to be his type.

Her class all went away for the bash in a London hotel. There was no obligation to go in couples but Rita and red-headed Jamie did because they were such good friends. After their lavish dinner, where teachers gave speeches, they headed to Rita's partner Jamie's house in Kent for a wild bash.

Witnesses there can't remember if Rita hit it off with anyone at the party, but years later she would reveal she did have the hots for someone who matched this other Jamie's complexion.

'When I used to go to school I fancied this guy and he was white and ginger.'

She would go on to write a song about her unrequited love.

'There is a song called "Unfair" about him. It's about putting a lot of effort into something nobody cares about.'

At least the party seemed a fitting end to their time at theatre school.

'We sneaked in drinks,' one of the revellers said. 'It was messy and lots of people were sleeping all over the house. It was our last memory of everyone together. It was sad, but I don't remember Rita crying.'

Rita had some fond memories of Sylvia Young but her burning desire to break through was the only thing she was focused on.

'When I left Sylvia's at sixteen, I thought a week later I'd be famous,' she confessed.

Confident that success lay just around the corner she touted herself around record companies, and came back down to earth with a bang when her meetings did not go as well as she hoped.

'I did get slayed,' she said. 'They said, "She doesn't know what she's doing. She just sounds like so-and-so." Everyone was putting their two pence in, I got really confused, I thought I'd messed up. When you don't know yourself, you think that everyone else is right. So you cry.

'I was sixteen. I thought I knew everything, but I didn't know anything. I was lost.'

She added: 'I'd sit around the house for days. I was really down.'

Vera and Besnik could not understand what was happening to their daughter. It was like she was rejecting all they had taught her about Albanian tradition, hard work and the rewards that it brought. Relations grew even more strained.

Rita asked for more hours at Size? and was grateful when she got them. For what she needed short term, the job in Size? was a godsend for Rita.

But it wasn't what she wanted to be doing. The cash she earned gave her freedom to do what she wanted and push boundaries with her parents. It was not the answer to her problems – which seemed to be mounting by the day. Rita, who had been so sure, so focused on following her dream, had fallen off the straight and narrow. After the promise of her production deal, her dreams of making it as a music star seemed further away than ever.

And she knew only too well the clock was ticking. If she didn't sort herself out soon those dreams might be dashed forever.

5

Good Girl Gone Bad?

AS soon as the woman entered the store, Antonio Fumarola knew she was not after a pair of shoes. She was beautiful but bore an expression of anger and concern.

'Where's Rita?'

It was Vera and she was frantically trying to find her daughter. Antonio had no idea what sort of trouble his young assistant was in but he knew it was bad.

Instinctively he offered to help. 'Don't worry,' he told her. 'I will look for Rita and if I know anything I will let you know.'

Vera was grateful for the help. When Antonio caught up with Rita he explained what happened and urged her to sort out whatever it was that was going on.

Rita warmed to his protective spirit – and a bond was formed between them.

'There was some kind of trouble,' he recalled. 'I can't remember exactly why. She wanted to make sure Rita was okay. I remember Rita went through a rough patch with her parents, especially her dad because he was a very strict guy.'

Rita confided in Antonio about her family background. 'She told me how her family moved to London because of the Kosovan war and I think her father was running a restaurant at the time,' he said. 'So they were hard workers. Rita's mum used to get mad when she was coming home late.

'I imagine having a daughter like Rita ... it probably wasn't the easiest,' Antonio said.

That episode wasn't the only time Vera – or someone else in the family – came looking for Rita. In Size? Rita was a formidable saleswoman – but she was burning the candle at both ends and her endless partying was taking its toll on her home and work life. Antonio got to know Vera and Elena and he could see how Rita was the rebel of the family.

'Elena was the good girl, Rita was the bad girl,' he said. 'I think her parents were happy she was working for Size? because they knew where she was and the environment was good and she was staying out of trouble. I think the problems related to her partying. It would have been an issue for any parent. I know the Albanian people are a traditional sort of people.

'She wasn't into drugs or anything like that – maybe smoking cigarettes. But she didn't get drunk too much. We had a couple of nights out together and she wasn't the girl who was drinking too much. I think it was her lifestyle that sparked the arguments – she'd be coming home too late or showing up in the morning. I remember on a Sunday she would sometimes come into work smashed from the night before. I remember sometimes she'd say, "I drank too much." She wasn't eighteen yet when we were working together.'

Antonio wasn't the only person to notice Rita was overindulging when she was hanging out with friends.

Yemi said: 'I did see her drinking. I remember seeing her when I was walking home one day and she was so drunk. She was with another girl and she was so drunk – she was like, "Heeey!" She was so happy. I think she was about fifteen or sixteen then. I never saw Rita smoke weed but the people she hung around with did smoke weed.'

Yemi explained why she never saw too much of her in their teenage years.

'We didn't party together because my mum was strict. Rita's parents were strict too so it always surprised me what they let her do. But Rita's mum has always been very supportive of her children. Her mum is very trusting of her,' she said.

'She knows Rita is a strong person and she can handle herself. She was very streetwise from a young age. She's a unique individual. Her experiences throughout life have made her who she is. She's always been mature. I think that's why her mum was able to say,

"Fine, you want to go out, you can go out," or whatever the case may be. Even at school Rita was always wanting to be a grown up, always wanting to be a year older.'

Another old friend from St Cuthbert's also ran into Rita years after they'd last met. Omar Hajaj, whose sister was once so captivated by Rita's talent and verve, admits he started to worry she was heading down the wrong path. Like Rita, he had experience of the music scene and saw the warning signs that all was not well.

'I saw her again when I was in Year Nine,' Omar said. 'I think she dated one of my friends. A lot of my friends lived around there [Ladbroke Grove]. I'd see her now and then in sheesha cafés.

'I used to do music at that time as well. I was going to do a collaboration with her. We were both underground then and we had plans to collaborate in a studio but it didn't happen.

'Ladbroke Grove is a bit of a rough area,' Omar went on. 'There is a lot of crime and lots of gangs. She was quite safe because she's a strong confident girl and knew how to speak slang. Because she was pretty she knew a lot of the older guys. Usually in gangs there's the young boys and the elders. The older boys gave her some security.

'She was very mature. She was very sexy. When you're that age you don't care about authority or school ... you get respect when you're getting yourself in trouble ... excluded in school or detention. She had friends who were like that. People around her would smoke cannabis. That was popular. She used to smoke cigarettes. I was under the impression she had lots of boyfriends. I did see her drinking alcohol.'

Omar went as far as saying that what he saw back then made him worry for her.

'I know she's a good person,' he said. 'I knew her when she was a child – she was very smart and a good-hearted person. To be honest, when I saw her as a teenager, it put me off. I didn't have that same interest in her. She was still a pretty girl, but it was the good character that had made me like her when we were younger. I think she is still the same person deep down.'

Omar, who is no longer involved with music, was close to making it back then. Under the stage name Ace, he was involved in UK grime and rap and was on the cusp of being signed by Sony, performing

51

with people like the rapper Chipmunk (now Chip), someone who would feature in Rita's life soon.

'I was involved in the same scene as Rita,' he said. 'There were lots of fights and gangs. Every time I'd go to a new postcode for a performance my guys would have to ... there would always be fights between different gangs. Too many problems with the police and crime. Rita was in mutual circles.'

It was against this backdrop that Antonio saw Rita when she came into the shop on the back of a heavy weekend or a bad experience. The caring colleague, who Rita would always call 'Tony' and tease fondly about his Italian accent, was like a big brother to her. He watched the sort of attention she got from male customers and Rita confided in him what was going on in her life. He tried to give advice when he could.

'She didn't have a serious boyfriend during the year and a half we worked together,' Antonio said. 'She was dating. She used to tell me stories about these guys.

'Even though Rita was seventeen she had a lot of experience [with boys] and she was very open about it. She wasn't innocent. I'm not saying anything bad but she and her friend had experience,' Antonio said. 'I would tell them, "Beautiful girls like you, just make sure you don't let guys abuse [use] you for sex." Some of those guys who were around were good guys but with some of them you didn't know what they were up to – some of those guys who used to come in were dealers, maybe selling weed. It's not some sort of ghetto but that area wasn't the best at the time. I'd try to tell them to be careful.

'Sometimes they would come in and be upset, telling me stories maybe about having had sex the night before. Not the specifics, but maybe the guy had upset them. We were very open – me, Mishka and Rita. I think it was sometimes guys she was dating and other stories were about random guys. I remember she was with this guy but somehow she ended up one night with another guy and she was worried about her actual boyfriend finding out. My only suggestion was, "You're seventeen, you don't need to stay with this guy and get married, so enjoy your life."'

It's a measure of how much Rita trusted Antonio that she was able to confide in him as much as she did. He told how fond he was of his star sales assistant – and would forgive her for her little failings.

'We were really close,' he said. 'I liked her a lot in terms of her personality. Maybe sometimes I would get mad at her when she wouldn't do the stuff I was asking her to. But she was one of my favourites. She used to be late for work – especially on a Sunday after going out the night before. Especially for the first few months, she was pretty much late every Sunday.

'Sometimes she would be entertaining people [socialising] too much downstairs. Sometimes in the day you would literally see her and Mishka surrounded by ten guys. Some of them were customers – but some of them were just trying to impress and meet these girls. I was like, "Come on guys, we're here to work." I would say, "You can talk as long as these guys come out with one or two pairs of shoes but please don't waste your time." And she was pretty messy in terms of managing the stock upstairs. So often I had to shout to her and Mishka, "Guys, please go upstairs to tidy the stock room because it's a mess." After a few months she started to get better. She started understanding what I wanted from them more. I would say, "All I want is for you to sell and make it tidy," and then I would let them leave early. They would always come to me and say, "Tony can we leave half an hour early?"'

Rita was by now very serious about fashion, and working in a store like that was perfect for getting her hands on the latest styles.

'Rita and Mishka wore very tight clothes. Skinny jeans. Sneakers, of course,' said Antonio. 'Jordans were popular. We weren't selling a lot of girls' shoes at the time and they would complain we didn't have things in their size. So we used to sometimes get them shoes from other stores. Nike Air Max, Air Force Ones and Jordans were all popular at the time. White was popular. Her and Mishka were obsessed with keeping their shoes clean. They were constantly going upstairs to wipe them off. They used to get annoyed when people stepped on their shoes. Sneakers were getting really popular at that time so it was a great time to be working at the store.

'Rita used to spend a lot of her money on sneakers and clothing. Sometimes she would ask me for more hours because she wanted to buy something nice to go out. I think Jordans were her favourite sneakers then.'

Rita and her friends created a party atmosphere in the shop.

'There was another girl who used to work with us who became friends with Rita. Karima – a tall black girl. And another guy – Josh. When the four of them were working together the store was like a party. They'd be playing loud music, dancing on the floor, singing and making jokes,' Antonio said. 'People were actually coming in to see what was going on. I enjoyed it because we were making money at the same time. It was really fun.

'There was another guy around – they were very close – Kyle,' Antonio added.

That was Kyle De'volle, a fellow style junky who Rita got talking to by chance because of their mutual appreciation of each other's taste. 'Rita and I grew up in the same area, Ladbroke Grove, and we have loads of mutual friends,' Kyle said. 'We really started talking when one day, it was around the time that American Apparel were doing their neon range, we walked past each other on Portobello Road; Rita was wearing the yellow fluro high-waisted skirt and I was wearing the matching jeans and I said to her, "Nice skirt," and she smiled and said, "Nice jeans," and we got talking. Ever since then we started having lunch together most days and became really close friends.'

Kyle and Rita have been inseparable ever since. As her personal stylist, he is now an integral part of her entourage.

She certainly had good friends around her, and Antonio recalled how Rita's family would pop into the shop often to see her – perhaps to check she was actually there! He even soon developed a soft spot for her sister.

'Elena – I had a crush on her,' he admitted. 'She was beautiful and a bit older than Rita. She was the clever one – you could see it. She was studying at the time. She was completely different. She was the good girl – while Rita and Mishka were the opposite. They were still good guys though. I think Elena was in a relationship so nothing happened [with me]. Her mum used to come in the store a lot with her little brother and also her dad. With her mum I was trying to be friendly and really kind. Rita would always say, "Oh, my mum loves you."'

Getting access to the family dynamic up close, Antonio could see there was friction. 'Sometimes there were some issues,' he said.

In September 2007 Rita enrolled at the British Academy of New Music, in a year-long Music Performance Level 3 Course, an A-Level equivalent, something that must have at least kept her dad happy. But again, she felt unsettled in the classroom and only stuck to it for a short time before dropping out. One of her fellow students Albert Gold said they were both there in 2007 but 'Rita didn't stay long, she was only there for two months'.

'She wasn't really interested in college,' Antonio explained. 'I don't think she was a good student. She was doing college because she had to. But I don't think it was for her. As soon as she finished she asked me for more hours because she just wanted to get some money.'

Rita was back to where she was after leaving Sylvia Young. However, this time her situation was a little different. She'd struck a deal with her dad. She had a year to make something of her music. It nothing came of it she would go back to college to complete her studies.

Now it was all or nothing, but Antonio recalls how Rita seemed to have lost faith.

'I don't think she was very serious about music at that time,' he said. 'I remember she was a very good singer. I was the one saying, "Rita, you should be a star." She was really into Chris Brown and Mariah Carey, those guys. She was always singing loud on the shop floor or upstairs in the stock room. I'd tell her she should take it more seriously.'

Sadly, however, it was like the light inside Rita was fading – she didn't seem committed any more.

'At the time I don't think she realised it was really going to happen,' Antonio continued. 'It was like a game. She wasn't recording or anything like that. She was focused on partying and having a good time with her friends and had forgotten about singing. It was a passion she had inside, but everybody was into music.

'Being ten years older than her I was the one who was focused on a career. But the majority of the time they were thinking about partying and enjoying life. I never heard anything from her about school. I'd ask, "What do you want to do with your life?" She never said anything like "go to university" or this or that. I think she said she wanted to be famous, but more like a joke, not very serious.'

Antonio detected something deeper was going on, as if something had happened to sour the musical experience for Rita.

'She told me that she was working with this guy,' he said. 'There was some issue with dating or some guy much older than her ... there was some trouble, something happened. She was talking about this older guy who was trying it on with her. I was like, "Oh, be careful, these guys are my age or older". At one point actually I remember she said to Mishka, "Fuck it", but she never really gave me any details.'

This man 'trouble' would have come around the time when Rita had her production deal. Through Martin Terefe she was working with a number of artists. Her invitation to sing on the Craig David demo had been a great success. Rita's textured vocals were the perfect compliment to Craig's soulful tune. The song 'Awkward' was going to make his new album *Trust Me*, released in 2007.

The album was launched in 2007 but came amid a torrid time for Craig in the press. Seven years after he had been the darling of the media, he found himself at the mercy of unflattering tabloid attention. Given he was someone who'd once sang how he made love four days a week, and had already dated a series of models including Sofia Vergera (now a star on *Modern Family*), who apparently dumped him in 2003 over his friendship with Beyoncé, the papers couldn't get enough once someone came forward to talk about his sexual prowess.

In June 2007 the *News of the World* reported how his glamour model girlfriend Danielle Mason, the sister of *EastEnders* star Jessie Wallace, had dumped him because he had been allegedly cheating on her.

Then a month later the same paper reported model Karina Holmes' claims that he'd been surfing Myspace for other girls to sleep with while he was still in bed with her. And just four months later escort girl Alex Wysocka told the *News of the World* how David, who had no idea she was a hooker, vainly played his own tracks while he had sex with her.

Then, by way of confirming one of their earlier stories, the *News of the World* in December that year carried an interview with model Taylor Ray who told how she had also bedded Craig and was one of the supposedly many women he had met through Myspace.

It was during this turbulent time Rita was working most closely with him.

When Craig's latest album was eventually released the reviews were less than enthusiastic. Although the music press seemed to be in agreement on one thing: in 'Awkward', he had a song worthy of his glory days and who was the female voice that so enriched this slick groove? Rita Ora's name was finally on people's lips. The listening media were sure about one thing – as the London *Evening Standard* put it, this girl was going to be a future star.

Trust Me got to number eighteen in the UK album chart – not the commercial success Rita was hoping for. Nevertheless, working with Craig had opened doors. She featured as a backing vocalist and performed live with James Morrison on his acclaimed album *Songs For You, Truths For Me*, which would come out a year after *Trust Me*.

She teamed up with Craig again – along with London rapper Tinchy Stryder – on a new song 'Where's Your Love?' for his *Greatest Hits* package to be released in 2008. Strangely though, given Rita featured in the video and appeared with Craig to perform the song on a number of occasions, most notably the MOBO Awards in 2008, her vocals were not credited.

That seemed stranger still given how much praise they heaped on each other when showcasing the tune.

Rita said of Craig's offer for her to sing on 'Awkward': 'Working with Craig was great. I wasn't signed then, I was just a girl trying to sing. From there things just escalated. I was originally meant to record the "Awkward" track as a demo and then it just came out and people really liked it. That's how I kept singing and then I met Tinchy and it just kind of escalated from there.

'Craig kept me on that track then the doors suddenly opened and people were like, "Who IS this? What's this girl ABOUT?" ... Which is something I'm still grateful to Craig for to this day.'

Craig said of Rita at the MOBO Awards: 'The beautiful Rita Ora ... I should intro Rita properly. She sang "Awkward" on the last album *Trust Me* but in my opinion is one of the best vocalists I've heard for a long, long time. I'm biased – she's eighteen years old, young, fresh, looks amazing and can sing. This girl is the next big thing.'

Even DJ Miotajam, who interviewed the pair backstage at the

MOBOs said: 'Listen, Rita, the first time I heard you was at a little industry listening party for Craig David's last album and they played this track "Awkward" and everyone was like, "Who the hell is that girl on there?" You smashed it to pieces.'

The common denominator, besides Martin Terefe, between Rita, Craig and James Morrison was Fraser T Smith (real name Fraser Lance Thorneycroft-Smith), an English Grammy award-winning producer, songwriter and musician. As well as Fraser helping out his more illustrious artists, he seemed to be turning his attention to Rita. At the MOBOs she appeared reinvigorated by what lay in store.

'It's good,' she said. 'Getting to know everyone Craig introduced me to and working with Tinch, it's just amazing and, like, it's finally my time. Craig's helping me out a little bit on some writing skills. I'm doing a couple things with Fraser too, Fraser's helping me out. So everything's finally fitting into place. Like, the package is going to come this way so you lot best watch out.'

Sadly 'Where's Your Love?' – despite being a favourite of samplers – limped to number fifty-eight when it was released as a single.

Rita's career seemed to have stalled once more before it really got started.

What happened to make it turn sour?

It seems curious that such mutual appreciation did not lead to something more substantial, either personally or professionally. Did Rita have feelings for Craig that weren't returned?

For the record Craig began dating former Miss Manchester Francesca Neill, who would go on to become a make-up artist for *The X Factor* and Girls Aloud, in 2007.

This was a period when Rita was discovering her sexuality, but as with many teenagers the path to love was not a smooth one. She spoke of this time in a very honest television interview broadcast in 2013 – the more explosive content from which will be explored in a later chapter. Speaking of other men, she told of her frustration at discovering guys whose respect she thought she'd earned only really wanted her for sex.

'I can't begin to tell you how confident I felt when a man was interested in me,' she said. 'I felt like I was sexy, I felt like I had a form of respect, I felt like he listened to me. Now I know he listened to me because he wanted to have sex with me. I felt good. I would wear low tops. I would put red lipstick on, I would make my hair blonder. My mum would just completely be like, "What are you doing?" I think that's what got me dressing crazy, why I love crazy clothes. Because my mum always let me freely express myself. Don't get me wrong, even to this day if someone fancied me I'd feel great.'

Despite her relationship angst, Rita tried to remain on the surface as bubbly as ever.

'I never saw Rita sad,' Antonio said. 'Even if something happened at home or with her parents, she would always find a way to laugh and be happy. Maybe she had a goal of wanting to be a singer. She wasn't insecure. Sometimes she would worry over being in a bit of trouble like over a guy. She was never very serious. She was very positive all the time.'

A more resilient, wiser Rita had emerged. 'I thought I might make it when I was fourteen, when I was signed to a production company,' she recalled. 'That didn't work out. A year later, I was signed to a management company, but that didn't really work out either. There were a lot of promises, but nothing came of them. The important thing is you believe that it's going to happen eventually, and that keeps you going despite rejections and other things coming to nothing.'

It might not have looked as though she was taking her music seriously but she was plugging away, hoping every time she performed someone was listening. She continued to sing at least, whether it was in a bar where she had to lie about her age, or in her dad's pub.

'Before I would sing [at dad's pub] and he loved it,' Rita recalled. 'He's asked me sometimes and I've done it for fun. We have great celebrations – my mum's birthday, Kosovan independence day. Sometimes I sing randomly but it's never like an organised thing. And then everyone leaves and it's just us in there.'

She sang at YoYo, a Notting Hill nightclub popular with industry types like Mark Ronson, and a place she attended regularly. She appeared vaguely on the radars of A&R scouts – the people who match artists with the right labels, producers and songwriters – but there was no grand plan.

Although Rita's predicament was only partly her fault, her parents were understandably upset. It was like everything that happened merely confirmed what they'd feared.

Rita and her parents regularly clashed – until one huge fall-out dwarfed them all.

She explained: 'My mum and dad were really disappointed 'cause they're very traditional. Albanian is a very traditional background. I didn't speak to them [properly] for a few years so I had to find my way and then I got enough money to travel, play guitars and go around bars and just sing. I would sing Destiny's Child songs, anything that anybody would listen to. I was like "I need to sing."'

Although she was trying to do music on her own terms the temptation to fall off the rails must have been massive. With little prospects, she could have blown her cash on drugs and wasted her young life like countless other disaffected youth. Certainly she came into contact with people who had gone down that route.

'I had nothing to do with drugs,' she said, 'but I was around it and in all honesty it's an experience that I don't really wish on anybody, but unfortunately some people are raised in that community and you have to really make the most of what you have at your disposal in a good, safe way.'

She had to do something – or risk falling between the cracks forever.

'It was just a moment in my life where it was I either do something with my life or I just sit on this block and just sell weed with the rest of my friends,' Rita said.

And so she continued to graft in the hope it would lead to something meaningful. 'It is all these little steps that make a difference,' she went on. 'At the time you think it is hell because no one is listening to you and no one cares. I was scared and thought, "What am I gonna do?"'

Around 2008, when her collaborations with Craig were released, she returned to Kosovo, to visit her grandmother's house in Pristina.

Being back in her homeland would have helped give her some perspective. She loved visiting not just her grandparents but also her other relatives. In particular she was developing a close bond with her cousin Amantina Tolaj, someone who would soon be by her side, thick and thin.

When she was back she was putting a brave face on her prospects. 'I told everyone, "I want to be a singer" and everyone was like, "Yeah, yeah," and I was like, "I swear I'm gonna do it, you watch."'

If that was going to be true she needed to take things into her own hands. Rita needed to be noticed.

For that to happen she had to do something desperate.

6

Making Her Mind Up

THE flowing curly locks were more blonde than brown, the lips though were not yet vibrant red. But the smile was unmistakable.

The viewing British public was getting their first glimpse of Rita Ora – and she dazzled.

It was a scenario TV audiences were well used to: the sparse room, the po-faced judges, the nervous hopeful desperate not to blow their one chance of fame.

'Next in is eighteen-year-old Rita from London,' announced Graham Norton's voiceover.

And there she was – Rita, singing her heart out for the chance to represent her adopted country in the Eurovision Song Contest 2009. She was actually still only seventeen when she auditioned but had turned eighteen by the time of broadcast.

If the first thing BBC One viewers saw was the fresh-faced beauty, stripped of any major style statements save for some bling in the way of huge gold earrings and multiple bracelets, the next thing they would have noticed was the voice. Stamping her own authority on 'Get Here', a song made famous by Oleta Adams, Rita showed astonishing control of a voice that was textured, vulnerable and rousing all at the same time.

First we saw her, dressed in a Fred Perry T-shirt going through her paces in front of producers. Next it was her turn to impress Andrew Lloyd Webber, whose song the winner would take to Eurovision, and here viewers saw Rita stripped down to a white vest top over a black bra.

'It's very scary but hopefully I can blow them away,' a visibly nervous Rita said to camera. 'We'll see how it goes. Oh my God.'

'She doesn't need gimmicks,' Lloyd Webber's sidekick said, while the impresario himself concurred: 'I wouldn't bother with any choreographer or anything with her.'

'I wish I could be in that room, like a little fly right now,' Rita said, as she awaited their verdict.

Looking back at footage it's fascinating to see Rita on the other side of the audition process, given her recent appearances as a judge on *The Voice* and now *The X Factor*. She knows exactly how the young hopefuls feel.

She needn't have worried. Blow them away she did. However there was to be a twist.

'Rita was offered the chance to sing for the country,' Graham Norton informed viewers, 'but decided this challenge wasn't for her.'

TV viewers, raised on a diet of reality shows, hadn't seen anything like it. A winner turning it down?

What the TV audience didn't know was that it was a deeply confusing time for Rita and she was in turmoil over what to do.

She'd entered the show out of desperation. After failing to make the breakthrough she reluctantly turned to that mainstream tried-and-tested route – reality TV. She looked at the big one – Simon Cowell's much maligned but success-laden juggernaut.

But Rita said: 'I was too scared to enter *The X Factor*. I had nothing else to do.'

Explaining the thinking behind auditioning for Eurovision, she said: 'I was at that point in my life where I really didn't know what was going to happen. I'd just finished college and I was working in a trainer shop. I didn't have a record deal, I wasn't signed and I got scared. I just wanted to do anything. Anyone can relate to me if they love something so much and will take any crack at making it somehow.

'I went in for the Eurovision Song Contest and did my first audition. It all went great. It had gone so well that I'm sure something might have come of it. I would have been representing Great Britain. But as soon as I walked out of the room after auditioning, I just knew it wasn't the right thing.

'Right from the start I was like, "What am I doing here?"'

Vera could sense her daughter's desperation – but she worried whether she was making the right move. She feared Rita appearing on reality TV could kill her career before it even started.

Both Rita and Vera felt she needed help. And there was someone they could call.

Back when Rita had been offered the production deal by Martin Terefe, she'd contacted SSB Solicitors, a company founded by artist agent Sarah Stennett and business partner Paul Spraggon. Since then Stennett had grown to become one of the biggest and most influential names in the music industry.

According to Stennett, what happened next was that Vera rang her asking for help.

'We met in a café,' Stennett recalled. 'She [Rita] was sat at a table, chewing her hair. I looked at her and felt immediately there was something about her. I said, "If you can sing like you say you can, I'd walk out of that show." She rang me the next morning and said, "I've walked out."'

Stennett remembers she had never heard Rita sing before telling her to quit the show.

Rita's version is slightly different. She goes back to that early music production deal and says their contact dates back to then.

'It really happened from when I was sixteen I think, fifteen, sixteen,' Rita said. 'I was in the middle of a very difficult production deal. I just wanted to do music. I didn't have enough money to really do a lot of things. You know, my parents were providing everything but ... I then bumped into Sarah through a lawyer of mine at the time who helped me do the contract for my old production company. And ... that's Sarah. Sarah works with Paul and he introduced us and she said, "Yeah, but I'm really busy, I've got something to do, I've got things to do, I'm really busy."

'I said, "Please, can we just have a coffee, I just want to talk to you just about my life, just for a second?" She was like, "Oh, well, alright then." So we sat down and literally in about fifteen minutes she put me in the studio. And she said, "Really, you want to do this?" and I said, "Yeah, I just want to record music and write."'

What they both agree on is that Stennett was in no doubt Rita had to quit the show if she was serious about her career.

It was a huge moment for Rita. 'I was incredibly nervous because I was just seventeen [when the audition was filmed] and I was making this really big decision to pull out.'

The repercussions were immediate. The show's producers grew frantic.

'I did my song and walked out,' Rita said. 'No one knew what to do. They started looking for me, calling my agent.' When finally they got hold of her they respected her decision. 'Amazingly, the BBC producers were unbelievably kind and supportive,' she said, 'which made me feel more sure of myself artistically. I wasn't going because I had another option, I was going because it wasn't right.'

She added: 'I thought, "I am a real musician and a songwriter, and if it is meant to be someone will see me."'

The following day Rita says she called Stennett up and told her what happened. 'She went, "Shit! Now I really have to do something with this girl,"' Rita quipped. 'I was like, "So, now what? I dropped out of the show so what we doing?" She was like, "Oh here we go."'

Stennett did get Rita into the studio and knew she could do something with her. Rita remembers Stennett getting right on the phone to one of her industry contacts. '"Hiya, I found this girl and I really think that it would be great if she, you know, do you want to give it a try?" So that's how we met,' Rita says. 'Literally it was that simple and a week later I just kind of harassed her and didn't leave her side and now I can't get enough of her.'

Rita had taken a huge gamble but one upside was that she now had one of the most powerful people in music in her corner – and one of the few women at the top. In Sarah Stennett, Rita – or her mother – could not have chosen a more formidable ally.

'She's got balls, and she's from Liverpool,' said Rita. 'She speaks her mind and is not afraid of any powerful person in the male-dominated music industry.'

Stennett's Turn First Artists, a management and development agency based in West London, was at the time snapping up some of the hottest new talent around. Her agency had been building ever since acquiring the Sugababes in 1998. Now she had Rita, Ellie Goulding, Conor Maynard and Iggy Azalea who would all soon become household names.

As well as co-founding the law firm SSB, which represented Adele, Sarah and her husband George Astasio set up the songwriting/ production team The Invisible Men, which co-wrote a string of chart successes including Girls Aloud's 'The Show', 'No Tomorrow', a number one smash for Astasio's own band the American rockers Orson, and 'Don't Upset The Rhythm (Go Baby Go)' for the Noisettes.

What made Stennett even more unique was that there was no one like her in the industry. Female A&Rs, managers and agents had all made their name but not doing all three jobs.

Vera and Rita hoped that Turn First, being female led, would mean it was equipped to look after her interests.

'It's a very scary business for solo artists, and (managing them is) a big responsibility,' Stennett said. 'I don't know if it's a gender thing, but there are times when a female approach is successful. It's a maternal approach. People fulfill their potential when they're not scared and feel supported.'

Stennett knew making Rita a success would not come down to just tying her down to a big record label. Today's artists had to be built with care. As much was down to image, a social-media presence and backing from all sorts of quarters, as the music. Radio play by influential DJs would be crucial, as would presence on Shazam, an app that let fans identify songs they heard playing.

'Before a major will commit, they want to see signs of life,' Stennett said. 'If you've got a record playing in a club, kids will Shazam it, and that shows on the Shazam chart.'

It wouldn't have been what Rita wanted to hear. She was desperate for something to happen immediately to compensate for bailing out of such a high-profile show. She had to be patient. Her career had to be managed carefully. She might only have one shot at making it. At least, however, she had one of the business's big beasts paying attention.

And, despite her rejection of Eurovision, Rita said she was still a fan of the competition.

'It's a great contest that has been going on for years,' she said. 'The Brits have a long history of having failed on Eurovision but I still watch it. My mum and dad watched it and we have followed it for years. I'm not knocking it. But it wasn't my thing.'

The task of representing Britain was instead given to Jade Ewen, one of Rita's contemporaries from Sylvia Young. She went on to finish a credible fifth in Moscow, later becoming a Sugababe herself when she replaced Keisha Buchanan.

A few years down the road Rita would incur the wrath of Ewen for suggesting she got a lucky escape by pulling out.

'Imagine!' she said in one interview. 'If I'd stayed, it would probably have been all over for me. At best, I'd be a contestant on that diving show *Splash!*'

Jade, who did end up on the Tom Daley-inspired diving reality TV show *Splash!*, wasn't happy. She tweeted a response on Twitter. The *Evening Standard* reported she posted: 'Easy to mock when you are enjoying success. Eurovision and Splash? Proud of both.'

Rita would get her five minutes of fame when the recording of the Eurovision series aired. But her TV appearance didn't immediately lead to offers. Time was running out on the deal she'd struck with her dad. If she hadn't made it as a singer she had to go back to school.

Elena, who by then was well into a degree at university, encouraged her to go back. Rita couldn't face returning to a specialist college so opted for a regular establishment the following autumn.

'There are so many people leaving there [from schools like that] each year as brilliant performers, plus all the other schools putting out the same amount of quality,' she said. 'I didn't want to go to another performing arts college after I'd done my GCSEs, although most of my friends did. I just went to a regular college and carried on writing my songs. I followed my gut, really.'

Rita enrolled at St Charles Catholic Sixth Form College, just north of Ladbroke Grove Underground station and a fifteen-minute walk from her house. She studied a Performing Arts A-Level and her teacher James Falconer remembers how she immediately made an impact.

'It was clear from the start Rita had a stand-out voice,' he said. 'But there's always talent at St Charles. It wasn't just Rita's voice or her having a certain kind of look that made her stand out, it was the fact that she was already taking small steps in the industry.'

She wasn't your average student. James recalled one day when he came into class to find Rita camped in front of a computer with some other students.

'They were watching her do backing vocals with Craig David on YouTube,' he said. 'The kids were well impressed and frankly I was too because I was thinking, "Good, she's actually doing something with that voice of hers."'

James was also impressed that Rita liked to be taken out of her comfort zone and wasn't afraid to take on new styles of music.

'One of the things I used to do in Performing Arts lessons – because I used to cover the music side of lessons – I used to play students the Amy Winehouse version of "Valerie". I used to give them the lyrics and get them to sing along,' he said. 'Some of the kids had never sung before and some of the kids were just taking up the subject for extra points. But most sang along with the track.

'Sometimes I followed that with Snow Patrol's "Chasing Cars". That was hard work because you've got to push the students out of their comfort zones – it may be a great song but the class didn't know it as well and would just want to do the Amy Winehouse number and move on to something else. But Rita quite impressed me because she seemed to understand what it was about. She understood the value of repetition and, more importantly, she wanted to try to do "Chasing Cars".

'While most of the students were saying, "Ugh, sir, what's this rubbish?" she was more like, "No, I like this, let's give it a try, guys." So, even though she wanted to get on with her peers, and she did, she was prepared to speak her mind musically when the easy option would have just been to follow the crowd. So that was one thing that really stood out for me about her time at St Charles.'

Even so, Rita was by no means a model student. Her time keeping was a constant problem.

'I'm sure she used Craig David gigs as an excuse for coming in late,' James said. 'But as a teacher, it doesn't matter if you're hanging out with the Queen the night before, you need to get in on time and you need to go to your lessons.'

It frustrated him so much that one day he reached boiling point and decided to pull her up about it.

When Rita turned up he marched her into his office. She had better have a good reason for not being in class. As a teacher he'd heard all the excuses under the sun. Rita's response had better be good.

She didn't disappoint.

'I've been in New York,' she said calmly. 'Meeting Jay Z. He wants to sign me.'

7

Roc the Life

GOING shopping in Boots for contact lens solution doesn't sound like a life-changing activity. It was in Rita Ora's case.

She was in Kensington High Street when her phone rang. She glanced at the screen. It was an international number. Thinking it was her grandma calling from Pristina she answered.

It wasn't grandma. It was Jay Brown, right-hand man to Jay Z, founder of the Roc Nation record label and one of the most powerful men in the music industry.

'What's up?' he said.

'What's up?' Rita replied, as if taking a call from one of her pals.

'Have you ever been to New York?' Brown said after he'd introduced himself.

Panicking, Rita stammered: 'No, but if you give me a few weeks, I'll build up some money.' In her head she was mentally clocking up how many extra hours at Size? she'd have to work to earn the cash.

Brown laughed. 'Can you get here tomorrow? Jay would like to meet you.'

Had she heard that right? Jay Z? Hip hop god, discoverer of Rihanna – the hottest rapper alive – and husband of Beyoncé, one of her all-time heroes? That Jay Z?!

Brown said it was.

Oh my God!!

Rita raced home. She had to tell her mum, she had to work out what to wear, she had to catch a flight ... to New York! To meet Jay Z!

Was this even happening?!

On the way home – which must have felt like one of the longest journeys of her life – she tried to compute what was going on.

Her mind flashed back to a gig some months ago in Koko, a hot music venue in Camden, one of London's trendiest neighbourhoods. Rita had gone there to catch Lykke Li, the acclaimed Swedish singer who was breaking new ground with her fusion of indie pop and electronica. There, Briony Turner, a scout for A&M Records, owned by Universal, came up to her. She remembered Rita from her recent recordings.

'What you doing?' Briony asked. 'I haven't heard anything since the Craig times.'

Rita shrugged. 'Just been gigging and trying to get my face everywhere, singing where I can sing.'

Briony was surprised nothing had come of Rita's recent exposure. She'd urged her to come for a meeting and give her some demos. Rita had duly obliged.

'I have a perfect guy I think would really work for you,' Briony said.

At the time Rita paid little attention. She'd heard it all before from A&Rs. Everyone promised the world. No one delivered.

But now she started thinking … could the man Briony was talking about have been Jay Z?!

She burst into her house like a raging bull.

'Mum, I'm out of here!!'

Vera had her work cut out trying to calm her daughter down. She was bouncing off the walls, racing around, rifling through clothes. When she finally got the story out of Rita she was bemused.

'She didn't even know who Jay Z was,' Rita laughed.

'You know, Jay Z!' Rita started singing lines from '99 Problems But A Bitch Aint One'.

'I know this song!' Vera said, still not really grasping who Rita was talking about

'Beyoncé's husband?!'

'Right!' Now Vera understood.

'Mum, I'm going to New York tomorrow, I'm about to meet Jay Z!! You don't understand. I'm really excited!!'

Vera couldn't believe it – but as much as she wanted to share in her daughter's excitement her mothering instinct kicked in.

'Then she just said to me, you know, the whole mum stuff,' Rita recalled. '"Do you have money, are you going to be alright?" And then she called my cousin up and was like, "Can you look after her while she's out there?"'

It was November 2008, two weeks before her eighteenth birthday. Rita caught a flight to New York's JFK airport the following day. It was her first trip to America and she was doing it alone. 'I didn't sleep 'cause I was so nervous.'

Her mind must have been racing. What would the meeting be like? In an office looking out over Central Park, or in one of the state-of-the-art studios where Jay Z works his magic?

By the time her flight landed she had no time to stop, change, sort herself out. She had to get to his studio. She was meeting him straight away.

'I was wearing a Run DMC T-shirt, my hair was wet 'cause it was raining, it was cold. I just didn't know what was going to happen. I landed and didn't even have a shower.'

Here was Rita, the girl who never went to school without her red lipstick perfect, on her way to the most important meeting of her life looking like a mess!

She couldn't let it get to her though. She just had to make a good impression. Her life depended on it.

'It was a moment I couldn't really believe was happening,' she recalled. 'I didn't have time to absorb everything that was going on. Because I was like, "Alright, I have to snap up fast and stay where I deserved to stay."'

The meeting would take place in Jay Z's Roc The Mic studios on 27th Street in Manhattan. The address might have meant nothing to Rita but it sat just four blocks away from 'Club Row', a section of 27th Street featuring some of the city's trendiest nightclubs like Bungalow 8 and Marquee.

Rita arrived at the studio for her audience with the man who could change everything for her. She was shaking with nerves.

'It was literally like meeting God.

'You know when you can feel someone's power? It was like that. You could just tell when you walked in the room that he was powerful and successful. It was so odd.'

She was led to a booth where he was holding court. 'I was tired and jet-lagged, it was not the ideal moment. I thought, "Oh, I've got to do it." I just went, "Hey" and held out my hand,' she said.

'He said hello and shook my hand. I couldn't speak for a few minutes, which is unusual.'

'You have a firm handshake!' Jay Z told her. 'I like that.'

'It was a real pinch-yourself moment,' Rita said. 'And the meeting we had when I met Jay Z was just unbelievable. It was so nerve-wracking, interesting, exciting and weird all at the same time.

'I walked in, shook his hand and then we were suddenly having a conversation.'

For Rita to be nervous was healthy. It showed how much she cared. But she needn't have been worried. They shared the same star sign, which meant, as well as having the same desire to entertain, they were both independently minded but fiercely loyal.

'We just clicked. He's Sagittarius, I'm Sagittarius,' she said.

Jay Z has a formidable reputation but in one-on-one situations those who know him say he likes to put people at ease. He had no desire to make Rita feel uncomfortable. He played her some music, allowed her to describe the type of sounds she liked. 'He played some music, I played some music – it was kind of like a DJ battle.' It was like hanging out with a cool cousin … just a ridiculously rich cousin – and one who had bodyguards! And Rita was to quickly find out how closely his minders stuck to him. Just after she had shaken hands with Jay Z one of the bodyguards stepped on her shoes. 'Brand new Air Jordans,' she said.

Rita's shoe-shop attitude instinctively kicked in – but Jay Z was about to give her a glimpse into another world.

'I knelt down to rub them clean, 'cause that's what you're supposed to do,' she said. 'But Jay Z grabbed me by the shoulders, pulled me up and went, "Don't ever do that. Come with me." And then … we went sneaker shopping. A whole suitcase of sneakers!'

She couldn't believe this was the world she was entering. She'd always believed she had the talent and deserved to be there. 'The good thing was they saw it in me,' she said. 'Other people did, but never had the balls to actually be like, "Let's do this." As soon as I met them I wanted to be a part of it.'

Part of it she soon would be. And Jay Z was equally gushing about his new protégée.

'You can see the potential,' he said. 'When she enters a room it changes ... and that presence – you can't duplicate it, especially at a young age. It was just infectious, like "Man, she loves this ..." She's driven in that way.'

Both were just as impressed with the other. Jay Z's gut feeling about her had been confirmed. His mind was made up. She was worth taking a risk on.

'They said, "You're a star" and offered me a record deal,' Rita said. 'I was so happy.'

Rita may now recount the story quite matter-of-factly but at the time she was flailing around in a tidal wave of emotion. Jay Z offering her a deal? It scarcely seemed possible. After two years of plugging away she had finally got THE break.

And in the end, after production and management deals, reality TV and performing at high-profile award shows, it was the old-fashioned route that got her there: a low-key gig, a chance meeting, a switched-on A&R, the one phone call that had made all the difference.

In time Rita would find out the other factors that came into play to set up that meeting.

After hearing about Rita, Jay Brown had called Sarah Stennett to help set it up. Demos were emailed and that's what prompted the call to whisk her to New York. The reason she'd been so nervous about meeting her idol was that, not only was Jay Z a hip hop mega star, he was also on his way to becoming one of America's richest businessmen, building an empire that would one day be worth over a billion dollars – and on first-name terms with US President Barack Obama.

Jay Z's rise was every bit as remarkable as Rita's. Born Shawn Carter and raised in Brooklyn by his mum after his dad walked out on the family, he could have stayed on course with an emerging life of crime before music proved to be his saviour. A crack cocaine dealer, he endured a bruising education on the streets of New York, being shot at three times and witnessing murder at just nine years old. But dealing drugs and covering the backs of friends taught him business skills and the meaning of loyalty. Rapping earned him the nickname 'Jazzy' which morphed into the name he's now known by the world over.

Under that moniker he had released ten albums by the time he met Rita, the latest of which, *American Gangster,* put him level with Elvis Presley in terms of number one albums in the US.

He was the former chief executive of Def Jam records and had launched the careers of Rihanna, Kanye West and Shakira among others. In 2008 he courted controversy by appearing as headliner at the Glastonbury Festival, a move that incurred the wrath of traditional rockers like Noel Gallagher and prompted Jay Z to open with a cover of 'Wonderwall'.

That same year he had founded a new label, Roc Nation, and by the time he summoned Rita to meet him was on the hunt for new talent.

Not only was Rita coming face to face with one of her idols – in April 2008 he had married another of her heroes, Beyoncé, turning them into America's most powerful showbiz couple. Would that mean she'd soon meet her too?

It was an incredible turnaround in her fortunes but Rita would find out later the meeting was nearly postponed. She has Sarah Stennett to thank for hurrying it along.

'Rita was super excited to meet Jay Z,' Sarah said. 'But it nearly never happened. As it was very close to Christmas we were supposed to postpone the meeting until the New Year. I had a conversation with Jay and said to him, "Look, you should get in immediately. It doesn't matter if it's just a quick meeting. Just do it and see what you think."

'They agreed and flew her out there and within forty-eight hours we did the deal. They were in absolutely no doubt the moment they met her. Jay Brown and Jay Z saw the potential and said, "Let's do it!"'

'As soon as I got there everything turned into a rollercoaster,' Rita said. 'It was crazy. I'm never going to forget it for the rest of my life. It was like walking into your own dream coming true. I knew this one person could change my life forever.'

With the offer of a record deal, Rita thought all her dreams had come true. But she did have one obstacle to overcome first. Her parents wanted to satisfy themselves that this was as good a deal on paper as it promised to be.

They might have been frustrated with how things had gone for Rita – and even by her own attitude at times. But they only wanted the best for their daughter and when she needed them they immediately stepped up. Vera, herself a formidable operator, wanted to meet Jay Z face to face. After everything Rita had been through, Vera wanted to satisfy herself that he had only the best intentions for her daughter.

And so, before long Rita returned to New York – this time with her mum. Jay Z responded with his own charm offensive – he brought along his superstar wife Beyoncé.

If Rita had been nervous the first time she visited Manhattan it was nothing compared to how she felt meeting a woman who more than most had reshaped the role of women in pop and R'n'B.

'The first time I met her I was so nervous,' Rita said. 'I hugged her and told her she was my inspiration.'

She might have been praying that everyone got on. What she wasn't prepared for was how her mum would crash her party.

'My mum is embarrassing around Jay Z and Beyoncé,' Rita said. 'She starts talking about when I was a baby and my nappy rashes. When they first met, my mum said to Jay, "Are you the one who sang, '99 Problems'? He said, "Yeah," and my mum goes, "You've got the baddest bitch," and points to Beyoncé.

'After that it was, "See ya later, Rita," and it was all about my mum and Jay!'

Jay Z and Beyoncé might be America's power couple but Rita was amazed how smitten they were with each other. 'They are so in love,' she said. 'They made me believe that true love really does exist.'

The big meeting went well. Vera was happy it would finally be the chance her daughter deserved.

Rita could now do what she always wanted to – devote her time to music. But, before she could embark on her new life she had some loose ends to tie up.

That's when she returned to St Charles Sixth Form College to explain why she'd been missing class.

Teacher James Falconer said: 'When a teenage student tells you something like that, it would be reasonable to have some doubt. But, I believed her. I knew she was doing other stuff anyway and why should she lie? She asked me if I knew who Jay Z was, which was a fair enough question. Of course, I did know who he was.

'It wasn't the normal thing you hear from a teenager and, of course, it turned out to be true. I didn't quiz her much about it. I was thinking straight away, "She must be destined for something to get a deal like that."'

As her teacher, James wouldn't have been doing his job if he didn't point out some hard truths to her.

'I would have no doubt said, "Obviously you've got some decisions to make, Rita. I'm really pleased for you but obviously if you want to do the A-levels you need to attend and put the work in."'

Rita probably appreciated the concern and the reality check but there was only one decision she had to make.

'I don't remember seeing her much after that,' James said.

Unsurprisingly, given how excited she was, Rita dropped out of her course. She had only been there for a few months.

At Size? Rita's manager Antonio had moved on to a new job by the time Rita's big break happened and she handed in her notice. But he revealed how he bumped into her after her meeting with Jay Z.

'I ended up in the same club with Rita a couple of times. She was like, "Oh Tony, we miss you." She was telling me, "Oh, things are happening, the music is getting more serious," but she didn't really go into details. Then after a couple of months these guys were like, "Did you hear about Rita? She met with Jay Z and he is going to do something with her," and I was like, "Shut up, man, what are you saying?" At the time it wasn't clear, it was just rumours.'

Antonio is delighted Rita made it. 'She is living the dream,' he beamed. And although she occasionally used to moan about her job he says her time in Size? helped her. 'It's a good job for young girls working at a store like that. I think it was the same for her. People were impressed when you told them you worked for Size? – I think she was pretty excited. For a young girl, having her first job in a sneaker store, it was a good deal.'

Rita returned to New York and Jay Z treated her to a night out, introducing her to some of his entourage. And there was a special surprise when Kanye arrived to meet her. Jay Z revealed he would be working with her at some point. Her boss also wanted her to appear in his latest video alongside then-hot producer Mr Hudson. 'Young Forever' would be released in January 2010. Her presence in the finished promo might have been one of those blink-and-you'll-miss-it appearances but Rita didn't mind. She was in dreamland. The invitation seemed to be an endorsement of his decision to hire her. She thought it would only build from there. She would surely be appearing on American chat shows soon. She was Roc Nation's new rising star. The singles, albums, TV appearances and all the other trappings and trinkets that came with that status were just around the corner.

What she wasn't expecting was that Roc Nation had other ideas.

'Rita, relax,' Jay Z told her. 'You've got us. Wait. Find yourself.'

Rita couldn't believe what she was hearing. What?!

His advice to her was to be patient, to find out who she was and what she had to write about.

Rita felt she'd been spending the last few years finding herself. She was itching to get on.

'It was a frustrating time,' Rita said, but that must be an almighty understatement. After several false dawns she was desperate for this to be her time. She had no choice but to be patient.

Jay Z's plan was for Rita to move to New York. They would find a place for her in trendy Brooklyn, where he grew up. By immersing herself in the community, Rita would be getting a crash course in the culture and street vibe of this foreign city.

'With Jay Z being from Brooklyn I had to go there and be involved, be a part of the beginning of a journey that I didn't know how it would turn out,' she said.

It was a huge move for Rita, who had never lived on her own before.

'I went from sharing one bedroom with my sister to my own amazing flat in Brooklyn,' she said. 'It was shit scary – I'd never lived alone! NY made me grow up very fast. It's full of energy, it makes you want to wake up and do something. Everybody's going somewhere.'

Taking on board Jay Z's advice, Rita spent time thinking about the type of album she wanted to produce.

'All I thought about was music. I couldn't cook, didn't care,' she said. 'I ate buffalo wings every day, didn't wash my clothes.'

Whenever she needed advice she could call upon Jay Z for guidance and his wife.

'Beyoncé is great too. She is such a great inspiration. She is one of my idols, so to have her physically in my face, being really helpful, is like a dream come true. It's a really nice feeling. One minute I'm singing Destiny's Child's "Say My Name" in my dad's pub and the next I'm sitting here asking Beyoncé does she think this song is right for my album?

'Even people who have never met her or don't know her can tell that she is one of the nicest people. She is one of the most genuine people I have ever met.'

Outsiders might assume Rita was given a huge signing-on cheque but in a fascinating interview with *hitquarters.com* Sarah Stennett revealed a lot more care goes into the development of artists.

'We try to do things quietly and not build any expectation of excess,' she explained. 'If you put £10,000 into their bank account every month then it sets an expectation. Manage the money, manage the artist; it's about not giving too much too soon. Quite often they're young kids that live off very little money, work in part-time jobs or are living off their parents.

'We generally give the artist a salary. We pay them monthly just like you would in any other job. We try to teach them to understand that the people investing in them are investing in their future and so they trust them to be responsible and act like an adult about the investment. The rock and roll days where you just show up at work and sell ten million albums are long gone. It's a trust thing. The money will come, but you have to do your apprenticeship.

'Roc Nation invested in Rita Ora's development and that's an investment of time, effort and resources,' she added.

In order to get her name out they sent Rita on a gruelling tour of the US, playing in some obscure venues. 'I played a funfair in Flint, Michigan,' she said.

It was exciting for her to see parts of America she never knew existed. But it could also be miserable. In one bar in somewhere she can only recall was 'the middle of America' she felt as low as she'd ever been on stage.

'No one was paying attention,' she said. 'Plan B was there and he told me not to worry because he had to sing to two people in some random place too. It's fine. I'll win them over one fan at a time if I have to.'

Rita might have been feeling down but that attitude showed how determined she was to succeed.

Jay Z's right-hand man Tyran 'Ty Ty' Smith took Rita under his wing and between them both set up meetings with some of the hottest acts in music as well as some collaborators to help her hone her sound.

'Ty has been incredible with her,' Sarah Stennett said. 'He's given Rita the space to develop into the artist she is now. I have the utmost respect for the whole Roc Nation team. Rita really needed the time and she was given that.'

Then Rita got the news she'd been waiting for ... Roc Nation wanted her to start recording – and they were lining up a host of top names to work with her.

Rita could scarcely believe the roster. In addition to Kanye, she was promised established rapper-producer will.i.am and Drake, a red-hot Canadian rapper fast becoming a household name in North America at the time.

'It was amazing to be introduced to loads of great songwriters and producers,' Rita said. 'I met Kanye West, Drake and will.i.am all through Jay.'

Regarding Drake, her timing couldn't have been more perfect as he was coming off a hugely successful year. 'Best I Ever Had', from his first EP *So Far Gone* had soared to number two on the American Billboard chart, denied the top spot only by will.i.am's Black Eyed Peas' 'I Gotta Feeling' and he'd had three further top-forty hits, including 'Forever', featuring Kanye West. In four short years he would become one of the hottest hip hop acts on the planet, racking up more chart number ones than even Jay Z and earning more than $40 million.

Hailing from Toronto, the rapper, whose real name is Aubrey Drake Graham, was four years older than Rita but musically he was light years ahead with his development.

'Drake was the first person I worked with,' Rita said. 'We met through work people. He was doing his first album at this point – "Best I Ever Had" was popping off.'

The pair struck up an instant rapport and Drake had a song he thought would work well for Rita. With a working title of 'I'm Ready For You', it was a tune he'd written for Rihanna to use on her *Loud* album but the Bajan superstar had rejected it. Her decision seemed strange. Not only was it a great song but she and Drake had been enjoying a close flirtatious relationship. For Rihanna, hooking up with Drake would have been a wise move after her tumultuous relationship with R'n'B singer Chris Brown, whom she'd split from after he became violent towards her. But things were complicated, and when it looked like Rihanna was going back to Brown rumours started flying that Jay Z had ordered Drake to give the song to Rita in protest at her choice in men.

Rita wasn't interested in the background to the track. When Drake played her a demo version she loved it. The song was renamed 'R.I.P.' and Rita saw it as a cornerstone to her debut album.

'As soon as I heard it, I said it was mine. I was going to fight for that song,' she said. '"R.I.P." wasn't written for Rihanna. But even if it was played to her, I don't care.'

In return for gifting her such a powerful song, Drake asked Rita if she would appear in the video for his single 'Over', to be released in March 2010. Rita was happy to help. The song was about how Drake was coping with his newfound fame and Rita seemingly played a good girl/former love who was on the rapper's mind at the same time as an exotic stripper who caught his eye. Style-wise Rita didn't look much different to how we'd seen her with Craig David. Her role was small but it was significantly greater than the fleeting cameo appearance she made in Jay Z's 'Young Forever' video.

'He asked me for a favour,' Rita said. 'I did that favour whilst we were writing.'

There was clearly a relationship building between Rita and Drake. 'It was a very, kind of, great, natural friendship like we just built it out of nowhere,' she said.

With such chemistry between them it was inevitable Rita would be asked whether anything more developed. Rita has coyly denied they ever dated but in those early days they forged such a close bond it sustained them through the rigours of pop stardom in the years to come.

And even amid the bedlam of living inside Rihanna world, Drake still found time to pay tribute to Rita, who at the time was still basically unheard of on both sides of the Atlantic.

'I love her to death,' he said, some months after they met. 'We worked together in the "Over" video. I wrote some songs for her album. She's just a great girl. I admire her very much.'

If romantic love didn't fully blossom with Drake then sparks certainly flew with her next songwriting buddy. Bruno Mars was a talented singer whose own first forays into the music industry weren't too dissimilar from Rita's, albeit a continent apart. Mars, whose real name is Peter Gene Hernandez, was a Hawaiian who'd moved to Los Angeles to pursue his singing dreams. Instead he'd had to make do writing and producing for other people. Five years older than Rita he was now turning his attention to her – in more ways than one.

Rita and Bruno started working together and quickly she developed a serious crush on the crooner – perhaps dispelling any chance of romance with Drake.

'It was love at first sight, such a great experience,' she said candidly. 'We met in 2009. I was starting out at Roc Nation. Bruno was unknown back then too. He was a struggling songwriter hired to write songs for me. I'm not a flirt, just very friendly. I thought, "Wow, that's just the world's greatest guy!"

'Our time together was wonderful. And when we were together we were so happy. But once we got famous, work got in the way. We ended it. But we remained close.'

Bruno was clearly Rita's first serious relationship. According to her it lasted until 2011, before she had released an album.

It wasn't all play and no work in those first twelve months though. Rita recorded a number of songs, including some she collaborated on with Kanye, her Roc Nation stable mate, as Jay Z had promised. The rapper was already dominating the industry but had further cemented his place in the world's consciousness by teaming up with Jay Z. By the time he started working with Rita, however, he'd achieved ridiculous levels of notoriety and fame; first in September 2009 by storming on stage during the MTV Video Music Awards while Taylor Swift was receiving her award for Best Female Video to announce Beyoncé should have got it instead. That was almost nothing to the press attention he would get in the future when he began dating reality TV goddess Kim Kardashian. It was a controversial character she was linking up with, but Kanye gave Rita a musical education.

'Kanye is Kanye, so yes, I was a little "Wow!"' she said. 'But I've learned so much from being in the studio with him. It's been an experience. He introduced me to Motown and so many great records.'

From all her different collaborations Rita crafted enough songs for an album. She was excited. It was all coming together. She believed she'd put together an eclectic mix of styles, which showcased her talent. She started dreaming of filming her own videos.

But when she took it to Jay Z and Roc Nation they hit her with a bombshell. The songs were fine but they didn't think they sounded authentic. They weren't powerful enough, they were watered down. They wanted the real Rita.

'Start again!' Jay Z had spoken.

Rita was gutted.

She'd worked so hard. And now she had to return to the drawing board. She couldn't understand it.

Her old doubts started to return.

If those songs weren't considered good enough did she have it in her to produce the goods?

What did they want from her?

She had been given this amazing opportunity. Suddenly a new fear started to take hold.

What if she just couldn't cut it?

8

False Dawn

THE curls had gone, replaced by more sophisticated waves, while the colour was now fully blonde. Gone too were the trainers. In their place were black Doc Martens-style boots. A white sleeveless denim jacket and blue denim hot pants completed the look. Only the bright red Gwen Stefani lips remained of the girl we'd seen before.

In June 2010 Roc Nation took the wraps off their latest starlet. The world was getting its first glimpse of the new Rita Ora.

Rita featured in a short YouTube advert – or 'webisode' as it was called – promoting Aviator headphones her label had produced with Skullcandy. In the slick minute-and-a-half video Rita formally introduced herself to the music listening public for the first time.

Shot on the streets of New York, she said: 'Hi, I'm Rita, and I'm on Roc Nation. Rita Ora, but you can just call me Rita. I'm nineteen years old and I'm a singer.'

The accent sounded almost contrived but anyone who has spent time in her company would recognise that 'Ree-ah' anywhere!

The film showed Rita singing and anyone closing their eyes would have been forgiven for thinking it was a young Beyoncé. Comparisons were also swiftly made with Rihanna.

Rita gave a potted history of her life, from singing at the age of six to getting noticed at sixteen. 'I was floating around for a while and then Jay saw me and that's a wrap,' she said, showing a fresh confidence.

This was to be the first of many short clips featuring Rita. Clearly a Roc Nation strategy was to get their artist out there so she could seep into the minds of the public before the music was ready to come out.

Rita's makeover was taking shape. All she needed now were the songs to match.

Since Jay Z's withering assessment of her first batch of songs Rita had gone back to the drawing board. After she'd had time to reflect she accepted the assessment of her first set of songs was the right one.

'They weren't right for me,' she said. 'I listen back to my early songs and just don't recognise that girl.'

It was still a troubling time for her, however.

'I doubted myself in the beginning, I'll admit it,' she said. 'I'm very honest, in the beginning I didn't know what I wanted to write about. I was writing about things that weren't really that important. And my friends and family were like, "These are cool but, Rita, this doesn't feel like you."'

At the time it was hard for her not to fear that this was yet another false dawn. Now she can look back on that time philosophically. 'I was signed at eighteen and had to grow up quickly,' she said.

At least her label was behind her, still believing in her – an attitude that seems almost unbelievable in this age of instant success.

'It's incredible to have that sort of business mind behind you. It's all very well thought through and he's patient,' she said of Jay Z.

'I had to take myself out of the zone for a second – luckily I had a label that were waiting for me.'

Rita had gone back to Kosovo for the Christmas holidays. She had needed to take herself out of the zone. Get back to her roots. If she was to make an album that was a truer reflection of herself and the cosmopolitan musical background her parents provided in her childhood, then she needed to reconnect with her earlier life. When she relayed her news to family and friends, though, people were still a little sceptical. They were excited for her but admittedly they had been there before. They hoped this wasn't going to be another of those occasions when her hopes were dashed.

Back in Kosovo she had hoped to find some inspiration. What she did find was perhaps a potential love interest.

Albin Gashi was a handsome young student who was also home visiting relatives. The son of prominent lawyer Tome Gashi, Albin was dark haired with dancing eyes. It would have been easy to succumb to his charm. He was working towards a future career in artist and event management – but he looked every inch the star himself.

He was reportedly studying in San Diego and spent time in New York, which is where Rita first met him. Like her, he returned to Pristina for the Christmas holidays.

She was snapped with Albin in a Kosovan newspaper in January 2010, sparking rumours they were together. Rita looked relaxed and happy, her style reminiscent of her appearance on *Eurovision: Your Country Needs You* a year earlier. Local media reported she was spending a lot of time in the Kosovan capital while she was waiting for her career to heat up.

Whether Rita and Albin were anything more than friends is unclear but a relationship with an Albanian is something that would have pleased her parents. 'You know how they are, right, marry your own kind and it's suddenly ten times better than anything else,' she sighed.

Rita flew back revived and refreshed and was teamed up with a fresh set of collaborators, most notably Chase & Status, the English electronic duo Saul Milton and Will Kennard, and Terius Nash, better known as The-Dream, whose hit-making pedigree was unquestioned. Nash had a string of smashes to his name, including Rihanna's 'Umbrella', in 2007, and 'Single Ladies (Put A Ring On It)' for Beyoncé in 2008.

Aside from songwriters, Roc Nation had assembled an impressive list of producers for her to work with. Stargate, the Norwegian duo of Tor Erik Hermansen and Mikkel Storleer Eriksen, had produced and co-wrote Beyoncé's global monster hit 'Irreplaceable', which topped the Billboard Hot 100 chart for ten weeks, and had also enjoyed a successful partnership with Rihanna.

'I look at the list of people I've worked with and it's crazy. I've connected with people like The-Dream and shared parts of my life with him in the writing,' Rita said.

For more than a year she worked on songs, continued gigging and honed her style. In the summer of 2011 Rita spent three months in Los Angeles putting the finishing touches to her album.

There was an altogether different feeling with this second throw of the dice. Rita had been strapped in so tightly on an emotional rollercoaster since first arriving in New York, at times she felt she couldn't breathe. Yet, this time, everyone who heard her music could actually connect with some of the sentiment in her words.

Still, all of that would amount to nothing once more if the man on the throne gave Rita the thumbs down. Jay Z was her judge, jury and executioner.

The answer came, and it was a resounding "Yes!"

Finally, the fantasy life that been playing out on repeat in Rita's head since she first discovered her voice was about to become a reality.

'I'm so excited for this album to come out, you have no idea,' Rita beamed. 'I've been working on it for two whole years and I've been working with some amazing people like Chase & Status, Stargate, Tricky Stewart, Dream, will.i.am, Drake ... the list goes on. It's an amazing album. I can't wait for you all to hear it. And I'm so honoured to be working with them,' she said.

One of the songs Rita wrote with The-Dream was inspired by a city that was fast becoming a favourite, Las Vegas, where she hosted a night at Lavo nightclub.

'Vegas inspired my song "Roc The Life" which I wrote with The-Dream. It's such a crazy city, my favourite city I've been to, and we wrote the song while partying,' she said. 'It took ten minutes to write and it's going to be a huge song for me. I can't wait for my fans to hear it.'

Once back in the UK, she released a sequence of video diaries as teasers for her new material. Future fans caught a snippet of what sounded like a thumping dance-fused pop track, as she explained the thinking behind the clips.

'I'm going to let you guys see everything that I do, even when I'm mad or when I have no Tabasco or my roots grow out or I lose my red lipstick. Everything. I want you guys to see it all so there's no hiding now,' she said.

'Rita's been hiding for too long. This is now time to show you lot why I'm on Roc Nation.'

The video showed her hanging out on Portobello Road, with her best friends Mishka, her former colleague at Size?, and Kyle De'volle. Rita had trouble talking because she was losing her voice. At the end of this first diary she appealed to fans to send her lyrics, songs and ideas for things she could sing in future diaries.

'Every week I will sing for you,' she said.

Rita's mention of Tabasco sauce meant that whenever she did an interview people wanted to know more. Why did she love it so much?

'It has to be Tabasco, it's so easy to get anywhere,' she said. 'I have to have it on my eggs, pasta, toast, on my Sunday dinner.'

As Rita did the rounds of radio stations in the US, one interviewer caught her out by asking if she loved it so much would she have it with custard? She duly obliged.

'I had to eat it,' she said, grimacing. 'It was good though. One day I'm going to have to try and make myself the face of Tabasco. It's my new thing.'

Rita revealed she always carried a bottle of it around with her and a friend had a spare in their car in case of emergencies.

Rita was showing she was up for a laugh and came across as open and engaging in those early chats. She was herself. And considering she didn't yet have a hit single to fall back on, those interviews must have been particularly daunting.

When asked if she felt under pressure to deliver after all the faith shown in her by her label, she said: 'It's good pressure. It's better to be anticipated than no one really caring about your project.'

Rita continued to give fans updates of her life but by the time she posted her next one she was unable to sing as promised because of a sore throat. 'I went to the throat doctor,' she said. 'They put a camera down my throat, through my nose, saw my vocal chords. They're dead sore so I'm on a week's vocal rest. I'm on these tablets, don't know what they are.'

Instead she gave fans a sneak look at a photo shoot she'd been on, where she was channelling Marilyn Monroe in full effect. Kyle, who she revealed was now her stylist, created her look.

He described Rita's style as 'very eclectic … She loves a bit of everything. She's the only girl where any vision that I come to her with she's always up for trying it.'

He joked that he would define her style as 'Gwen Stefani meets *Where's Wally?*' – something she took exception to.

'She loves a red lip and a beanie with a little bobble on top,' he said. 'Gold, long nails, studs, anything, Rita's into it and I love working with her.'

By her third video diary, posted just after Halloween, she gave an insight into the side of being a celebrity to which many fans wouldn't give a second thought – the glamour photo shoot. Rita posed with two friends for a shoot with *The Independent*, which had them lying provocatively over a dinner table, 'drinking milk through a straw, as you do.'

This clip was also significant because Rita was filmed singing a stripped-down acoustic version of the Outkast classic 'Hey Ya!' which she sang in response to requests fans had put in over Twitter. Not only did it show Rita had versatility but it also helped attract the attention of someone who would have a dramatic influence on her career.

While she was posting the clip on YouTube, English producer Daniel Stein, better known as DJ Fresh, was in the studio with Jessie J, a new songwriter acquired by Rita's management Turn First who had recently emerged as a singer in her own right to huge success. Stein was remixing Jessie's 'Who's Laughing Now?', and her song-writing team, The Invisible Men, wanted him to pen a hit for her. Stein did have the hook for a new song 'Hot Right Now', which he hoped might score him his second number one after his dubstep track 'Louder' hit the top spot in July. The trouble was he wasn't convinced it was right for Jessie.

'They [The Invisible Men] said, "We know this amazing girl,"' Stein recalled. 'They showed me a YouTube video of Rita and I went, "Oh my God, that's the girl." I just knew straight away. She's just got the most amazing energy. She just is … she's hot right now.'

Rita loved the track but before she could record it they had to get a green light from Roc Nation.

'So we sent the track to Jay Z and he loved it, signed off on it and it was just like a really perfect match,' Stein said. 'We never actually finished anything for Jessie.'

The pieces of the jigsaw were falling into place for Rita. Expectation was building.

Rita secured a guest appearance with DJ Fresh at Alexandra Palace in London on the eve of her twenty-first birthday.

'My twenty-first birthday. Where am I? On a tour bus, about to go on stage,' she said. 'I was so nervous because I haven't performed for a while.'

She need not have worried. Once Rita took to the stage it was like a returning hero. The fans clapped, they whooped, and caught the moment on their camera phones. They even sang 'Happy Birthday' to put Rita on top of the world.

Once she'd caught her breath after her performance she said, 'It just went by so quick. It was the best feeling ever. I had so much fun doing it and it reminded me of what it's like being on stage and to see all them faces and those eyes.

'Everyone's watching you and it's, like, just a great feeling to know that you can entertain a whole lot of people. There was like four thousand people there so it was just an amazing thing. The impact was crazy, the vibe was crazy, everyone had their hands up, and what made it so brilliant was it was my birthday as well.'

There was no let up in her schedule. In December 2011 she flew to Los Angeles to catch her boss Jay Z in concert with Kanye West promoting their joint album *Watch The Throne*. It was an amazing show but Rita was almost as thrilled when back stage she met the stars of the reality TV show *Keeping up with the Kardashians* – Kim and Kourtney and little brother Rob Kardashian.

'I was like, "You guys are all so hot in real life." I was acting like a proper fan,' said Rita.

She wasn't alone in her love for the Kardashians' TV show. The whole of America, it seemed, and the rest of the free world, had been enthralled by the antics of Kim and her family since the reality series first aired on the E! channel in 2007, turning them into instant stars. In the years that followed, Kim, her sisters, their shrewd manager, mother Kris Jenner, and other relatives had built a billion-dollar fortune.

Rita hit it off with Rob, who seemed to be a reality TV stalwart after a semi-successful stint on *Dancing with the Stars* in the US that year. It seemed like she'd found a new friend. Whether he would play a greater role in her life than that remained to be seen.

That night in LA was special for another reason, however. Not only did Rita come face to face with the Kardashians but she also met one of her all-time heroes – Stevie Wonder. The soul legend came back stage during the interval to meet Jay Z and Kanye. And all Rita could do was sit and watch in amazement.

'It was an epic moment. It was so amazing and surreal. I'm a girl from West London, born in Kosovo, watching Stevie say "Hi" to these sensational artists.'

Back to her own music though, and Roc Nation and Sarah Stennett were in agreement. With 'Hot Right Now' they had the song to launch Rita Ora.

'When we got "Hot Right Now" we knew this was our chance,' Sara said. 'You can only keep people's attention for so long. If you have people's enthusiasm you want that ball of energy to move forward. Once you smell that chance, it's the right chance.

'Once you are confident with the record and that the artist can deliver it, that's when you have to pull everyone together as a team and say, "Right, we are pressing the button." I've said that to several artists that I've been involved with. When I say that, what I mean is, this is it. Start running! We are moving forward.'

This was it for Rita.

Things were moving at last.

All she needed to know was whether the reaction she'd been getting was all an illusion or whether she had what it took to be a genuine star.

She would now find out.

They were pressing the button.

9

Cometh the Ora

GRAFFITI-covered back streets, LA sun casting long shadows, Rita stepping into the light in a customised spray-painted leather jacket, as chiming house chords give way to breakneck beats … Rita Ora had arrived with her own starring role in a music video – not playing eye candy alongside Jay Z or as an uncredited extra next to Craig David or Drake.

Here she was front and centre, gathering hipsters in all shapes and sizes for an impromptu dance off as she stripped down to a pink bra and blue hot pants, conducting proceedings with a huge Eighties-style ghetto blaster and megaphone.

London director Rohan Blair-Mangat's fast and furious video was the perfect promo for 'Hot Right Now'. The song itself, credited to DJ Fresh featuring Rita Ora, was frantic, the beats relentless, the hook catchy. The production – with slight auto-tune vocals and Rihanna-style 'eh-eh-ehs' – felt like nothing had been left in the studio.

When the button was pressed the public responded – and then some. The song shifted more than 128,000 copies in its first week, making it the fastest selling single of the year so far when it hit the shops on 12 February 2012. It went straight to number one and ended up selling 480,000 copies. As if anyone doubted otherwise.

Rita had done it. Fifteen years after she first realised she could sing, seven years after her first production deal, and more than two years since signing for Roc Nation she was sitting on top of the pile. And, man, it felt good.

She'd made history in the process. Incredibly, 'Hot Right Now' was the first drum 'n' bass track ever to reach number one in the UK. Years after being pioneered by Goldie and championed by BBC Radio 1 DJ Grooverider (London disc spinner Raymond Bingham) the scene had its first chart-topper. Yet for DJ Fresh it was his second ground-breaker, after 'Louder' had done the same for dubstep. 'For me that's a massive, massive achievement,' he said of 'Hot Right Now'.

'So many of us – Goldie, Grooverider, Andy C [English producer and DJ Andrew John Clarke] – we've all been pushing so long to get the music taken seriously and to be seen as a platform that anything can be done on so it's a massive feeling of achievement.'

Rita's joy was total. And while she was thrilled to be part of history, her feeling was far simpler. 'It's the first track I've ever had on the radio so for me I'm like, "Arghhh!" I'm just really happy that it's done so, so well.'

What must have been amusing – and frustrating in equal measure – was that people assumed Rita was an instant success story.

'Some people think that it just happened over night,' she said.

It didn't matter that people didn't yet know her full story. That would come. She was just delirious. And if she felt this ecstatic just guesting on someone else's track imagine how it would feel to have a number one all on her own.

'I don't even know how I feel. I feel really, really happy. Like, genuinely happy,' she said. 'The funny thing is, it's not my own full song – it's a feature and that makes me happy already. So, if I feel like this now, if I get another number one with my song, I think I'll just, I don't know, faint.'

Suddenly it seemed like the world wanted to know her name. The requests for interviews, appearances and invitations tripled over night. Finally, as she allowed her success to sink in, she could appreciate the wisdom in getting her to hold off until the time was right. Over the course of those two years she'd been the dutiful protégée, never throwing her toys out of the pram when told her first stab at an album wasn't good enough. She'd sucked it up, got her head down and worked harder. Only now did she give voice to some of those frustrations.

'I never believed people when they were like "be patient," because I was so confused on why I wasn't out,' she said. 'I didn't know what I wanted to put out. I just knew I wanted to sing and be out. This is my first record deal. When they got in touch with me they really, really were like, "Rita, wait, just wait." And now I cannot thank them enough. I used to be like, "Why they making me wait, I don't know why they are making me wait, why don't they just do something," but they were waiting for me. That's what I didn't realise. They were waiting for me to find myself and to find something worth expressing. If I play you something from three years ago to now, it will sound completely different.

'I finally feel ready,' she added. 'I'm so grateful my label had patience and the money 'cause there's no money left in the music industry. The fact that they waited for me, that doesn't happen nowadays any more because there's no money to develop an artist. You've got to know who you are nowadays. I knew who I was, I just didn't know what I was.

'I just feel that I have to keep putting things out there that's gonna make people feel happy. This has been an amazing stepping stone, for me, with DJ Fresh, who I really admire. It's an amazing introduction for the people that don't know about me 'cause I haven't really done that many things apart from the Craig David stuff, "Where's The Love" [sic], which is cool. It was little features but it still wasn't me.'

The biggest upside of being number one was that it finally removed any lasting doubts from the minds of her parents that Rita had made the right choice in pursuing her dreams.

Just like their daughter, there must have been times during that period after she signed for Roc Nation when Vera and Besnik feared she might never make it. As parents they might have wondered how they would pick her up after another setback. Thankfully though, despite the ultimatums, the deals over going to college and the periods when relations strained so much they didn't speak, it looked to them like Rita might get her happy ending after all.

They still might not fully understand how the music industry worked and what it was their daughter actually did but her success helped heal their fractured relationship.

Confirming they were all talking to each other once again, Rita said: 'My parents are my blood. They're happy which is all that matters.'

One thing it would take Vera and Besnik a while to get used to was that people now knew their daughter's name – and, by association, who they were too.

'When they started to see people and they were like, "Yo, your daughter's Rita" and they were like, "How do you know my daughter?" and they were like, "Well, she's all over the radio." Slowly but surely ... they never leave your side. It might take a few years but they never leave your side.'

Having said that, however, Rita wondered if they'd ever get what she was doing. 'Mmmm, nah! In the beginning they were like, "Alright, cool," but now they are like the biggest, biggest supporters without a doubt. Without them I don't think I would know what to do. My mum is like my inspiration. She influenced my whole album, she's such a strong woman and my dad is just a go-with-the-flow kind of guy.'

Rita's relationship with her parents took on a new dimension in early 2012 as she entered a new phase of her life. After returning from the States, she moved into a place of her own in London. At first she thought living on her own would have multiple benefits. For a start she'd be able to play her music as loud as she liked, after years of having to listen to it in the bathroom so her sister could study. 'Now I have my own place, it's like ... I don't even have to be quiet.'

But within a few weeks of moving into the flat in Kensington she shared with her stylist Kyle she was noising up the locals. 'My neighbour said he saw me in the paper and asked me not to make too much noise,' she explained. 'I said, "I'm nice and spend my time watching movies."'

Another drawback was that her schedule was so busy she hadn't had time to kit out her new pad with furniture. 'I literally haven't even been able to sit in my house,' she said. 'I just moved into this new place so there's no furniture, just a beanbag and a table, but you know it's been good.'

'Hot Right Now' was not released in the US. Clearly Jay Z had a different strategy in mind but with his latest starlet at number one in the UK he seized the moment to introduce her to an otherwise ignorant American public.

Dropping by influential New York radio station Z100, which syndicates throughout America, he allowed the station to premiere another Rita song, then called 'Party And Bullshit'. Making out it was all a spur-of-the-moment decision he nevertheless turned up at the station's studio in TriBeCa with a glammed-up Rita, camera crew and entourage.

'I have Miss Rita Ora. This is all very spontaneous,' Jay Z announced. 'We just came to see some great friends over here and play some music. They liked what they heard and said, "Just throw it on the air", which is great. I love that. That's what radio is all about – feeling and emotion and not scheduling or any planning. Let's do it right now.'

Rita looked a little like a rabbit caught in the headlights but she performed admirably, telling listeners: 'I'm from London but I love America so I'm usually here.'

The song was more mainstream pop than 'Hot Right Now' and drew its hook from 'Party And Bullshit', the debut single by New York rapper The Notorious B.I.G. – then known as Biggie Smalls – who was murdered in 1997.

It was a surprise, personal intervention from Jay Z, who only a month earlier had celebrated being a dad for the first time. Beyoncé gave birth to their daughter Blue Ivy on 7 January and Rita was one of the first to send them a gift. 'Beyoncé is this massive star, but she's incredibly humble,' Rita said. 'But it's weird because even though I love her, she's my boss's wife.'

To outsiders it seems strange that Roc Nation wouldn't capitalise on the global appeal of 'Hot Right Now'. It could be argued that drum 'n' bass was a more British phenomenon but the LA setting for the video made it perfect for an American audience and with YouTube video views approaching seven million she was showing she had potential for an international fanbase.

Instead Roc Nation went with 'Party And Bullshit', although by the time it was released in the US in March it had been renamed 'How We Do (Party)'. Rita claimed the change 'made it easier for people to get it'. It was more likely Roc Nation decided to censor the chorus to maximise radio and video music station plays.

Initially, 'How We Do (Party)' only came out in the US, New Zealand, Australia and Italy. It went top ten in Australia and New Zealand but, despite being launched in such fanfare in New York, it failed to register with the music-buying public in America. It limped into the *Billboard* Hot 100 at ninety-six and peaked at sixty-two.

It was a blow. Although it could be argued that Britain and Europe were her main markets, Roc Nation obviously signed Rita believing she had crossover appeal.

There was no time to lick wounds, however. Her schedule was so hectic she barely had a chance to catch breath. First, she had a short set to perform for her first ever London gig as Rita Ora, the artist.

As fate would have it, it was to be at YoYo, the club in Notting Hill where Rita would go with her friends. In the build-up to the gig, the enormity of how far she'd travelled in three years since she'd left for New York to meet Jay Z sank in.

'I'm just so nervous, man. I'm like, really, really nervous,' she confessed, just before going on stage. 'I'm listening to my tracks back and back and back. I'm only doing five. And I know when I get off stage it's probably not even going to be a big deal, but because it's my first show I'm just really nervous. I've done a week's worth of rehearsals.'

At least she had some friendly faces with her, including Royston Legore, a choreographer who now counts Victoria's Secret models Jourdan Dunn and Vas J Morgan as his close friends and hangs out with Rita's clique.

'We have the best MD and the best band. I call them LDJs cause there's three boys and there's Royston,' she said. 'We always get into our zone. We don't let no one come into the room. I'm kind of a perfectionist so I really wanted it to be perfect.'

To mark the occasion, her management invited some music biz movers and shakers – the type of people who could make or break a singer. That made it even more vital for Rita not to mess up.

'The pressure in general is always stupid pressure and everything,' she said, 'but the fact that it's gonna be industry people as well as, hopefully, some of my fans will be there ... my family and my friends, 'cause it's gonna be in my hood. It's in YoYo so I live down the road from there. So it's gonna be a good venue this time, but it definitely puts pressure ... but I'd rather be spoken about than not be spoken about.'

Despite her nerves, she was able to laugh at one absurdity about the venue for her big night.

'The last time I performed here I was seventeen,' she said. 'The doorman threw me out because I was underage.'

One of the songs Rita premiered in London that night was 'R.I.P.' She'd fought for the song – the one given to her by Drake – to be one of those that stayed on the album after so many were discarded. Going by its early airing it sounded like a shrewd move on Rita's part to get her hands on it.

The night in YoYo was significant too for another reason. Not widely reported was the fact that watching backstage was a new admirer. Rob Kardashian, the brother of Kim, had flown in especially for the gig.

In March she attended the *NME* Awards and after-show party at London's swanky Sanderson Hotel, also with Rob. He was now being referred to as her boyfriend in newspaper gossip columns and he was certainly keen enough to jet in from the States to be with her.

In April, however, she joined Drake on the UK leg of his European tour, supporting him on selected dates. Interestingly, Drake's other support act of the European leg of his Club Paradise Tour – the most successful hip hop show that year – was rapper A$AP Rocky, who Rita would hear a lot more from in years to come. But playing to ten thousand fans in Glasgow as Drake's support act gave her a glimpse of what she still had to achieve to be in the big league.

The Canadian rap superstar was fast becoming a close confidant but in Newcastle, where they were also appearing together, it seemed they took the concept of collaboration to a whole new level. *The Sun* reported they were seen kissing back stage.

A source told the newspaper: 'Rita and Drake have been good friends for a while now but things seemed more serious this week. They were all over each other backstage at the gig on Monday and weren't trying to hide it.'

Appearances can be deceptive, and it could be that what looked like a passionate embrace was just two really close friends hugging. But Rita did not hide the fact she found Drake 'hot' and it's understandable if she found him irresistible. He was supremely talented, a man's man but someone who placed as much importance on family as she did. Also, just as his career was sky-rocketing, he was looking out for her.

On one of Rita's video diaries from April 2012, Drake was shown hanging out with Rita backstage. Rita and Drake hug, while her mum takes photos of them. Rita tells her to stop it. 'It's embarrassing,' she says.

As Vera insists she's not taking pictures of Drake, just taking them of her beautiful daughter, the rapper tells Rita: 'It's your moment.' It's a sweet statement and anyone witnessing would be forgiven for thinking they made a perfect couple.

There had to be a downside and there was. Drake came with Rihanna-shaped baggage. Back in January 2010 Drake and Rihanna appeared to be dating, speculation he later confirmed to be 'semi true'. They had been sparking 'are-they-aren't-they' rumours ever since she split from Chris Brown seven months earlier. However, by June 2010 Drake told the *New York Times* she had used him.

In reality, Drake and Rihanna have been on-off lovers since her split with Brown after he assaulted her in 2009. Rihanna and Drake were apparently spotted kissing in May of that year.

Drake confessed: 'I was a pawn. You know what she was doing to me? She was doing exactly what I've done to so many women throughout my life, which is show them quality time, then disappear. I was like, "Wow, this feels terrible."'

But then in September 2010 Drake announced he was working on a great new song with Rihanna – and in October that year they released 'What's My Name?' The accompanying video showed them getting very cosy.

Rihanna returned the favour by appearing on his song 'Take Care', released in February 2012. A month later she watched his show in London. Discussing their relationship status in April 2012, Drake said he and Rihanna had a 'connection established for life'.

So with all that in mind, it was into a confused situation that a brave Rita was venturing. Keeping quiet and letting people draw their own conclusions was probably the safest policy.

And drawing conclusions is what some were doing.

An insider told *mediatakeout.com* that Drake – whose nickname was 'Drizzy' – and Rita were dating, after she had ditched Rob. The source claimed Rita had been pressurised to end it with Rob because Roc Nation didn't view him suitable.

'The two musicians have reportedly been flirting for months,' the website said, 'but Rita didn't hook up with Drizzy until she and Rob called it quits. She was allegedly getting pressure from her handlers to dump Rob because the relationship wouldn't be good for her career, and MTO [mediatakeout] not-so-subtly implies that Jay Z was the one responsible for pushing her to be with Drizzy instead.'

That Rita and Drake had been flirting was not really news. But the idea that Rita's label could be taking such a close interest in her personal life was an intriguing one. Certainly they might have something to say if she hooked up with someone who could tarnish her reputation but going by her public pronouncements there was a world of difference between the way she talked about Drake and the way she referred to rumours regarding Rob.

Shortly before 'R.I.P.' was released she referred to Rob as an 'ex-boyfriend'. Whether Rob had yet even achieved 'boyfriend' status was open to question. When it was then put to her that she and Rob had been snapped coming out of a London club she said: 'Look, "R.I.P." went to radio and a whole bunch of friends came to Mahiki to celebrate. That was it.'

At the same time she was batting away queries about her private life, she was getting a crash course in the art of social media when what she thought might have been an innocent comment threatened to blow up in her face.

Rita claimed 'Call My Name', a song penned by Scottish DJ and producer Calvin Harris that was to be the next single for Cheryl Cole [now Cheryl Fernandez-Versini], had been offered to her first. She said she passed on it because it was too dance orientated for her tastes.

'I heard "Call My Name" quite a while ago because I was offered it,' she said. 'I turned it down. I do like the song but I didn't want to sing it 'cause it's not really me. I don't want to go down the dance route that a lot of other pop stars are doing. I prefer to have my own sound and do my own thing.'

That prompted an angry rebuke from Calvin, who announced on Twitter: 'For the record, Call my name was never given to Rita Ora to sing … she made that up, don't know why.'

Rita appeared to backpedal, insinuating her words had been

twisted, when she responded: 'So for the record, don't believe media when they twist sh*t.'

Calvin urged her to 'calm down', adding, 'I was setting the record straight as you didn't at the time. It was a disrespectful comment to make, that's all.'

And she backtracked completely when she offered to explain all privately, saying, 'I hate beef and fighting. So I love u all @calvinharris call me ill explain wat [sic] actually happened they twisted it and congratulations. X'

Some clearing of the air must have happened because Rita later said: 'I love Calvin Harris, it was such a stupid misunderstanding. I feel silly for even commenting on something I wasn't clear about. The truth is I heard this song and I was like, I want this song and I didn't know Cheryl had it already. It is such a small industry, there's no point in fighting or beefing with anyone. I spoke to Calvin, cleared it up and laughed it off.'

Rita had managed to set the record straight but that little run-in with the straight-talking Scot might just have created a frisson of tension between them that would play out further down the line.

Rita was learning fast that any comment, any tweet, any photo could be jumped upon and blown out of proportion.

She must have been grateful therefore for a chance to return to London and get back to her roots with a low-key show in the east end of the city.

'I had a gig at the Hoxton Bar and Grill. It was a whole bunch of girls. I literally sat down there with them and we had a conversation and I sang them a song and it was basically just singing in my living room,' she said. 'I did a show before that when I was supporting Drake in Glasgow to a huge crowd – biggest crowd I've ever performed at – and coming back home and performing in front of like three hundred people it was just the best feeling ever. I sat on the edge of the stage, I sang the song and I would talk to them.'

Her intimate gig gave some journalists the chance to check her out up close but though she got the thumbs up, some labelled her 'Britain's answer to Rihanna'. It was a comparison she'd have to quickly get used to.

That versatility – and an ability to perform whatever the

circumstances, drawing on her roots as a pub singer – would stand Rita in good stead as she prepared to embark on the busiest period of her career to date.

And Jay Z was quick to appreciate Rita's power as a live singer. 'The first time I truly saw her on stage was at the Cartier event in New York City. To have that sort of stage presence and that sort of energy. The music went off and she still was like "more" she still wanted to go. She jumped off the stage at one point and was dancing with the crowd. It was a great moment. Being from London and all, she has that bit of Brit rock. That kind of feeling to her, which I love. To have a new artist pay homage to what's come before them is great, that's an amazing thing.'

Jay's comments came during an intense period of promotion for Rita in April 2012. She was the second act in the UK – and the second Turn First act – to benefit from Vevo Lift, after Jessie J. What that meant was that she was given preferential status on Vevo, the video hosting service, operated by Universal, Sony and Abu Dhabi Media in partnership with Google.

'The idea of Lift is that we take a new artist and we give them, for want of a better phrase, the superstar treatment,' said Nick Jones, international senior vice president at Vevo. 'Over an eight-week period we do five pieces of original content. What we don't want to do is ask all the obvious questions, so it's bespoke original content that we work up with Rita, with Sarah [Stennett], and make sure what people who are watching Vevo get the opportunity to do is to really understand what's behind who Rita is and what she wants to do.'

In a digital age many people might be forgiven for thinking all Rita needed was a good video to put on YouTube. But Nick Jones said: 'Digital's fantastic but there are so many options, so many places you can go.' What he hoped to achieve with Lift was give certain artists the ability to build a career. Rita was delighted with the opportunity for such a concerted promotional campaign but at first she was baffled at what she was expected to do.

'I didn't know how I wanted to come across,' she said. 'Vevo and the team said to me, "You know, pretend like we're not here. This is what people want to see". I was like, "Really? You want to see me sharing a room with my sister, where I grew up, that's interesting?"'

It was. Indeed the videos that showed Rita in her home and neighbourhood were far more intriguing than the initial introductory clip, which had her stiffly reciting a scripted story of her discovery.

In one, where she showed a camera around her family home in Foreland House, Rita's bemusement at the way everything was unfolding was plain to see.

Talking about how much she loved coming back home she did admit things had changed. 'It's a bit different now with my neighbours and that, kind of like, knowing. The block is all going, kind of like, mad and things like that but it's just so funny to be in here now there's cameras in here. It's really weird because I never thought anyone would care about where I used to live.'

She showed the cameras her memory wall, inside two cupboard doors, where she had posted photos and mementos. It had grown somewhat in the last few years. Rather sweetly it showed that alongside ticket stubs of gigs she'd paid to enter there were guest passes for live events she'd been to even after she was making it as a singer. Included among them was the first Jay Z gig she went to at the Roundhouse in Camden, clearly as a guest of Roc Nation. In Rita's mind she was still teetering between being a wide-eyed fan and a fully-fledged member of the pop star club.

The wall, she said, was not completed, because she had moved out. It was the only evidence – save for a large portrait of Marilyn Monroe on the wall – that she'd lived there at all but her bed was still made, ready for her if she ever needed to come back at a moment's notice.

'I get recognised a bit right now but because of the number one and stuff, things just kind of exploded,' she said as she toured her old neighourhood with her camera crew.

But by far the most touching moment was when Rita, while filming a piece to camera, noticed her grandma sitting in the park chilling. Amid all the scripted scenes and after months of careful planning, according to her manager Stennett, it was this little intimate moment, as she hugged her grandma, that said so much about Rita Ora. Besa still had a home in Pristina but increasingly was spending more time at her place in Ladbroke Grove.

'That's so random, it's like we organised it,' Rita said, 'but we didn't. She was literally just coming to read her newspaper.'

Her grandma could not speak much English but managed to say 'thank you all', to the crew and viewers.

The focus of the campaign was the first single bearing Rita's name as the main artist, the Drake song 'R.I.P.', due for release in May. But the videos allowed Rita to introduce herself to people who might have missed 'Hot Right Now' or wanted to know more about the vocalist on that track.

More discerning viewers might raise a cynical eyebrow at the big corporate sponsorship of the Lift clips and how clever marketing would tailor it to users' tastes and preferences. Rita, herself, speaking at the annual Midem music conference in 2014 as part of a panel talking up Vevo Lift, let slip a slightly sinister corporate comment when she said: 'I love it how the Internet and the media is completely controlling everything we do.'

But there could be no denying the impact Vevo Lift had on her career. At the end of the campaign Rita had achieved over twenty million views of the Vevo videos and her Twitter followers had doubled to 3.5 million. These were astronomical numbers and demonstrated what reach such exposure could bring.

'Honestly, I can say Lift definitely changed my life,' Rita said. 'We have the acoustic sessions, which is really exciting for me because that's where we can kind of play with the songs, you come to the studio, you listen to how we sound, literally, live, raw, guerilla style and that's what it's about. It really does just change everything.'

One of those 'guerilla style' clips Rita mentioned went behind the scenes of the 'R.I.P.' video shoot, giving a flavour of the gruelling shoots that are necessary to create these visually stunning promos. At the helm was Emil Nava, an acclaimed director who was fast becoming the go-to guy for slick music videos. Rita had countless costume changes, ranging from a look that resembled a sexy mechanic to Eighties Madonna through to pure Rihanna. That was hardly surprising given the song had been written with the 'Rude Boy' star in mind. But Rihanna's loss was Rita's gain.

'When he [Drake] first played it to me I thought it had a strong message to come out with as a new artist,' Rita said. 'It shows such confidence in a female and I wanted a song that women can feel strong with.'

Producers of the track also made room for a strong male cameo in Tinie Tempah, who was more than holding his own on the British hip hop scene.

'It features Tinie Tempah who is a legend, it's great to collaborate with such an amazing UK artist on the track too,' Rita said.

She was also thrilled to be working with Chase & Status who had a double connection to the track. They were ideal producers, given Drake had sampled their remix of 'Heartbeat', a song by Nigerian singer Nneka, and Rita adapted the hook for her version.

Being linked to Drake meant she was quizzed again about their closeness as the buzz around 'R.I.P.' grew ahead of its release.

'He's a great guy,' she said, denying any romance. 'We're just friends. We've built a great relationship. He wrote an amazing song. So it's an amazing business and personal relationship. He's just such a smart guy and he's doing great and I feel like he's gonna be around for a long time, so he's also a voice that I listen to.'

She added: 'I just was a fan of his music. And he sings songs that make women feel good about themselves. Women love an honest man. An honest man that isn't afraid to say, "Men get hurt too." And a lot of men don't admit that.'

With Drake, as she had been with Jay Z, Rita wasn't shy about name-checking the men who had influenced and helped her. That led to unkind suggestions she might be more than a protégée to some of them. Rita understood what was being suggested.

'The new meat?' she said. 'I get it, but it's not been like that for me. I know my boundaries. I've been brought up really well. I know how to earn my respect.'

It'd seemed unfair to brazenly suggest she hadn't found herself in this position solely on talent. After all, how many male stars are asked the same question?

But, again, it would be something Rita would have to get used to.

Shrewdly, she kept her cool, though, and managed not to rise to any bait during interviews. Rihanna? Was it true she threw a tantrum when she learned her song had gone to Jay Z's newest star? 'Rubbish,' Rita rebuked. And what of those comparisons? 'It's an honour,' she confessed. 'Who wouldn't want to be compared to her?

'I like the comparisons,' she added. 'It's a compliment. It's better being compared to her than anyone else. She's so hot and beautiful. The good thing about her is we've all seen her grow as an artist. I relate to her story. Rihanna has gone from Barbados to world domination. Now I want to follow the same path.'

Did that mean she wanted to be the next Rihanna?

'I don't think there will be a next Rihanna,' she said. 'But I think [Jay Z] definitely sees me as someone who could be as big as Rihanna. She's a superstar now but they first knew her as a small-island girl – and they want to repeat that success.'

Thanks to the boost she got from Vevo Lift by the time 'R.I.P.' was released the buzz around her was huge. Maybe that ambition to make her as big as Rihanna wasn't so outlandish after all.

Rita was nervous though. Despite already knowing what it was like to have a number one, the failure of 'How We Do (Party)' in America must have been playing on her mind. Plus she was apprehensive about what solo success would mean.

'I'm scared,' she admitted, as she watched her life being dragged further away from normality with every passing day. 'I'm so excited that I'm getting to do what I want to do. I worked so hard towards this. I am scared, but it's part of the game. I have to suck it up.'

She launched her new single in style, hiring out Asprey diamond shop on New Bond Street, one of London's most up-market roads, for a star-studded bash. Tinie Tempah arrived with flowers for her and she had the amazing news that she was topping the download charts after just one day.

It seemed like the inevitable was going to happen – Rita was going to get her second number one.

The chart that mattered would be revealed on the Sunday and Rita said: 'If I get to number one, I will proper cry.'

She needn't have worried.

'R.I.P.' shot to the top of the charts, selling 104,592 copies in its first week.

Rita celebrated by partying all night with Mishka and some other girlfriends in London. Impressively, she still managed to look bright as a button the next day when she attended the Sony Radio Academy Awards to hand out the Sony DAB Rising Star Award with The Script singer Danny O'Donoghue.

'I've only had three hours' sleep but it was so much fun to be out with my girlfriends,' she said. 'After all, it's my first solo number one.'

She had done it. Proved all her doubters wrong and proved it to herself.

Everything was falling into place.

There was just one subject that needed to be addressed.

Rob was keen to share in Rita's glory.

'You did it,' he posted on Twitter. 'I love you and you're my girl.'

Clearly he was doing his best to make it official. In his eyes he was Rita Ora's boyfriend.

If that was the case, though, why was another man wearing her ring?

10

A Secret Favourite

HE had helped change her life. And Rita wanted to give something that said how grateful she was. She chose a ring from her grandfather – something she had cherished for years. It was a gold-plated ring with a black gemstone.

In a private moment she presented it to Drake, the man whose song had put her on top of the world. He didn't have to wear it, she said, just take care of it and know what the gesture meant.

Drake was so touched, however, he put it straight on.

The gift speaks volumes about the fondness they have for each other. In the fleeting world of pop, collaborations come and go, writers pen songs and artists have hit records. It happens. But something deeper occurred between Rita and Drake.

Rita explained: 'I had a ring, since I was young and it was my granddad's ring. I've known Drake for so many years. He was the first guy I worked with on my album because I've been doing my album for literally like three years because I scrapped it. But Drake always kept his songs on the album because we really connected and he's one of the most genuine people I've ever met.

'I have so much time for him, I love his family, I love what he stands for and he's so genuine. So when "R.I.P." went to number one it was a moment for me. It was my first number one and I kind of shared it with the right person. He wrote it for me and it just all made sense. The least I could do was give him something important to me.

'If you think about it, he changed my life so I gave him a ring. A friendship kind of ring and I was like, "You don't have to wear it", it was more of a sentimental gift. But he wears it, so it's cool.'

The gift led to questions over whether there was something more to their relationship but Rita denied it. 'Don't get me wrong,' she added. 'He's hot … but he's more than that. It's just like family.'

Drake described the ring as 'one of the greatest gifts I ever received in my whole life'.

'I wear it every day,' he said. Drake wanted to keep the story behind his new piece of jewellery secret. But eagle-eyed fans started speculating whether he had married a former childhood sweetheart, so he felt he had to set the record straight.

'They tried to talk about this ring the other day and say I got married to somebody, which I didn't. Rita actually gave me this ring. We're dear friends. "R.I.P." is a song that I originally wrote for Rihanna [and she] actually didn't take the song … Rita expressed interest in it and anything I can do for Rita, I will do.'

He added: 'I've known her for years and this is one of the most important things in my collection. First of all, it's vintage. It's just beautiful to me. It means a lot. Rita's like one of the first people to ever just be genuine and embrace me and show me love. She was in my "Over" video.

'She was always there to talk to. Her personality brings joy to my life. So it was a great gift. I usually wouldn't put her out there like that but I hate that they assume/associate it with some other girl so I really want it to be clear that this is a gift from a dear friend of mine. Her name is Rita Ora and I'm not married and I'm very single.'

Rita was also forced to further deny anything romantic was going on.

'No, I'm not dating Drake,' she said. 'I'm a hundred per cent single. I honestly haven't got time for a relationship. The only relationship I'm involved in is with my bed and I don't get much time to commit to that. I've known Drake since I was seventeen. We are great friends but are not together.'

The denials were strong. In a way it was a pity they weren't together. Rita might have said Drake's songs remained on her album.

But what fans didn't know was that they worked on a song together that didn't make the final cut.

The tune – intriguingly entitled 'What If I Kissed You Right Now?' – wasn't finished in time to make the album. The lyrics told the story of secret admirers unsure of how to take their feelings to the next level.

'Trying to imagine how it might sound if I just yelled out "take me I'm yours."' Rita sang. How would they explain it, how would they keep it a secret? Don't tell anybody and let them wonder, went the lyrics. Where did they get their inspiration from, fans may wonder?

'We wrote a song called "What If I Kissed You Right Now?", which is one of my secret favourites,' Rita let slip. 'It's not going to be on the album, unfortunately. I would have loved it but we didn't have time to finish it.'

Drake did record the song as a demo but to date it hasn't appeared on an album.

'I love her to death,' Drake said about Rita. 'She's just a great girl. I admire her very much.'

How all this, including her comment that she was 'a hundred per cent single', went down with Rob Kardashian we would soon find out. He clearly believed they were in a relationship.

In the aftermath of Rita's chart glory, he continued to behave like the dutiful boyfriend.

'Rita is beautiful,' he gushed. 'Her best music hasn't come out yet. I just want to get her music over to the States 'cause I know people at home would love her.'

Rita made no more public comments about Rob that summer, except to say she'd never be appearing on *Keeping up with the Kardashians*. She did however reiterate how much Drake meant to her.

In one magazine interview she said: 'We're great friends. If he ever needed me I'd fly out. He's one of the nicest guys I've ever met and if anyone talks shit about him, I get protective.'

Rita did find herself attracting further headlines for kissing, but this time it wasn't Rob, or Drake … it was Rihanna. The Roc Nation stable mates joined actress Gwyneth Paltrow, the Olympic 2012 British team uniform designer Stella McCartney and Rob's sister Kim at a bash thrown by Jay Z and Kanye West – who by then was dating Kim – for their manager Ty Ty's fortieth birthday at London's trendy Dstrkt club. The *Daily Mirror* said Rita enjoyed a smooch with Rihanna, who had such a good time at the party she missed her flight back to the States.

'You know life is great when you wake up at 9am drunk!' Rihanna tweeted. 'How did I get in my bed? Did I walk? Stumble? Get carried?'

Rita might only have had one number one in her own right but she would have been forgiven for feeling like pop royalty – not only for the company she was keeping but also with some of the invitations she received.

She landed the coveted slot as support act for Coldplay – fronted by Gwyneth's then-husband Chris Martin, a friend of Jay Z's – beginning later in May.

Then Simon Cowell asked her to appear on *The X Factor* as a guest judge. Cowell needed urgent replacements after Beyoncé's former Destiny's Child bandmate Kelly Rowland announced she would not be returning.

Just three years earlier Rita had been a budding reality TV hopeful who wasn't even brave enough to audition for ITV1's hit show.

There wouldn't have been many singers who would have relished opening for Coldplay one night in Switzerland then catching a flight to London to make her debut as a reality TV judge. Yet that was the task facing Rita – herself still effectively a novice.

'I didn't have to audition by singing for Jay Z,' she said, 'but I was given just three minutes to make a first and last impression that I was worth signing, so I know what that feels like. I felt that pressure and I think that is how I could relate to the contestants on *The X Factor*.'

As she turned up for her leg of the tryouts at the O2 Arena in Greenwich, it seemed she was almost as nervous as the singers! 'Im [sic] here ... I can't breathe! X-Factor ... I'm just like you – remember that. I've just started, too. I'm here to help!' she tweeted.

Fellow judge Tulisa Contostavlos gave the rookie a thumbs up. 'Rita is great for the panel. Despite just breaking the commercial scene, she's been in the industry for years and knows what she's talking about,' the ex-N-Dubz star said.

Take That's Gary Barlow, who had clashed with the previous guest judge Spice Girl Geri Halliwell, gave Rita a smoother time and graciously allowed her to find her feet by commenting first. That might have had something to do with Rita's comments about him.

'He's actually hotter than I thought,' she said. 'I think Gary's a really good-looking lad.'

A source on the show said: 'Rita did brilliantly despite only having two hours' sleep because she played with Coldplay in Switzerland the night before.'

Rita performed well, and even when the audience laughed at her asking identical twins if they were the same age, her natural charm won everyone over. She looked such a natural in front of the cameras that Simon asked her to stay on for another day. When she told him she needed to be in Coventry for her next gig with Coldplay that night he laid on a private jet to take her there on time.

'Simon and the show's producers were really impressed by Rita,' the series insider said. 'She was warm and funny, and gave everybody constructive criticism. The audience responded really well to her.'

Simon's desire to keep her an extra day led to speculation he might make Rita a permanent fixture.

'By December, she could be a much bigger star so picking her now could be a masterstroke,' the insider added.

Rita didn't want to look too far into the future – but she had fun on the show.

'When you say "no" to people, the audience feels sad for them. But there were some people who were really bad and some people who were just funny and singing weird songs. As far as becoming a permanent judge goes, I don't think I am ready for that right now. Maybe once I have a few years more experience, then I'll be a better judge.'

Hold that thought!

However, her increased exposure led to further comparisons with Rihanna. Already she must have suspected that this was a charge that was going to be levelled at her throughout her career.

One paper compared their outfits, nails, style and tattoos, concluding they were 'increasingly difficult to tell apart'.

Back to the day job, and her gigs with Coldplay opened her up to a new style of live performance – not to mention more fans than she'd ever seen before. After two smaller concerts she opened in front of 50,000 people during the stadium leg of their tour.

'It was straight in at the deep end, which is just how I like it,' Rita said. 'The stages were huge, so I went out there with my band and ran as much as I could. I was inspired by watching Chris Martin every night.'

Jay Z had told her Coldplay were masters at wowing audiences, without gimmicks.

'The best advice he gave was, "Have you seen Chris Martin perform? It's literally just him on a stage. He rocks it out. You don't need dancers and stuff around you."'

And when she'd seen them for herself, she agreed.

'It's ridiculous,' she said of the band's stage show. 'Can I just tell you it's like the most surreal thing in the world. Everything is lighting up. Neon lights everywhere. The great thing about them is they're so cool because there's only four of them on the stage. They just rock out. Like, Chris lies on the floor. It's just a great show. I've been a fan of them for ages. I only did two intimate gigs before I did the stadiums so I was very, very nervous. But I went on there and it all went out the window. It was great. And the catering was so great on the tour, no joke.'

Jay Z and Beyoncé joined Gwyneth and Ty Ty in a box for the band's gig at the Etihad Stadium in Manchester and Rita joined them after her set.

Rita found Chris Martin to be generous with his time and advice. As she was putting the finishing touches to her album she sought out his opinion. He went through it track by track telling her what he liked and didn't, and gave her some useful tips.

'He told me to stand by my music and have fun with it,' she said. 'And to not worry what anyone else says, although I'm still working on that. He was lovely.'

And Rita was grateful that her boss made it happen.

'Jay Z does use his profile to help me,' she said. 'He has been great getting me to meet all these fantastic musicians and artists. The tour with Coldplay was absolutely amazing and Chris was really nice. Jay Z is great to give me the platform and the opportunity. But at the end of the day I have to put the hard work in and deliver the goods, otherwise he wouldn't be putting his name on the line.'

Once her Coldplay duties were completed, Rita embarked on a summer of festival appearances that would include Wireless and T in the Park. First up was the Capital FM Summertime Ball at Wembley Stadium where she was on the same bill as Cheryl Cole, whose 'Call My Name' – the song Rita claimed she'd been offered – had just been released. Thankfully her comments didn't lead to any bad blood between them.

But if Rita survived embarrassment there, she was only delaying it. At Lovebox, in Victoria Park, East London, Rita suffered her first wardrobe malfunction – in full view of the watching media... and her dad!

Rita had been wearing a Pucci embossed, beaded bralet with a white blazer over it.

Stylist Kyle did warn her: 'Rita, you can't wear that, your tits are gonna fall out.'

But Rita shrugged off his concerns. 'It'll be fine, I won't jump around.'

'She went on stage in it,' Kyle said. 'The next day it was all over the papers that her tits came out. She's the type of person that makes a joke out of everything though, so it wasn't any big drama for her.'

Rita did indeed joke about it, taking to Twitter to blame it on the bralet coming in a sample size that wasn't big enough.

'It's not a size that fits me boobs!' she tweeted. 'I got t**s everyone. LOL my secret is out.'

Her dad was less amused, however.

'My dad sent me an email saying, "Please don't let this happen again, thanks,"' she revealed. 'So I bought some nipple tassles and said, "Don't worry, Dad, that won't happen again. I've got a whole bunch of nipple tassles." And he said, "No! Buy bras."'

What might help Rita avoid any future mishaps was having Elena join her team full time. Having finished her degree course, she joined her little sister as her assistant and effectively her manager, although being paid by Turn First.

With Rita's second single about to be released, followed by her album, she was entering into another hectic period.

'How We Do (Party)' was released in August and Rita was praying it did better in her homeland than it had done across the Atlantic. Promoting the release, she declared herself a 'big Notorious B.I.G. fan' suggesting she came up with the idea of turning his sample into a pop song, gushing: '"Party And Bullshit" was one of the first rap songs I heard. And I loved what that song represented about having a great time so I turned it into a pop song – a great summer jam. It's a song that reminds me of barbecues and having a beer, sat in the sunshine.'

Yet out of twelve writers credited on the track, Rita wasn't one. Instead she had people like Bonnie McKee, a songwriter who has co-written eight number one hits and enjoyed a successful partnership with Katy Perry. The song was Rita's most commercial to date but the B.I.G. sample provided some 'dope', as one critic put it.

The video was entrusted to the mega-experienced Marc Klasfeld whose past promos read like a roll call of the pop and rock hall of fame, from Jay Z, 'N Sync, Bon Jovi and Foo Fighters to Destiny's Child, Britney Spears and Aerosmith.

Shot in Coney Island, New York, Rita was seen in a stars and stripes jacket, jiving about with a host of eccentrically dressed boys and girls.

The whole vibe was fun and frolics, glossing over the general tone of the lyrics, which were more about taking a shot in the morning to get over the excesses of the night before.

'How We Do (Party)' shot to number one, giving Rita her third chart topper and third song with first week sales topping 100,000. She was also the only UK act with three number ones that year – an incredible achievement for someone unheard of less than twelve months before.

'I can't believe I'm the first artist this year to have three number one singles in a row!' she told the V Festival crowd in Chelmsford where she was playing when the news came through.

When she had a proper chance to celebrate she did it in style – reportedly blowing £10,000 on a booze-fuelled bash at VIP club Mahiki in London's swanky Mayfair.

She partied with one half of Rizzle Kicks, Harley 'Sylvester' Alexander-Sule, and quickly tore into expensive vodka and £650-a-head cocktails.

'She had the biggest table in the house and covered it with magnums of posh Ciroc vodka,' one source was quoted. 'Rita also ordered a few of the infamous Mahiki Treasure Chest cocktails, which are £650 a go. Halfway through the night, management had to call for extra security to surround her table as she was getting a lot of attention from overexcited male fans.'

The tear-up was part of a week-long celebration that included other get-togethers with friends and family. Now that Rita was experiencing incredible success she could finally appreciate what had happened to her.

'It feels amazing,' she says. 'I'm so chuffed. Stardom, it's a funny thing. You never know what it's like until you're in it. I knew what I had to do, what I had to sacrifice and it's not a problem. With the right team around you, you can control it. I've had this dream as long as I can remember. My mum and my dad are the sweetest couple. They can't sing to save their lives, but they have great taste in music.'

She was looking forward to her album finally coming out – and for her chance to show fans her full range.

'I can't wait for people to get the album,' she said. 'It's going to make sense. I wanted to make sure I made a record which everything was different on as I never grew up listening to one type of music. I like to do things people don't expect. I'm not one-sided – I'm human too. I love partying, but I'm also up for great music.'

Coming swiftly on the back of 'How We Do (Party)', the album – which Rita must have thought would never see the light of day – was finally here.

'I'm just gonna call it *Ora*. Ora, it's obviously my surname, but it also means time in my country, in Kosovo, and it took me a long time to get this album done – three years to be exact.'

The album certainly boasted a host of collaborations, guest appearances, writers and producers. Rita's original batch of songs had been rejected because they didn't sound authentic enough. But with input from so many different quarters it was inevitable some of the themes expressed on the songs didn't really ring true.

'There's a track on my album called "Unfair,"' said Rita. 'I haven't yet been through a heartbreak so I don't want to talk about it. I hear they're very tough though.'

Rita was on far stronger ground when it was party songs like 'How We Do (Party)', as fans could imagine that was how she lived her life.

Old-school critics in the UK national press seemed to be in agreement that the album was a mix of hits and misses. *The Guardian* said it felt 'more like a collection of other people's songs than a cohesive album', while *The Independent* said it was hard to see Rita 'as anything but the UK's own Rihann-alike'. In the new media, however, the reviews were kinder. *Digital Spy* accepted the album sounded like 'a highly calculated exercise', but added 'that doesn't mean she hasn't turned out some genuinely well-crafted songs'. *Contactmusic. com* claimed that despite its shortcomings *Ora* was 'still a worthy introduction to the world of arguably the UK's most credible and slightly left-of-centre pop star in years'.

While reviews were a necessary part of promotion, Rita would say the only critics that mattered were the ones who paid to hear it – and the public gave it a resounding thumbs up.

Ora shot straight to number one in the UK selling over 41,000 copies in its first week alone. It was an amazing achievement and after all her false starts was justification of her label's strategy.

'Jay Z told me to be patient, which is the best advice I've ever been given,' Rita said. 'He was looking at the long game. I thought I was ready, but I wasn't.'

Her boss flew her to Philadelphia, where he was hosting his first *Made in America* festival, and laid on a huge party to celebrate hitting the top spot. Rita was growing used to the limelight but she must have pinched herself when, clutching her glass of champagne, she looked around and saw Beyoncé, Kanye West, Drake and Kim Kardashian toasting her success.

To illustrate what sort of company she was now keeping, President Obama sent his own message of congratulations to Jay Z for his festival, heralding the hip hop star as someone who 'refused to quit'.

Rita could finally take a breather to bask in her own glory, having confirmed she was worth the money and time invested in her. But amid the revelry there was one rather large elephant lurking in the room. Despite what now amounted to years of promotional work making herself known in America, a surprising decision was to be made not to release her album there.

Perhaps it was the lacklustre performance of 'How We Do (Party)' in the US, or maybe Roc Nation executives simply felt Rita still wasn't ready for the more critical audiences stateside. Whatever the reason, it was further evidence her trek to the summit was incomplete.

She would later assert the choice was all hers, echoing the reason behind the collapse of her original album: 'I said to myself, I will not release an album in the States unless I know one hundred per cent that by the end of it people will say, "That's Rita."'

Nonetheless, Rita wasn't going to let the glitch dampen her spirits. It only meant she'd have to continue as she had been, refusing to quit just like her boss.

After the celebrations were over, Rita started to look to the future and spoke of trying to use her success to help people in her native Kosovo.

Her homeland continued to suffer from ignorance – and bad press thanks to films where the baddies were Albanian such as *Taken* (2008), which had been so successful it eventually turned into a franchise in its own right.

'There aren't a lot of well-known Albanians or Kosovans, so when someone makes it in another country, it's a big deal. The actress Eliza Dushku [Faith in *Buffy the Vampire Slayer*] is one – people are so proud of her,' Rita said. 'There's a perception of Albanians that we're all like the kidnappers in *Taken*, that film with Liam Neeson. But it's a great place, a beautiful country, full of cool people with talent. I will always big up my country, whatever I'm doing.'

As a result of her success, Rita and her parents met the president of Kosovo, Atifete Jahjaga, the first female head of state in the modern Balkans.

'She said that everyone was proud of me, and to ask for anything I want when I come back to Kosovo. My dream is to start a music school in Pristina. There are so many talented singers, but not so many opportunities.'

She made plans to go back to perform a concert and film the video for her next single there. Not only would it be her chance to give

A young Rita and her sister Elena pose with their beloved grandfather Besim Sahatçiu.
(courtesy of Shaqir Poniqi / 22five Publishing)

The flat in Pristina where Rita's family lived before they fled Kosovo.
(© Selvije Bajrami / 22five Publishing)

The photo Hana Hajaj snapped of Rita after she impressed in the Year Five school play.
(courtesy of Hana Hajaj / 22five Publishing)

Rita's class photo from Year Six at St Cuthbert with St Matthius Primary School. Rita (back row, third from right) stands behind her friend Yemi Akintoye-Dedier. Omar Hajaj is in the middle row, second from left. (courtesy of Ilona Buttinger/22five Publishing)

St Cuthbert with St Matthius Primary School in Earls Court, London. (© Rosie Hallam/22five Publishing)

A headshot of a 14-year-old Rita taken while she was a pupil at Sylvia Young Theatre School. (© John Clark Photography)

Foreland House in Notting Hill, London where Rita spent her teen years. (© Rosie Hallam / 22five Publishing)

Rita's first crush Jamie Blackley who is now an up-and-coming actor. (© Rex Features)

Size? shoe shop in Portobello Road, London where Rita had her first job.
(© Rosie Hallam / 22five Publishing)

Rita poses with Craig David at the 2008 MOBO Awards. (© Getty Images)

A proud Rita with a young fan during an
early signing of her first album.
(© Rex Features)

Rita with her mum Vera at *Glamour* Magazine's
Women of the Year Awards in 2013. (© Rex Features)

Excited fans mob Rita as she films the video for 'Shine Ya Light' in Pristina, Kosovo. (© Getty Images)

Rita performs with pal Iggy Azalea at the Budweiser Made In America music festival in 2014. (© Rex Features)

Rita poses with 'wifey' Cara Delevingne backstage at the British Fashion Awards in 2012. (© Rex Features)

Rita meets her idol Gwen Stefani during a guest appearance on *The X Factor* in 2012. (© Rex Features)

A loved-up Rita poses with then-boyfriend Calvin Harris at the Brit Awards in 2014. (© Rex Features)

Rapper Drake gives Rita a cuddle at an MTV VMA after party hosted by Jay Z and Diddy in 2013. (© Rex Features)

Rita and Chris Brown at the MTV Video Music Awards in 2012. (© Rex Features)

Rita and her sister Elena chat to Rita's Roc Nation boss Jay Z at a pre-Grammy brunch in 2014. (© Getty Images)

Rita poses with US President Barack Obama and family at the Christmas in Washington party in 2014. (© Rex Features)

The newest *X Factor* judge before auditions in London in 2015. (© Rex Features)

Rita with her fellow *The Voice* judges – Tom Jones, will.i.am and Ricky Wilson. (© Rex Features)

A stunning Rita performs 'Grateful' at the 2015 Academy Awards. (© Rex Features)

something back but it would be an opportunity to connect with people she hadn't seen for nearly three years.

She had much to tell her relatives back home. So much had happened in the intervening period. It seemed she had everything she wanted out of life. Just one thing was missing however – a meaningful relationship.

Rob Kardashian had been in Philadelphia for Rita's party but in her eyes as nothing more than a friend.

Mixed messages continued to come from both camps.

They tweeted a photo of them holding hands, their knuckles tattooed with 'Rita and Rob K' but Rita still insisted it meant nothing.

'That's not real. It was just for fun,' she said. 'Loads of our friends were out and we all got them. Rob has got loads of sisters and he gets along with girls. He has got a lot of girlfriends. We just get along.'

And when he travelled to London to see her?

'He was here with his stepdad, Bruce [Jenner], for the Olympics,' she said. 'I have a lot of friends in LA because I was out there for a long time, so whenever he is here we hang out.'

Kim Kardashian also seemed to suggest her brother was not in a relationship, tweeting that he needed to find himself a girl.

'When out to dinner w my brother @RobKardashian every gorgeous persian/armenian girl stares at Rob! I think that's what he needs in his life!'

As interviewers demanded to know what was going on, Rita said: 'I'm single, but me and Rob are friends and he's a really cool friend and we chill a lot together. To me, I don't really care about where you're from or what you are or what you do, he makes me laugh. We're not a couple. I love Rob, but we're not a couple.'

Just a few weeks earlier she had been talking about having no experience of heartache, but now it seemed Rita did know about pains of the heart. She was suffering the heartbreak of loneliness.

'I'm so lonely. I just want to be in a relationship,' Rita said. 'This album, to me, was just about making people feel happy. I wasn't going through any kind of heartbreak, so I didn't want to write about that. But in this next album, I am. I think I'm going through a heartbreak right now'

119

Her comments would have chimed with Rihanna, who said only a few months earlier: 'Single life is so overrated. It sucks.'

Rita might have thought she was letting Rob down gently by trying to set the record straight on their status but he was anything but gentle.

Privately he was seething – and he would get his revenge.

11

Rocky Horror Show

IF Rita thought she was disentangling herself from one awkward situation with Rob she was innocently stumbling into another dose of boy trouble.

There didn't seem much in it when Rita tweeted in June 2012: 'A$AP Rocky. I Need You. Dope.'

She was just bigging up a fellow artist's song she was feeling at the time, right?

Or was there more going on behind the scenes?

Was her tweet a more direct appeal?

A$AP Rocky – real name Rakim Mayers – was one of the A$AP Mob, a self-styled hip hop collective of rappers, producers, video directors and fashion designers from Harlem, New York, whose moniker stands for 'Always Strive And Prosper'. He shared a connection with Rita to Drake – as A$AP also appeared as support to the Canadian rapper on his European tour earlier that year.

He was two years older than Rita but probably seemed far more worldly to her than the slim age difference suggested. Hardened by life's challenges (he was twelve when his dad was sent to prison for drug offences and a year later the older brother he idolised was shot dead) it was to his credit he'd been able to turn his life around and forge something creative from his anguish.

A$AP was setting his own rules, and it's easy to imagine how this hot young rapper must have appealed to Rita, who from a young age had been drawn to rougher characters.

If something happened between these two – and three years later

Rocky in a shocking and public way would claim it had – it might well have been in those early months of 2012.

As with Rita and Drake, there would be complications.

Around the same time A$AP was the object of someone else's desire.

A female Australian rapper called Iggy Azalea was also creating a buzz with a style that was in-your-face, sexy and raw. Videos of her live shows were going viral and when Rita bumped into her in New York at the time of 'R.I.P.' she was immediately impressed.

'I remember the first time we really actually met was at the Soho House in New York,' Rita said during a joint radio interview with Iggy in 2014. 'And you walked in and you looked a bit stressed because I think you flew in from somewhere. I remember it and I was like, "Who is this really pretty girl", and then I found out she was Australian and then we just kind of connected 'cause that was when I released my first single and she had this massive viral following and I just kind of loved her.'

Iggy Azalea's story had a lot of similarities with Rita's. Although born in Australia, Iggy would also find fame in her adopted homeland, having lived in America as an illegal immigrant when she travelled there as a teenager. Like Rita, Iggy had suffered at the hands of industry men who made big promises to launch her career but never delivered.

But when Rita met Iggy would she have known the beautiful blonde rapper had the hots for Rocky? It would have been hard for her not to – as in the summer of 2012 Iggy bore the name of his break-out mixtape *Live. Love. A$AP* tattooed on her fingers. She also suggested he had a similar tattoo of support for her, adding: 'I'm just the only one with it on my fingers.'

Nothing is forever, it seems, in the pop world and by July 2012 Rocky was distancing himself from Iggy, announcing: 'No, I'm not dating her. But I do like blondes.'

What other blondes could he be referring to?

A$AP seemed calm about the situation at the time – but something was to happen that would enrage him so much he would seek payback in a lyric three years later.

Did Rita have a role in the break-up between Iggy and A$AP?

Did she reveal something of his behaviour to her new friend? Did she set him up?

Whatever the detail, the fallout from whatever happened between Rita and A$AP would play out in the summer of 2015, but it certainly seems the seeds were sown for the rapper's fury back in 2012.

In the short-term Rocky's split from Iggy hit her hard. So much so that when Rita's manager Sarah Stennett tried to bring her into the Turn First Artists' fold, she couldn't care less.

'I didn't even want to meet her,' Iggy said. 'I came to the lunch forty minutes late in gym clothes, purely for the free food. Sarah was like, "What is wrong with you, luv? Are you just really rude or are you heartbroken?"'

It was the latter. 'I'd just broken up with my boyfriend and nobody would return my calls,' Iggy said.

Sarah told her: 'We're going to show them.'

Show them she certainly would. The incredible rise of Iggy Azalea – now one of the world's most influential female performers with a staggering hit rate – charts back to that moment. And Rita also played a huge part in her success story. She wanted Iggy to support her on her first official tour – a five-date run of gigs in the US before the end of the year. The Ora Tour would start in Santa Ana in California on 23 October and end in New York seven days later. Hanging out on tour together would form a bond between Rita and Iggy that would boost both their careers. And it gave Iggy the push she needed to break out on her own.

Like Roc Nation had done with Rita, Stennett believed the best move for Iggy was to take her time. She hooked her up with songwriters The Invisible Men and told her to go to Wales over Christmas that year to write.

'I wanted her to get really away from all the glitz and glamour and really back to basics,' says Stennett. 'It was harsh – it was very cold and very dark in deepest Wales at a very faded-glory studio, but it became a hugely important part of the process.'

Iggy's writing retreat would prove fruitful. One of the tracks they worked on became 'Fancy' – a song that would eventually become a huge number one for her in the US.

Signing Iggy would prove to be one of the shrewdest moves of

Sarah Stennett's career as she turned a virtual unknown into an international superstar. Back then, however, Rita was the much bigger star. Yet even she was to get a shock to discover just how popular she was.

12

Hero to Zero?

THE president, prime minister and mayor stood proudly to attention. Behind them hundreds of people lined up to catch a glimpse of their returning hero.

It was the sort of reception usually reserved for a visiting dignitary. Who they were waiting for might not have been a world leader but she'd done more than most to help put Kosovo on the map.

Rita could hardly believe it. Her mother, who kept abreast of what was happening back home, had warned her daughter her success was big news – but she hadn't taken her seriously.

'I never really thought it was a big deal,' she said. 'I was like, "Nah, don't believe it." But my mum was like, "Ree-ah, they are going crazy for you in Kosovo." So I said, "OK, let's go to Kosovo."'

And so Rita flew home to Pristina to film a video for 'Shine Ya Light', the third single to be released under her own name and fourth from *Ora*, if you include 'Hot Right Now', which had been added to the album as a bonus track.

Never in her wildest dreams would she imagine the reception. To have her country and city leaders there to welcome her was unheard of. But, aside from them, the sight of so many people gathered just for her blew her mind.

'All the planes stopped so we could come through and there were six cars waiting for me,' she said. 'I got off the plane, it was like millions of heads. The whole country was outside. I couldn't see the floor. I'm not even exaggerating. It was the most surrealest [sic] experience I've ever felt.'

She had no idea her music was making such a difference.

'It made everything that I've been doing make sense,' she said. 'I realised how many people are out there who I can inspire and help. I had been inspiring and helping them without even realising. It really opened my eyes to what I can do. Imagine having enough power to change one country? It's great!'

Sparking memories of how dishevelled she looked when meeting Jay Z, Rita panicked slightly when she realised she was hardly dressed for meeting dignitaries.

'It was like Obama being there or something – it just doesn't happen, does it?' she said. 'I had no idea they were coming so I looked really bad. Suddenly we were in this private room and they were sitting there saying how proud they are as a nation.'

The plan was to film Rita moving through the streets of the city of her birth, mobbed by fans. Usually these shoots require the hiring of dozens of extras. For Rita, the locals were happy to oblige. She was amazed to meet so many people, hear their stories, see how they lived, witness the hope in their eyes.

'I felt like Princess Diana of Kosovo,' she said. 'You know how much attention she got in her life? That's what it felt like. I've never had a reception like that before.

'It was a shock. I didn't realise how people lived there. Children ran after me in the street. Men were crying.

'They are so proud that someone from there had succeeded, and came back to see them. It gives them hope.'

Rita filmed the video, directed once more by Emil Nava, which captured the essence of her return home. In addition to being mobbed she was shot cavorting on top of a building in just her underwear and a bomber jacket and rode a motorbike [licence plate 'ORA'] through the city. Rita's makeshift biker gang featured some of her cousins who still lived in Pristina.

One of the video highlights included Rita rocking out on the city's Newborn Monument – giant letters spelling out 'Newborn'. They were unveiled on 17 February 2008, the day Kosovo declared independence from Serbia. The yellow letters were coated in graffiti and the signatures of delighted citizens – one of which belongs to Rita.

As she bounced around atop the letter E in a baggy jumpsuit, bomber jacket and woolly hat, her legions of fans chanted 'We love you Rita'. The adoration was so overwhelming that during a break in filming Rita collapsed in tears.

The song was a self-empowerment anthem – and the perfect soundtrack for what she was trying to achieve in her homeland.

'It was more than a music video,' Rita said. '[It] was a moment in our history as Kosovo, it was a moment for people to see us: how we live, our landscape. It was my duty to do my video there.'

Many artists fly into locations, do their job and fly out again, but Rita, although her schedule was tight, took time to meet with inspiring individuals and listened to what else she could do to help make a difference.

'I realised that with my level, I could help them,' she said. 'I met local leaders and I'm involved in projects to help youth, the construction of reception centres and orphanages.

'The thing I can do today is to be a voice for my country. I firmly believe that to know where we come from and to not forget it helps to know who we are.'

Besides promoting Kosovo, Rita was keen to build bridges too – even with the country that subjected her people to so much hardship and misery. She knew it might be difficult for some Kosovans to accept but she said she would be prepared to play a concert in Belgrade, capital of Serbia.

'What I'm going to say could be very political, and it could become a huge thing, but being from Kosovo and knowing the hunger and the desperation we had as a country to just be individual and be independent and stand on our own two feet. We fought for that. And I know that people in Serbia know what that feels like, to fight for something,' she said.

Her trip was a welcome distraction from speculation surrounding her private life but, although she managed to achieve much in her time there, her star status meant sacrifices had to be made.

'Sometimes I see people writing the most ridiculous things about me,' she said. 'It's all about me being with this person, or that person, and no one realises. I'm in Kosovo shooting a video and that's what matters. The fact is I'm not able to be Ree-ah, the regular twenty-two-year-old girl. I'm never in one place for long enough.'

Before the single was released on 4 November 2012 Rita's 'Ora Tour', with Iggy Azalea, kicked off in America. Their west coast dates went off without a hitch but when they travelled east trouble struck. They hit New York just as the city braced itself for the arrival of Hurricane Sandy. The storm would cause widespread devastation and chaos the likes of which New Yorkers hadn't seen since the terrorist attacks of 9/11.

'It's like Independence Day in NYC right now,' Rita tweeted, comparing the scene to Will Smith's infamous 1996 disaster movie, just before the storm hit as people tried to evacuate the city. 'I'm actually gettin a little bit nervous.'

The show had to be postponed until December. Rita managed to avoid the hurricane but a personal storm was brewing just over the horizon. Oblivious to the gathering clouds she threw herself into a whirlwind schedule.

Rita returned to the UK and – as part of her promotion – performed the single on *The X Factor*, Simon Cowell returning the favour after her stint as a guest judge. By the end of October 2012 the show was onto the live finals stage and Rita was reacquainted with hopefuls she'd helped put through, including one of the favourites, James Arthur, a performer she'd get to know a lot better over the coming weeks.

Rita was appearing on the show as the bona fide pop star but she turned back into an excited young fan when she came face to face with the woman responsible for so much of her style, image and attitude … Gwen Stefani. They say never meet your heroes but Rita was thrilled, particularly when the No Doubt singer turned out to be as charming as she'd hoped.

'I was like, "Hi, Gwen, what's up?!" and we just sat there talking, it was amazing,' Rita said. 'I was a bit nervous to meet my idol, but I'm a bigger fan now than I was before.'

Next she had two massive awards ceremonies. First up was the MOBOs where Rita was hopeful of picking up at least one award after being nominated in four categories – Best Newcomer, Best Female, Best Album and Best Video for 'R.I.P.'. And she was thrilled when she collected a gong for Best Newcomer.

Given it was the MOBOs that had given Rita her initial introduction to music fans it was fitting this was where she picked up her first major award. And she used the event to showcase her unique sense of style – wearing firstly a fitted white Mugler peplum dress before changing into an equally stunning floral Alexander McQueen pouffe. 'I couldn't breathe or believe it that I've won my first ever award,' she joked at the sacrifices she was making for fashion.

She might have wished for a wardrobe malfunction in the super-tight outfit but by the time of her next public appearance she would have been thankful if her clothing had been as well fitting.

Rita was at two gigs in one night and at the first, at Wembley Arena, for the Red Bull Culture Clash, her zip slipped and she revealed another flash of her chest.

Thankfully by the time she appeared at a special gig at the IndigO2 in London, where her mum was watching, all went well. Continuing her theme of giving something back to the industry that made her, Rita fronted a band of ten young community musicians at the O2 Think Big event, where volunteers also helped with make-up and roadie duties backstage. The audience was largely made up of kids too, something Rita loved.

'It's a simple project, by young people, for young people,' Rita said. 'The project was set up to encourage kids to do creative stuff. I love performing for kids as they scream the loudest.'

Before Rita had time to catch her breath, she was off to Frankfurt to open the MTV European Music Awards. And she was on cloud nine when she bumped into Gwen Stefani's No Doubt once more at the event – and Gwen stunned her by remembering her name.

'They are my idols and I let them know that. Now she recognises me, which is crazy.'

Even though Rita had her mini tour behind her she admitted she still got anxious before big events. 'I'm scared,' she said. 'I still get nervous but I turn it into adrenaline.'

By the time she took to the stage, spectacularly lowered, suspended in a cage, before launching into a power performance of 'R.I.P.' all nerves were gone. Once again Rita looked incredible, on this occasion channelling old-school Hollywood in a red lace Marchesa princess gown.

Fans were thrilled but if showbiz columnists were to be believed one watcher wasn't amused. Rita's gown, it was claimed, was too similar to one Rihanna had worn two years earlier. And when Rita used an umbrella to shield herself from on-stage pyrotechnics, it set even more sparks flying. *The Sun* quoted a source saying: 'Rihanna was furious when she spotted Rita Ora's dress for the VMAs, a rose gown that looked like one she wore in 2010. But she was even more annoyed when Rita went on stage using an umbrella as a prop. When Rita started her career, Rihanna thought it was cute that she was copying her look. But now she's getting p***ed off, especially as Rita is getting a following by using her old tricks.'

The Sun then also reported Rihanna was furious that Rita bagged a movie role she was after. Rihanna had apparently been lined up to play a villain in the blockbuster sequel *Fast and Furious 6*. But Rita, who had also cast for the part, equally impressed and landed it.

'Rihanna impressed movie bosses with her role in *Battleship*,' the paper reported. 'But schedules didn't work out and Rita really shone during castings. They loved her look and her attitude.'

One of Rita's new friends also found herself the subject of claims that Rihanna wanted a piece of her. Rita had befriended up-and-coming model Cara Delevingne, who was crowned Model of the Year at the British Fashion Awards in November. But Cara, it was said, had also become friends with Rihanna after meeting her at a Victoria's Secret fashion show in Manhattan.

Whether Rihanna was genuinely unhappy or whether the rivalry was something dreamt up by the tabloid, or their label, to generate interest was open to question.

Further claims that Jay Z had presented Rita with a £30,000 personalised Rolex watch for her birthday only heightened the feeling that the two singers were being played off against each other. Whatever the truth, the constant speculation must have been irritating for Rita – and she tried to set the record straight on the reality of the situation.

'To tell you the truth, I don't really care,' she said, insisting they were just both sisters under Roc Nation. 'My music's different, we sing differently, we're from different parts of the world. Plus, we've seen each other lots of times and we hang out. So if people are trying to create a feud, it's not going to work. Even if that was the case, Roc

[Nation] would be like, "What are you guys doing? You're part of the same family!"'

At the British Fashion Awards, while most eyes were on Cara, style watchers couldn't have failed to catch Rita, who again conjured up yet another look, this time reminiscent of Marilyn Monroe in a blue corseted gown by Vivienne Westwood.

Rita was everywhere, but her hectic schedule was putting a strain on her voice and with her first major tour looming, she was advised to take care of her throat. Distressing for her, though, was the doctor's warning that her favourite Tabasco sauce was damaging her vocal chords.

Rita couldn't believe it. After championing it repeatedly and making known her desire to be the face of the hot sauce brand, the company had been in touch. Now her dreams would be shattered. 'I've been told by my doctor that Tabasco is bad for my voice so I can't have it any more – but I absolutely love it,' she said. 'The head of Tabasco even sent me a bottle with my name on it. My whole team were emailed within an hour of me being told with orders to keep me away from it.'

All this meant Rita's tastes were a lot less spicy – much to the shock of backstage caterers at the top music venues who were used to excessive and eccentric requests from pop and rock stars. 'All Rita ever asks for is teabags and a packet of biscuits,' staff at a venue in Manchester revealed. 'There's no booze.'

Rita's next engagement was one she definitely wouldn't need anything to get in the mood for – celebrating one hundred years of Albanian Independence Day. On the same week as her twenty-second birthday, Rita flew to Tirana to headline a festival marking the historic occasion on 28 November. As fans queued for hours in the rain to catch a glimpse of her at the open-air concert, Rita dined with the Albanian president Bujar Nishani. And when the time came for her to take to the stage she wowed the audience with a high-octane performance. She pranced around in a gothic-style period dress and boots as she stormed through her hits. After her thrilling set Rita took to Twitter to express her gratitude to fans who braved the elements to see her.

'ALBANIA U WERE UNBELIEVABLE U ARE A DREAM COME

TRUE, I KNOW IT WAS RAINING BUT WE STILL ROCKED IT! HAPPY 100TH INDEPENDENCE DAY #IMHONOURED,' she declared.

As 2012 drew to a close Rita was able to reflect on what an incredible year it had been. She had gone from relative obscurity to one of the country's most prolific chart stars. As she looked to the future she saw herself branching out from music and capitalising on her popularity. One of the things she aimed to do was launch her own clothing line.

'I would absolutely love to,' she said. 'I don't know what it would look like yet but it would definitely be different.'

She added: 'I love flamboyancy and glamour and elegance. I love that over-exaggerated style. I'm a boy-girl. I love my trainers and mixing comfort with sleek, clean lines.'

These were exciting times, yet while she wasn't entirely sure what the future would bring one thing was certain ... Rob Kardashian would not feature in it.

The writing was on the wall when Rita revealed she had yet to find love. And as she denied again being in any kind of relationship it looked like Rob's hopes of anything developing with him were dashed.

'In twenty-two years, there's been nothing,' she said. 'I've had young fascinations but never love. I think it's my only weakness. I'm scared of letting my guard down, and if I fell in love with someone now, he'd have to try ten times harder to break it down.'

She revealed she only needed three things from a boyfriend: 'For him to make me laugh, tell me I'm beautiful once in a while, and be there for me.'

She wasn't looking for much, but Rob wasn't that guy.

'He's a great friend. But the only relationship I'm having now is with the tour bus.'

Rita might have claimed they were nothing more than friends but she must have said something to change his status because no sooner was it being reported that they'd split than Rob was demonstrating his disgust. In the modern version of tearing up photos, burning love letters and binning mix tapes, Rob unfollowed Rita on Twitter and deleted all tweets and pictures of her on Instagram. Speculation was that Rob had been due to fly over for Rita's birthday celebrations at Dstrkt nightclub but after serious talks they'd decided to call things off. In a show of unity, none of the Kardashians tweeted Rita birthday greetings. His sisters might largely have been staying silent but Rob was doing anything but. Just a day after news of the split broke he took to Twitter to unleash a torrent of fury.

The *Daily Star* reported that Rob tweeted: 'I'm actually disgusted a woman could give up her body to more than 20 dudes in less than a year.

'How can a woman who is so busy trying to start her own career have time to be with so many dudes all while in a relationship? She cheated on me with nearly 20 dudes while we were together, I wonder how many she will sleep with now that we're apart. But I mean 20?!'

The Sun claimed he also wrote: 'When a woman cheats on you with one man I can live with that.

'People make mistakes, trust me. I have forgiven numerous times ...

'But when a woman disrespects herself by messing with more than 20 men, all while being in a relationship with a faithful man ... I just don't get how a woman can do that to her body, and your career hasn't even launched yet.

'I don't put up with sloppiness. LOYALTY.

'This is a lesson to all the young women out there to not have unprotected sex with multiple men, especially while in a relationship.

"RESPECT THY SELF!"'

Both papers said he deleted the tweets quickly after publishing them, but not before they went viral.

In response to comments he received, Rob later appeared to be backtracking, saying: 'Just so we are clear, I never once mentioned 'Rita Ora' in any of my tweets or even used the word 'whore' and I never would. I respect women.'

If Rob hoped that would smooth things over with Rita and other female observers shocked at his use of language he had another thing coming.

Caitlin Moran, writing in *The Times* in her humorous 'Celebrity Watch' column (CW), spoke for many when she said: 'Since breaking up with her boyfriend Rob Kardashian, yellow-haired songstress

Rita Ora has been on the unpleasant end of Kardashian's bitter dumpee tweet-feed. "She cheated on me with nearly 20 dudes while we were together," Kardashian alleged in a classic "flailing spiteful derogatory misogynistic bullshit" tactic.

'CW suspects that there is no truth in the allegation, not least because Kardashian later deleted all the comments. But let us, for a moment, humour Kardashian's question: "How can a woman who is so busy have time to be with so many dudes?"

'That would simply be down to a woman's natural ability to multitask, Mr Kardashian. Ora has probably one of those big, planny calendars, with a "20 dudes" column in which to plot dates. Or perhaps she has an iCal app on her iPhone, in order to juggle "starting her own career" with "20?!!!"

'Well DONE on your schedule admin, Rita Ora — or "Rota Ora", as CW will call you from now on.'

Rob allegedly made a further slur, seemingly claiming on Twitter that he had got Rita pregnant but backtracked when he realised he was being set up by a fake account.

Rita maintained a dignified silence and made it clear to any interviewers that questions about her personal life were off limits.

She wasn't complaining about the coverage she was getting, however.

'You have to suck it up, because it goes hand-in-hand with what you're doing,' she said. 'At the end of the day, the media are helping you.'

Amid the furore, however, there was some amazing news. Rita announced her first UK tour, eight dates starting in Manchester on 28 January and ending in Leeds on 13 February. Within minutes of the tickets going on sale all dates sold out.

Rita then had a triumphant return to *X Factor*, performing live at the final, held that year in Manchester. Belting out a stunning medley of 'R.I.P.' and 'How We Do (Party)' she showed just why she was the country's hottest talent. James Arthur, one of the early hopefuls Rita put through, won the series and as well as a guaranteed number one single and a lucrative record deal he walked away with something equally as precious – Rita's phone number!

An end-of-year holiday to Dubai with her family around her, so she could bring in 2013 with a spectacular firework-laden performance, couldn't have come at a better time. It was just what she needed to take stock. The recent comments about her had been unsavoury but they wouldn't take the shine off twelve months that had seen her become one of pop's hottest properties.

Photos she posted online showing her lying on the beach looking stunning in a white bikini sent out the message she was relaxed and happier than ever.

In a fitting end to a year of firsts, she took a leap into the unknown with a daring skydive alongside Elena – 'the bravest thing I've ever done'. She then brought the curtain down on 2012 with a rousing performance at the Downtown Dubai New Year's Eve Gala. Her headline slot followed a spectacular fireworks display accompanied by music from the Prague Philharmonic Orchestra, which organisers claimed was the 'biggest show on Earth'.

It was the latest glittering highlight in a year packed with them. Her album, one she feared might never see the light of day, had topped the charts and sales had reached 240,000 since its release. 'That's definitely the most surreal thing that's happened to me,' she said. 'The success of the singles, and the tour selling out within minutes of the tickets going on sale as well – all of last year was crazy.'

She looked forward to 2013, excited at what lay in store. Even bigger and better things awaited her. And she didn't know it then but the first seeds had been sown for a new romance.

Was Rita about to fall in love at last?

Or would she have to kiss a lot of frogs before finally meeting her prince?

13

Meet the Trouble and Strifey!

'I have no time for the opposite sex at the moment. Strictly none.'

So said Rita Ora on the eve of her first-ever British headline tour.

Strictly, it was true … at the time. But before long Rita would be linked to SEVEN men – but only one woman!

In the aftermath of her so-called split from Rob Kardashian she was being linked to all manner of male pop stars and actors.

But what wasn't widely known was that away from the headlines and prying eyes, Rita was getting close to people who, for a short while at least, held her fascination.

One of these was Ledri Vula, a rugged Kosovan rapper, musician and producer from Pristina, four years her senior. Rita, according to Kosovan sources, met him while staying in Ulcinj – a picturesque and southernmost seaside town, with a large Albanian community, in Montenegro. Rita's parents own a cottage there on the banks of the River Buna.

Ledri has something of a reputation in his homeland, both for his music and his colourful personal life. He had a long-standing on-off relationship with Dafina Zeqiri, the darling of the Kosovan Albanian scene affectionately known as Duffy, with whom he performed on a couple of singles.

By all accounts his reputation as a bit of a ladies' man meant he was known as much for his relationship status as his music and in 2012 he had stepped back from the industry to focus on directing.

Rita cryptically posted a photo of Ledri on Twitter and said she wanted him to make her pallaqinka [pancakes]: 'This dude right here needs to come over to my house for breakfast anytime and cook me those delicious palaqinka [sic]. Don't make me come there where u at LOL HAAAAA'

Another photo appeared of Rita and Ledri larking around with her wearing what looked like a sailor hat.

Ledri wasn't the only Albanian linked to Rita.

Another handsome singer, Armend Milla, was also snapped with Rita and her family as they holidayed in Ulcinj. He hails from the town but it seems he visited the Sahatçius while studying in London and even worked at Besnik's bar, the Queen's Arms.

After Rob Kardashian's ungracious comments, Rita would have to endure a flurry of speculation over her private life. She was linked to Diana Ross's actor son Evan when the pair were seen chatting at DJ Jonny Lennon's Funday party at Goldbart in SoHo. That followed a suggestion she was getting close to American actor Jonah Hill.

Rita initially saw no reason to address any of the surrounding speculation but, after weeks of keeping silent over Rob's outburst, she was forced to speak out when another outrageous comment was posted about her on Twitter.

Holly Hagan – one of the cast of *Geordie Shore* – an MTV reality television series, brought attention to herself by claiming there was more to Rita's relationship with Jay Z than work.

Rita was understandably furious.

'Neva eva will any1 includin a red head dum z lister try talk s*** about me & my family holly wateva ur name is. Anyway I only speak when I have to and that was just f***** ridiculous that's why I spoke,' she reportedly tweeted before deleting it.

Such a slur didn't merit a response but Rita was so outraged she felt she had to say something to reassure her fans, who were now proudly calling themselves 'Ritabots'.

'Anyway I only speak when I have to and that was just f****** ridiculous, that's why I spoke now I need to get back to my movie bots, I love you,' she added.

Hagan quickly backtracked. 'Oooopsy getting told off,' she tweeted, before claiming she had received 'sick' death threats for her unfounded comment.

It wasn't what Rita wanted to be doing. Mostly, she preferred to adopt the old Hollywood mantra of 'never explain, never complain'.

'Sharing my life with people is just part of my daily routine,' she said. 'But I don't take any notice of the things people say – it's just white noise. I know the truth. I don't feel I need to explain anything. Silence is the most powerful response. I know it's contradictory to put yourself out there and then not want to deal with the responses, but that's just how it is. You can be forgotten very quickly. So I am aware that I need to stay current, keep connecting and keep bringing things to the table. Otherwise you can just disappear.'

You couldn't blame her for wanting to take a break from men but at least Rita was able to laugh about her recent boy trouble. When asked during one interview who, out of screen legend Robert De Niro, Twilight star Robert Pattinson and her ex, who she would marry, hook up with or shoot, she replied: 'I would marry Robert De Niro, I would sleep with Robert Pattinson and I would definitely, definitely, shoot Rob Kardashian.'

Rita's recent comments didn't stop people trying to hook her up with various celebrities. The next available young man she was linked to was recent X Factor winner James Arthur. They had grown friendly during the series and James – who shot to number one with 'Incredible' and was bathing in that post-series glow – obviously followed up their number swap by giving Rita a call.

She played down any romance: 'It's funny. Just because I'm a female, people think that I have to be doing something. He's a good friend. It's really cool. We get on really well.'

If James had taken a shine to Rita during her stint on the show he wasn't the only one. Simon Cowell, who'd raised eyebrows after hiring Rita as a guest judge, sounded her out about joining the panel full-time for the next series in 2013.

'There were talks,' she confirmed. 'But if I was to take on that role, it would have to be at a point when I could give it my full attention. I feel like I have so much to accomplish first before I take on another job and it's kinda a full-time job being a judge on X Factor. It's not like a 9–5. It's constant, for months. Not that I have anything against it. I watch it and I love it but if I was to take on a full-time role, it would probably be when I'm loads of albums in. Being a guest judge is so much easier – you can say yes to people and not have to mentor them.'

When the nominations for that year's Brit Awards were announced Rita could concentrate on her own music once more and she was celebrating because she was up for two gongs – British Breakthrough Act and British Single of the Year, where remarkably both 'Hot Right Now' and 'R.I.P.' were in the running.

After the run of press she'd had, Rita was selective in who she spoke to at the nominations event but she said: 'I went to the Brits last year and no one even noticed I was there, no one took a photograph or anything, and a year later I'm up for some awards.

'I try not to think about it too much because I don't want to jinx it. To win would be a great achievement for me and my fans, but we'll see.'

Before the ceremony Rita had some big decisions to make – like who to invite. Her mum was an obvious choice but Rita said she wanted to make room for her new best friend Cara Delevingne, who she had taken to calling 'wifey'. 'My mum is coming along to the ceremony and I will also see if wifey wants to come – I'll ask her.'

Rita might have turned coy when it came to talking about men she'd grown close to – but there was no holding back when the topic was her hot model friend.

Rita had known Cara for months but since they'd been reacquainted at the end of 2012 they'd grown to be bosom buddies. 'She's officially mine,' Rita said. 'She's, like, untouchable. I've taken her off the market. We call each other "wifey." You know what a wifey means? It's like your other half. Like when you get married, like, that's your wife!'

Rita fans had cause to wonder who was this model that had made such an impact on her life?

From nowhere she appeared to be everywhere, on giant Burberry billboards to images of London streetlife for a Pepe Jeans campaign, Cara was fast becoming THE face of fashion. She seemed destined to follow in the footsteps of Twiggy and Kate Moss as a model who became a household name. After being crowned model of the year the twenty-year-old would grace the cover of *Vogue* in March 2013, with ten pages dedicated to the new star.

'Sometimes someone comes into the industry and just knocks everyone sideways,' said Sam McKnight, a hair stylist who regularly worked with her. 'Cara has an energy about her that brings an edge to every job we do. She is unthreatening, playful, warm and lovable – and is up for anything. The camera loves her, and she is a complete natural in a very uncontrived, cool way. In that, she is very like Kate, but they couldn't be more different.'

Cara was the daughter of a self-made property developer and a Selfridges personal shopper who enjoyed a privileged childhood where she wanted for little – a stark contrast to Rita's upbringing.

While Rita had to scrape and network to build her contacts, Cara's extended family and personal connections read like a *Who's Who* of London society life. Her grandfather, Sir Jocelyn Stevens, was chairman of English Heritage and her grandmother was lady-in-waiting to Princess Margaret, while her aunt Doris was a friend of Winston Churchill. Joan Collins was her godmother, Georgia May Jagger was her flatmate, Harry Styles of One Direction was an ex, while indie music darling Jake Bugg was said to be her current love interest.

'She's the kind of girl that you just want to hang out with,' makeup artist Charlotte Tilbury told *The Observer*. 'She's witty, intelligent and there's never a dull moment with her. Her face is strikingly beautiful with those dark eyebrows, defined features and piercing blue eyes. She reminds me of [Sixties model] Jean Shrimpton, but has great range as a model: she can go from classic beauty to quirky, from commercial to conceptual, with ease.'

Despite her lofty connections, Cara was someone Rita could connect to. 'I met Cara a long time ago at a festival. We hung out because we have a few mutual friends,' Rita said. 'We didn't see each other for a few months, then I saw her again and our careers were getting busier at the same time. We are really similar but come from totally different backgrounds. I found someone who is exactly like me who isn't really from my world. We just kept seeing each other and naturally started talking more and more. And now we're always together.'

As she embarked on her first headline UK tour, she made her comment about not having time for the opposite sex, adding: 'I've only got a wifey!'

Rita might have had her UK tour to rehearse for, but that didn't stop her taking time out to travel to Thailand with Elena in January to feature in a video alongside Snoop Dogg. Following the rapper's conversion to the Rastafari movement after a trip to Jamaica, he had changed his name to Snoop Lion and specifically asked for Rita to sing on 'Torn Apart' for his soon-to-be released *Reincarnated* album. Rita got to hang out in lavish resorts, dance with traditional Thai dancers, frolic on the beach and ride an elephant. And she couldn't have wanted a better person to hang out on a remote beach with than Snoop, whose real name (Calvin Cordozar Broadus Jr) was the inspiration for Calvin Harris's adopted stage name.

'He's much cooler than I expected,' Rita said. 'He is so experienced with everything. He's so funny. There were all these little crabs biting at our feet when we were filming on the beach. We built a race course for the crabs and watched them race while we were waiting to shoot. It was really fun.'

There was a minor drama when the tide went out, leaving them stranded. 'The boat couldn't come to the shore and we couldn't get off the island,' Rita said. 'Everyone had left except me, Snoop, my sister, the camera guy and the lighting guy. I was like, "Are we ever going to get off alive?" We had to walk all the way to the boat because the tide had gone out and the boat couldn't get to the shore. We had to wade through the sea to the boat. I don't know what was touching my toes! Slithery things, stones. I was holding Snoop's hand and he was squeezing it so tight I lost all circulation. It was hilarious.'

Snoop's chilled philosophy rubbed off on Rita. Their time in Thailand would always be special to her. She would go on to share a number of photos from her Thai adventure, including one that showed them with huge suspicious-looking roll-ups in honour of 'National Weed Day'.

'Miss you @snoopdogg #besttimeiveEvahadinThailand #tornapart,' she tweeted.

Back in Blighty it was back to the old routine. Just twenty-four hours after landing in London she was out partying with 'wifey' Cara and Radio 1 breakfast host Nick Grimshaw in the private members' Groucho Club.

Fans didn't have to worry that Rita wouldn't be on fire for her tour. Her ability to party hard and work even harder was becoming legendary – as Nick testified. 'I don't know how she does that,' he said. 'I've never met anyone like it. She's a machine.'

Rita's tour kicked off with a rousing opening night in Manchester. No expense was spared in the stage show, which was more befitting of arenas as opposed to the music theatres and halls she was playing.

Making her entrance inside a nuclear safe pod marked 'Quarantine', while hazardous waste lay all around, she launched into 'Radioactive' – a track which was going to be Rita's fourth solo single released just before the end of the tour. Shortly after the intro, the glass walls crashed down and she emerged in a skin-tight space-age foil cat suit. She raced through hits like 'Hot Right Now' and 'Shine Ya Light' before changing into a loose-fitting multi-coloured jumpsuit and slowing things down with an acoustic interlude that included her version of 'Hey Ya!' – a nod to her pre-breakthrough days. Rita made time in her set to serenade a fan each night and then she cranked up the pace for a kick-ass finale. Returning to the stage clad all in leather, she took to the drums for 'Uneasy' before a pumped-up 'How We Do (Party)' and sent her fans home happy with a stunning encore of 'R.I.P.'.

After years of playing second fiddle to other artists, or playing short festival sets, it was amazing for Rita to finally connect with her fans on her own terms. And they responded in kind – her Twitter followers soaring to 2.3 million during her tour.

As the tour continued she narrowly avoided what was now a near-customary wardrobe malfunction, just preventing at the last minute a flash of flesh by grabbing her silver foil dress as it slipped. Rita didn't want to risk another dressing down from her parents – and she explained how much she still referred to them for guidance on how much she should be revealing of herself.

'I've never been offered to pose naked but I need to ask my parents first,' she said, before opening up about her own sex appeal. 'It's either in you or it isn't. I feel like it's not something like you go, "OK, it's time to be sexy now." I feel like if it's part of your persona and you love being that flirtatious character, then I don't ever find anything wrong with that.

'It's just a personal choice, I think. If you start thinking, "Will everybody like this," you'll never do anything.'

The tour – and the press attention she'd had over the past year – showed Rita was no longer just a singer … she was a bona fide celebrity. And becoming a famous face was something she was still getting used to.

'I'm not complaining about fame. It's something I don't think I will ever understand but I can get with it,' she said. 'The confusing part was the celebrity element. I have always been a musician before anything so I think once the celebrity mixed in, it was a bit more confusing. But it's not something I have mixed in with the reality. I know what the reality is and the difference. As long as you don't get sucked in.'

Rita was speaking ahead of her two nights at London's Shepherd's Bush Empire, a venue not far from where she grew up, and she needed to pinch herself that the fans queuing outside were actually there to see her.

'That's so amazing,' she said. 'I mean, I lived down the road. I always used to look at people's names on the wall up there in the lights to see who was performing and now it is me.'

There might have been elements she would change but Rita was having the time of her life. Her raw energy and work ethic continued to amaze her support act Iggy Azalea.

'Honestly, I do not understand how you can go out and party all night long and not sleep and then wake up and be in sound check and do a show. I can't do that. I go to bed,' Iggy said to her in one joint interview.

Rita also gave some insight into life on tour: 'We've been partying on the bus,' she said. 'We put some music on and have the final drink of the night. There's me, the whole band and the backing vocalists on my bus – thirteen of us. I'm on a top bunk and I love it, I sleep like a baby.'

She said the worst thing about being on tour is waking up at a new place. 'We're at the venue and you come out and you haven't even washed your face yet,' she said. 'I have fans waiting outside and I really don't want them to see me. I hide my face. There's also the smell on the bus – like a big waft of morning breath.'

143

After her triumphant eight nights, Rita signed off the 'Radioactive Tour' with a lavish party at Mahiki with a star-studded guest list that included Tinie Tempah, TV presenter Caroline Flack and her mum of course.

Sadly for Rita, however, her 'wifey' couldn't make it. 'Cara's in New York for Fashion Week so she couldn't make this week. I'm a bit sad. Of course, we talk all the time – she was just texting me now.'

She had a double celebration – 'Radioactive', her final single from *Ora*, climbed to number eighteen, giving Rita her fourth top twenty hit. A slice of power pop fused with disco and house, the track was written by Sia Furler, who'd co-written 'Diamonds', a recent hit for Rihanna, and Greg Kurstin, who'd enjoyed a fruitful writing relationship with Lily Allen.

With her tour such a success, Rita was buzzing – and she even broke her code of silence to finally give her perspective on those ridiculous tweets from Rob Kardashian. Asked if those messages hurt her, Rita said: 'No. Nooooo. To tell you the truth I don't put energy toward things that don't need light. You don't need it.'

She was putting her energy to other things and, with her tour commitments over, she headed back up to the Midlands to meet James Arthur, who was in the middle of his *X Factor* tour. Rita might have been supporting a friend but she was the talk of the gossip columns once more when it emerged she'd hooked up with James three times in a week. On one night he was clocked arriving at her hotel and leaving the next morning in the same clothes. On another he allegedly took Rita to a strip club in Leeds, where it was said they stayed for four hours before getting into separate cabs and heading for the same hotel. The tabloids were having a field day, claiming James and Rita had met up after their respective gigs in Sheffield and York.

A source told *The Sun*: 'They were desperate not to be seen. They entered the strip club via the back door and left separately to avoid being snapped together. James made a big effort to spend time with her. He's smitten.'

He told *The Sun* his success on the show had transformed his luck with women, but his own management had told him to raise his standards.

'I'm not exactly Brad Pitt, but *The X Factor* has got me a few birds,' he said. 'I'm told by my management that I need quality control.

'I know I get attention from women I would've been punching above my weight with before. But if I bag a supermodel on the strength of my voice I'm not gonna complain. I'm under no illusion that I'm some kind of big shot or heartthrob but it's nice to get female attention.'

Whether James thought Rita represented the sort of step-up his management were after was irrelevant. She didn't stick around long enough for him to find out.

Rita's attention was diverted by London Fashion Week, when Cara took centre stage. Wearing a T-shirt bearing the face of her 'wifey' and the legend 'Queen Delevingne', Rita joined Cara as she dazzled the audience with a star billing at the Burberry Prorsum show. Cara's presence loomed large over the whole event, featuring in seven shows, prompting some to suggest it should be renamed 'Delevingne Fashion Week'. That came after she'd wowed onlookers at the New York Fashion Week just days before, when she appeared eleven times.

Rita might have enjoyed the company of men but this was a period when she kept returning to Cara. She posted a provocative photo of them about to kiss, prompting speculation there was more to this than meets the eye. Friends seemed convinced there was, but Rita and Cara appeared to revel in the 'are-they-aren't-they' guessing game.

And just when it seemed like no man could come between them, soon there were two!

It was party time in London with Fashion Week and the Brit Awards approaching, and Rita and Cara joined a host of other celebs at the Shepherd's Bush Empire to catch rockers Muse. They sank drinks with One Direction's Harry Styles, a one-time ex of Cara's, and were part of a group that included will.i.am, Kate Moss's husband Jamie Hince and football agent Dave Gardner, better known as David Beckham's best pal. Rita hit it off with Dave as the pair were seen holding hands and whispering into each other's ears. 'They looked very sweet together and were really flirty,' one onlooker said. 'At one point Dave squeezed her bum and gave her a kiss on the cheek as they waited at the bar. Rita looked very smitten with him.'

After the gig, Rita and Dave joined Cara and Harry at the Dazed and Confused party at the Café Royal. The foursome headed back to Gardner's West London home for a house party. It was said to be her second all-nighter but Rita brushed off any suggestion she was caning it too much. 'When you're young and you work hard, it's nice to have fun, too,' she said. 'I think I'm just one of those people who doesn't need much sleep. Obviously it's not wise to stay out late all the time.'

Rita's PRs were staying silent on whether anything serious was going on but at least with Dave there was little chance of him talking out of turn. As the former husband to actress Davinia Taylor, he was used to dating a famous woman and, as godfather to the Beckhams' eldest son Brooklyn, knew the virtue of maintaining privacy.

Rita had her own place by now – the fancy pile in West London not far from her parents. But although she loved having her friends drop by, she wasn't the most contentious homemaker. 'I still haven't done the curtains yet,' she said.

What she was desperate to do was hand the key to a new house to her parents who had sacrificed so much to give her every opportunity. She'd identified a house for them but her mum hadn't seen it yet. 'This is the craziest thing that I am about to buy,' she said. 'They love it. They are so happy. My mum has a little connection with the flat she lives in now but when she sees the house, she'll think it's great.'

For Rita to be able to repay her parents made all those years of struggle worth it. And for them to watch as their daughter, in a year, amassed enough wealth to buy herself and them houses must have surpassed even the wildest dreams they had for her.

Also beyond their dreams would have been the sight of Rita taking a seat at pop's top table, as she did at the Brit Awards 2013, held at the O2 for the third year. Rita had Vera with her as she went, hoping to scoop at least one award. A year earlier she had been there but slipped down the red carpet unnoticed. Now everyone wanted to grab her for a few words or take endless photos. It wasn't surprising given she'd chosen a sculpted full-length salmon pink Ulyana Sergeenko gown to wear for the occasion.

Sadly the event did not live up to the glamour Rita supplied and it was a year best forgotten, not least because Rita failed to win a gong. Despite being odds-on favourite, she sadly missed out on British Breakthrough Act, which instead went to Ben Howard, an English folk singer-songwriter who few people outside the music press had heard of – and who had scored just one hit single that only reached number thirty-two. Howard also won Best British Male Solo Artist, which had been on the cards but his double triumph confounded bookmakers. In the British Single category both her nominations lost out to Adele's 'Skyfall', the theme from the James Bond movie of the same name.

The Times reported that the ceremony 'contained few surprises, with all but one of the bookies' favourites winning their categories. Howard won the Breakthrough Act award at the expense of Rita Ora, the odds-on favourite.' Even Howard said: 'This is bizarre, isn't it? I didn't really expect it.'

After the year she had it was an inexcusable snub. Rita put on a brave face but her friend and fellow Turn First artist Conor Maynard said: 'She was really upset about not winning anything. But I told her not to worry about it and just to chill.'

If it was any consolation to Rita, pop fans slammed the bash as the most boring ever. Six and a half million viewers tuned in – the Brits' biggest audience for ten years – but most branded it bland.

One viewer, recalling the raucous behaviour of bands like Oasis in the past, said: 'How boring is The Brits? I'd rather have a p*ssed Liam Gallagher any day.' Another said: 'Most boring collection of average musical talent ever to be lauded. Disappointing.'

Taylor Swift was criticised for her 'awkward' performance and live acts Muse, Robbie Williams, Mumford & Sons, Justin Timberlake and One Direction also failed to thrill.

On ITV's *Loose Women* Janet Street-Porter said: 'When I looked at the list of winners, I mean Emeli Sandé is a great singer but not very exciting. She's no Adele.'

Rita, after a quick change into a slinky black dress, consoled herself at the Roc Nation after-show party, held at the exclusive Hakkasan restaurant. Calvin Harris, who had just secured a deal for a residency at the MGM Grand Hakkasan club in Las Vegas, was on the decks. He posed with Rita and Ellie Goulding.

Dave Gardner joined Rita at the bash, where he met her mum for the first time, but although his presence made it look like they were ready to take things to a new level she was having doubts.

Rita was developing feelings for one person at the party – but it wasn't necessarily Dave.

At least Rita didn't have to hang around and wallow in self-pity at her awards snub. She was off to Australia to take part in a Future Music Festival in Sydney. And the reception she got from the Aussie Ritabots eased her disappointment. She said she was amazed by how 'crazy, fun and naked' the fans were. After one female removed her top during Rita's performance, the singer was prompted to do the same, stripping down to a cropped vest top.

'I saw boobage,' she said. 'But I love it. It made me take my top off. I didn't take my actual bra off, just my top off. It was fun. I love festivals. You get to do things like that and get away with it.'

After her 'marry, sleep with, shoot' comments, she joked that she had her sights on Robert Pattinson after hearing the handsome actor was also Down Under, filming his latest movie. 'I never even knew he was British, he's dreamy,' she said, inviting him to another appearance she was making in Adelaide. 'I thought he was American.'

Rita needed to be careful what she said, though. After her experience with Rob and her Twitter spats with Calvin, Jade Ewen and Holly Hagan she realised she had to censor what she put out there.

'You should have to sit an exam before you go on Twitter. To see if you're mentally stable,' she said.

Then, directly referring to Rob Kardashian, she said: 'When you are involved with someone for a while and they decide to express their feelings to the public, well, that's not my personal way of therapy but I guess everyone takes split-ups differently.' Rita added: 'I never actually thought it was a relationship in all honesty. I never mentally defined it as boyfriend/girlfriend. When I split up with him I said, "It's because I'm never there, I don't know how to do it." That's all I said ... then the rest happened.'

Rita was having a great time Down Under but sadly had to cancel some of her gigs after contracting a throat infection. 'I woke up this morning with no voice,' she tweeted. 'I hate this. I hope you forgive me. Without you I'd be nothing. Scariest thing for any artist When their instrument doesn't work you can't help but worry.'

And she had yet more grief to deal with when she found herself on the receiving end of an unexpected outburst from rapper Azealia Banks. The outspoken Harlem star had been at the same Future Music Festival as Rita and took offence at her fellow performer taking some photos.

'Lol Rita Ora is so thirsty,' she tweeted. 'She climbed over the wall of my dancers' dressing room to snap photos. She's been TRYING IT on this tour man ... She's mad she's Rihanna's understudy.'

She went on: 'Ever since I arrived on this tour, Rita's been going out of her way to try and intimidate me. Taking all these candids of me when I wasn't looking, then posting and deleting them like a weak b****.'

Given how touchy she was about having her photo taken it was then somewhat surprising that Azealia then posted her own picture of herself with Rita online. Calling Rita the 'third lady of Roc Nation', she placed her below Rihanna and Beyoncé.

Rita responded in a private text, which Azealia then made public. The message allegedly said: 'At the end of the day I don't know who the f*** you think you are.'

Which was precisely what her fans must have been thinking. Whereas Rita had only ever tried to make friends in the industry since breaking, Azealia seemed content with creating beef with other acts. She had pops at everyone from Iggy Azalea to the Stone Roses. It seemed no one was safe from her acid tongue.

Sources said the background of the outburst was that Banks was jealous of Rita's relationship with Cara. Azealia, who identifies with being bisexual but has said she doesn't like to live by labels, seemed to think Rita had stolen the model from her. Banks might not have been happy then when Cara took Rita's side and tweeted that she missed her wifey.

Thankfully, aside from Azealia's dwindling fanbase, no one paid much attention to her rant. Rita had better things to concern herself with. She was unveiled as the new face of über-trendy Italian trainer brand Superga, replacing style queen Alexa Chung. The move represented a changing of the guard somewhat.

There was no denying it now – Rita was not only the hottest new thing in music, she was also making waves in the fashion world.

'I've always loved fashion as much as I love being on stage, although it's different,' she said. 'But I never really followed trends or cared what people thought about my outfits. I always bought and wore what I wanted. If I wanted to wear a mask on my head, I'd do it. If I wanted to wear an Audrey Hepburn hairstyle, I'd wear it. I like to be comfortable but I don't always take it into consideration. I really like latex clothes, for example. But latex dresses ... people come up to me and go: "Are you comfortable in that?" And I'm like, "I don't care." How does it look? It looks good? All right, cool."'

Rita is famously indecisive – which creates problems. 'Sometimes, my team get anxious because I can change my mind at the last minute,' she said, before adding that she was still getting used to the fact that so much attention was given to what she was wearing.

'Recently, I went to get some smoothies and I was wearing my gym shorts and a T-shirt and I got completely hammered for it,' she said. 'I was like, "Could someone please tell me what is wrong with this outfit before I go out?" Being in the public eye has definitely made me more aware.'

Rita also revealed how she and Cara inspired each other with fashion-themed sleepovers. 'A sleepover for us involves a whole lot of crazy clothes we put together. I love dressing her up because she is like my little doll. Most of my wardrobe is crazy, so I always put her in stuff she would never wear,' she said. 'She always has fun and she's like, "How the f*** do you wear this?!" And then we take pictures.'

Being recognised for her style was a fantastic boost, but music was Rita's bread and butter and she was next heard featuring with a new Roc Nation talent. K Koke (Kevin Georgiou) was an English rapper and 'Lay Down Your Weapons' was his second single release. With Rita's vocals he achieved his first chart placing, the song reaching number eighteen in March.

Rita's air miles were going through the roof as no sooner was she back from Oz than she was jetting to New York for the filming of an advert and then to Monaco for the Bal de la Rose du Rocher in Monte Carlo, where she got to hang out with fashion designer Karl

Lagerfeld. Next stop was Brazil for a C&A commercial, before heading to Las Vegas for a party in the Tao nightclub.

Eventually she ended up in Austria – at a health clinic dubbed 'the world's toughest fat camp'. Rita stayed at the £1,500-a-night Viva Mayr clinic, home to one of the most gruelling detoxes imaginable.

As well as taking regular doses of diuretic Epsom salts, she knocked back magnesium powder in warm water four times a day, exercised regularly and ate only organic food.

A source told the *Daily Mirror*: 'It's the most opulent weight-loss and detox clinic in the world, and pretty hardcore. Rita wants to get in perfect shape for the summer and her forthcoming promo appearances. The food is mainly boiled potatoes and broths, and guests are taught to savour their food by chewing it a minimum of thirty times per mouthful. The programme set for Rita was designed to be a blueprint for the rest of her life, helping her keep on the straight and narrow.'

The Viva clinic overlooks Lake Wörth near the border with Italy and Slovenia. Rita, however, described it as being in the 'middle of nowhere' as she tweeted a picture of the lake on Twitter.

After her punishing schedule it's little wonder she needed to take some time out. Yet it seemed an extreme measure for someone used to burning the candle at both ends. It was as if she had been schooled in how to live a healthier lifestyle by someone for whom quitting the booze and getting fit had produced amazing results ... someone like a Scottish DJ who'd transformed from geek to chic practically overnight.

Rita had spent the last five months living the high life and enjoying hanging out with different company. Now though, she'd met a man who literally put the others in the shade.

Who was he?

Rita summed him up perfectly. He was 'six foot sex!'

14

The Gentle Giant

IT all started with the theft of a cupcake. A trivial action but it sparked a romance that saw Rita fall in love for the first time and would both bless her with one of her biggest hits – and curse her with a career setback from which it would take her months to recover.

The setting was the Jingle Bell ball, way back on the weekend of 8 and 9 December 2012 at the 02. Rita was on the same bill as Conor Maynard, Tinie Tempah and Calvin Harris, the DJ with whom she'd had a sparky connection since their Twitter spat.

Backstage, Calvin helped himself to a cupcake meant for Rita. Capital FM's Max Akhtar, another Turn First stable mate, alerted Rita. She didn't care about the stolen baking but did remark to Max that Calvin was looking 'hot'. Max, playing Cupid, told Calvin what Rita said. Calvin – born Adam Wiles – could have played it cool, appreciated the compliment and said no more. Instead he decided to act on it.

'He said, "I heard you think I look hot,"' Rita revealed. 'And then, boom, it happened.'

That was Rita's recollection of how she and Calvin got together but it wasn't quite as straightforward as that. Yes, sparks flew before Christmas 2012 but it would take them five months – and a few little dalliances on her part – before they went public with their relationship.

Rita added to the intrigue further when she seemed to confirm that she shared mutual feelings with Ledri Vula before she got close to Calvin.

In a response to whether she liked Ledri, Rita reportedly tweeted:

'Yaaa there USED TO BE chemistry, ONCE UPON A TIME BEFORE I FELL FOR ADAM FUCKING ugh.'

Rita's original tweet is no longer available for verification but it was also said that Elena had endorsed the sentiment, adding, 'all these years' they had 'sought an Albanian man'. Whether this was just wishful thinking on the part of the Albanian media – eager to see their biggest international star hook up with a fellow countryman – remains to be seen.

But whatever it was, one thing was clear. Rita was completely blindsided by her feelings for the Scottish superstar. At the time she got close to Calvin, he was at the peak of his powers. Not just a disc spinner, he was the world's hottest songwriter and producer with two number ones of his own, and another two as a featured artist. The latest of which, 'We Found Love' selling ten and a half million copies, gave Rihanna her biggest-ever hit and topped charts all over the globe.

Calvin was also celebrating making chart history. When 'I Need Your Love', his song with Ellie Goulding, rose to number seven in April 2013 he became the first act to score eight top ten hits from a single album, beating Michael Jackson who achieved seven hits twice.

The feat prompted Martin Talbot, managing director of the Official Charts Company, to brand Harris 'THE modern day hit-maker'. 'Many artists only achieve a handful of hits in their entire careers, so for any act to secure three or four from one album is an excellent achievement. Eight Top 10s from one album is not just impressive, it is absolutely remarkable,' he added.

Calvin's run began in June 2011 with 'Bounce' featuring Kelis (which peaked at number two), followed by 'Feel So Close' (three), 'We Found Love' (one), 'Let's Go' featuring Ne-Yo (two), 'We'll Be Coming Back' featuring Example (two), 'Sweet Nothing' featuring Florence Welch (one) and 'Drinking From The Bottle' (five).

Not bad for a former fish factory worker and M&S shelf stacker from Dumfries, in southern Scotland. His unprecedented success swelled his already sizeable £6 million fortune. And it was about to grow even larger still. While Rita had been drowning her sorrows after leaving the Brits empty handed, Calvin was celebrating landing his twenty-month residency at Hakkasan club in Vegas.

So he was hugely successful and massively in demand but, more important than all that, Calvin had undergone a remarkable transformation from lanky pseudo rock star to groomed buff pop god. For years Calvin had trawled around Europe dragging a motley crew of mates with him playing his brand of electro pop live. At the end of 2010 though, in a move that was like a modern equivalent of Bob Dylan going electric, he ditched the live musicians and switched to DJing live full-time.

At the same time, he threw away his bottle of black hair dye, moved to LA, quit drinking, hired a personal trainer and emerged as a stubbled, blonde black-suited hunk, at last looking comfortable in his 6ft 5¾ in. frame, who would go on to model underwear and prompt women all over the world to go: 'Where did he come from?'

So it's little wonder that when Rita found out Calvin liked her, she forgot about Albanian pancake makers and footballers' chums, for a while at least. For his part, Gardner didn't seem to bear any grudges. He always maintained a respectful silence and went on to meet and fall for Hollywood siren Liv Tyler, with whom he had a child and became engaged to.

Calvin didn't waste any time in staking a claim for Rita's affection. He flew her on his private jet to Vegas, to join him in his booth while he spun the discs. He was as prolific on Twitter as Rita was and when he posted a photo online of Rita boarding his jet captioned 'You again!' the cat was out of the bag.

Rita had a new man in her life. But as ever that didn't necessarily mean things would run smoothly.

Calvin treated Rita to a series of cosy encounters at Hollywood's famous Château Marmont hotel and when they were back in London, she took him to the Electric Cinema in Notting Hill to catch a movie – a favourite haunt of her wifey Cara.

But while Rita was enjoying that buzz that comes from meeting someone new and exciting, Cara was having a spot of bother. Snapped coming home with a friend by waiting paparazzi she gave photographers a much more lucrative set of shots when a small sealed packet containing white powder fell out of her bag as she searched for her keys.

Photographers told *The Sun* newspaper, which published the

photo, she tried to hide the sachet beneath her handbag as she bent down to pick it up. One said: 'She found it hilarious but her friend was really edgy about it. Suddenly Cara dropped something and bent over to pick it up. Very discreetly, she just put her foot on it and then rolled her handbag across so it looked like she was just kind of bending over.

'The friend kept saying, "Can you stop taking pictures?" The friend definitely realised they were in trouble once that little packet had dropped on the ground.'

Rita wasn't around but had been with Cara the night before, at The Box nightclub in Soho, along with, incidentally, Kate Moss.

There was no evidence that Cara had done anything wrong but publication of the photos had fashionistas thinking back to 2005 when Kate had been embroiled in a drug scandal. Then the super-model was dropped by a host of high-profile clients before staging a remarkable comeback.

Cara had a £1 million deal with H&M and featured in other campaigns for Burberry Body Tender fragrance, Pepe Jeans and Yves Saint Laurent Babydoll makeup.

As the fashion world waited to see if there would be any repercussions, Cara responded perhaps in the only way she knew how. Both she and Rita were due at the Met Ball fashion gala in New York. Rita looked stunning in a white cutaway dress. But centre of attention was Cara, punking it up in an equally revealing studded Burberry number. Rita posed with Cara and Pixie Geldof, saying: 'Man I love bad bitches, that's my f***ing problem.'

It would be easy to assume this was just a cheeky throwaway comment on Rita's part considering Cara's recent predicament. But the star's words had an ironic undertone. They were actually lyrics from one of A$AP Rocky's most popular songs 'F**kin' Problems' featuring Drake. Small world. By now he had split with love interest Iggy Azalea who embarrassingly had the A$AP tattoo on her little finger crossed out.

Was Rita still in regular contact with him? Or was it just another show of support for an artist she admired? Either way, in time Rita would likely come to regret her association with the rapper.

Back to the present and Cara remained tight-lipped about what was in the bag but she diverted attention in fine style by puckering up with Sienna Miller. The English actress had arrived in a similar studded outfit and Cara, posting the image later, captioned it: 'Studded love.'

It was a perfect response – but was there an ulterior motive to her actions? If Cara's kiss was also designed to remind Rita what she was missing, it had little effect. The singer was preoccupied with business of her own.

While at the Met Ball she was cornered by Madonna. Rita sat stunned as the pop icon revealed her daughter Lourdes was a huge fan of hers. Not only that but she wanted Rita to be the new face of her clothing range Material Girl. Rita could hardly believe it. Being endorsed by the Queen of Pop was amazing on its own but being involved with such a high-profile brand could only help her break America, something she was still desperate to do.

It was yet further proof that Rita had something unique people just wanted to tap into, or grab a piece of – something Calvin could relate to.

They couldn't see enough of each other and one pal said: 'They are having a great time and are really into each other.'

It was an amazing turnaround after their first introduction – that spat over 'Call My Name'. Their war of words had obviously created a fizz between them that was impossible to ignore.

Rita wasn't the first celebrity Calvin had been linked to, but now he was dating one of the most talked-about singers in the country he was to discover what being in a relationship in the public eye was all about. Their first public appearance together in the UK was a gift for showbiz hacks and gossip columnists.

The occasion was the playback party for Daft Punk's new album, *Random Access Memories*. The location was the sixty-ninth floor of Europe's tallest building, the 1,016-foot-high Shard, by London Bridge. Until its opening London had only one building that worked as a euphemism for a sexual act. For years blokes were able to boast how they'd taken their girlfriend 'up the Oxo Tower'. Now people were posting that they'd been 'lucky enough to be taken up the Shard'.

Rita now knew what that was like too! *The Sun* joked that Calvin certainly knew how to impress a girl on a date – 'by showing her one of Europe's biggest erections'.

While Calvin chatted to their mutual friend Tinie Tempah, Rita took snaps of the capital's skyline. The pair then slinked away to the low lit, deserted top floor of the seventy-two-storey skyscraper for a private chat. 'They looked more interested in each other than watching the sunset,' an onlooker told *The Sun*. 'Rita hung on Calvin's every word and laughed hysterically at almost everything he said. He was lapping it up and seemed to enjoy being the centre of her attention. But when people came up and started to notice them they got a little shy and scurried back downstairs to the party.'

The highs just kept coming for the couple. Rita's deal with Material Girl was signed. Worth £600,000, it would mean Rita appearing in a campaign throughout America, where the Eighties-themed brand, aimed at teenagers, was sold in Macy's stores. She would be following in the footsteps of Kelly Osbourne and Georgia May Jagger.

Hot on the heels of that news Calvin was named 'Songwriter of the Year' at the prestigious Ivor Novello Awards, something he claimed was his 'greatest achievement'. He and Rita celebrated at London's trendy Nobu restaurant and Rita tweeted: 'Ivor Novello's eh? Songwriter of the year. No big deal just pretty f*cking awesome!! @calvinharris :))))'

Rita wasn't shy about praising her new man's talents. But he revealed she didn't really like his music! As he announced dates for his biggest-ever tour, he said, 'Rita doesn't really like dance music. She doesn't really like my music – but I like hers! We're not together for musical reasons, which is great.'

Calvin's tour would take him to most of the major cities in the UK and Ireland in December, supported by fellow DJ Tiësto. Demand for his tickets was on a par with Rita's, and his show at Glasgow's new Hydro Arena just before Christmas sold out in three minutes.

Rita might not have been a fan of his music, but being with a trend-setting songwriter meant it was natural she was bouncing around some ideas for new tracks. And she revealed she was going to use her recent relationship experience as inspiration for lyrics. 'My next album is about me being 22, growing up in this industry really fast and being in a really s****y relationship, and all the s*** I had to deal with,' she said.

The tactic had worked for American country-turned-pop star Taylor Swift who famously unloaded on her exes through her songs. Rita might not have had much heartache to draw upon for her first album but she had relationship stress by the bucket load now.

Rita and Calvin hit it off amazingly well. He was a gentleman and, unlike other men she'd been with, didn't have an agenda. For the first time in her life Rita was feeling something deeper than a crush.

At Café de Paris in London, as she showcased a new song during a MasterCard Priceless gig, she said: 'This song is called "Out Of Love Not In Love" – even though I am right now.' Calvin was waiting backstage in her dressing room and took her out for a romantic meal afterwards.

Both had such hectic schedules they had to see each other whenever they could. And Calvin demonstrated how smitten with Rita he was by clocking up an incredible 5,445 miles in just one weekend to be by her side.

After flying in for Rita's London gig, he popped into the studio before using his jet to take them both to Derry-Londonderry in Northern Ireland, where they were both on the bill for Radio 1's Big Weekend. He flew to Vegas for his DJ stint at the MGM Grand Hotel before finally jetting to LA, where he'd just bought a new £4.6 million home.

They had to part ways. Rita had her third gig in eight days when she joined a host of women taking over Twickenham rugby stadium, in West London, for a special charity event organised by Beyoncé, actress Salma Hayek and Gucci fashion designer Frida Giannini. *The Sound for Change Live* event aimed to raise three million pounds to promote education, health and justice projects for women around the world and also featured Jessie J, Iggy Azalea and Florence and the Machine.

But Calvin was back in London at the next available opportunity, flying in to take Rita to dinner with American movie star Will Smith. When Calvin wasn't in town Rita hung out with Cara. When she and top celebrity photographer Rankin devised a theme for a video to accompany her album track 'Facemelt', Cara came along for the shoot, joining Rita in one of the director's cuts.

As one London party organiser put it: 'If you can get Rita to an event then you are made. Cara usually turns up and the two of them like to be outrageous so the paparazzi are kept happy.'

Cara was happy to be snapped wearing a vest proclaiming her to be 'Rita's Wifey', but she liked to keep her options open. Keen to pursue a singing career of her own, she had been seeking advice from Rita and her other Roc Nation pal Rihanna.

Rita saw no reason why a model couldn't make the crossover. After all, she was going in the opposite direction herself with her Material Girl campaign.

'I love how music and fashion are so similar,' she said. 'At the moment music feeds off fashion and fashion feeds off music and when they get together they fuse perfectly.'

Rita had the luxury of having her favourite people by her side at her next public event. Calvin and Rita's mum accompanied her to the *Glamour Awards*, a ceremony honouring inspirational women, in a Mayfair marquee. And it was Cara – who else? – who presented her with her gong for Best Solo Artist. Running through Rita's incredible achievements, Cara gushed: 'I genuinely don't know anyone who deserves this more than she does – and she doesn't even know it. So give it up for *Glamour*'s Solo Artist of the Year and my best friend and I love you, Rita Ora.' However, despite Cara's fulsome speech, Rita celebrated by joining Calvin back at his pad in North London. Cara was left to wander home alone the morning after, bearing the hallmarks of having had a messy night, clutching the shoes she'd worn at the event and wearing just a bra under her jacket.

Rita wasn't discarding her friend, but her feelings for her gentle giant Scot (he's actually just a quarter of an inch from being a certified giant!) were so strong one wondered if she might add his name to the growing amount of body art she was getting. Rita was so into her tattoos that she had even learned how to ink others.

Her new favourite tat artist Bang Bang – real name Keith McCurdy – revealed Rita liked to strip off whenever she was getting a new tattoo. 'Rita Ora just can't keep her shirt on around me. I must just have that effect on her,' Bang Bang joked. 'She's always pretty topless around me. She has wardrobe malfunctions the whole time. I'm in love with her, she is so awesome. She is just a really great spirit with a fantastic smile and so much fun. It's rare to meet somebody you click with so quickly, but with Rita I did. I tattooed her and taught her to tattoo so she did me back, then we went out for dinner. Now we text all the time. I'm really proud to be her friend.'

Bang Bang and the singer shared such affinity that, not only did he let her loose with the needle on him, she also got to dictate the design. 'She put boobs on the tattoo because I kept seeing her boobs, and never wanted to forget them,' he said. 'I didn't ask her to put the boobs on, she just did it on the stencil and I was like, "Yeah, OK," even though she was just joking.'

Bang Bang was the go-to guy for many celebs. 'Her tattoo, and Justin Bieber's, on me were both pretty bad but I didn't ask for a perfect tattoo. I just wanted a tattoo from them and I'm totally happy. But they definitely couldn't charge as much for their tattoos as they do for their music.'

Rita was so impressed by his work she introduced Cara to him but, interestingly, it was Rihanna who discovered the body artist originally and booked him for her first tattoo – a lion on her index finger. 'Rihanna's the one who called me,' said Bang Bang. 'I ended up going to their hotel suite around midnight and was there until three a.m.. Ri was getting her hair done in the other room, Cara was getting tattooed, we were drinking Dom Pérignon.'

Rita might have needed a bit more practice if she was to pursue a sideline career. Plus, if there was going to be a secondary profession it was most likely going to be acting. *Fast and Furious 6* hit the screens in May 2013. Rita's role in the movie might just have been a small, uncredited cameo but her appearance as a kick-ass race starter was appreciated by franchise star Vin Diesel.

'I was out one night and was introduced to her,' Vin said. 'We were looking for someone to kick off the most quintessential race in the movie. We wanted somebody who represented today's London and have that presence to kick off a race of that style and she was just perfect and she was game to do it. We were lucky to get her and we were lucky that she came in and kicked butt.'

The movie also starred stunning actress Michelle Rodriguez, who too had been the subject of speculation about her sexuality.

As summer approached, Rita looked like she had it all. The love of a good man and a wifey on the side!

Both were putting demands on her time, both wanted her full attention. She was treading a tightrope. Could she keep everyone – including herself – happy?

Try as she might she was about to discover there were many things she could not control.

15

Wrong and Strong

RITA was in the zone. She'd performed 'How We Do (Party)' countless times but each performance demanded focus. She always gave her all.

Out of the corner of her eye she was aware of someone taking to the stage. Like every performer, she held a fear of that particular element of the unknown, being on guard, in case a random nutcase was on the scene.

She turned and grinned. 'Phew' – it was only Cara. She'd joined her friend on stage at the DKNY Artworks launch party in London and was dirty dancing. Rita had to admit it was funny, watching the model jiving badly. She played along, kept on with the song and went with it. Cara came up behind her and started bumping and grinding. She was crazy – but it was still fun.

Then Cara wrenched the mic out of her hand. The audience had heard enough from Rita Ora. The model wanted to showcase her singing talent. What the hell was she playing at? Rita tried to grab the mic back but Cara wasn't having any of it. She screeched into it, like a bad karaoke singer.

'It was a lot of fun,' one onlooker said, 'but she was singing out of key and it was a bit embarrassing for everyone watching. Rita tried to take the mic back a couple of times, but Cara kept hold of it, turned the other away and carried on singing.'

Eventually, after a ticking off from one of her handlers, Rita grabbed the mic back and rescued the performance with some killer vocals, reminding the assembled crowd who the singer was. But it was too late – videos of the sloppy performance would soon be all over the Internet.

It wasn't the first time in recent days that Rita had witnessed Cara's increasingly erratic behaviour. Less than a week earlier the pair headed to the Electric Cinema in Portobello Road but Cara looked 'eight times more sloshed' than Rita, according to witnesses.

Was Cara just reacting to being in the limelight a bit too much? Rita, after all, knew all about what it was like to go from obscurity to everywhere in next-to-no-time. But she had a relationship to focus on. She couldn't split herself down the middle.

Cara's antics were putting a strain on their friendship. And she was about to test it further by reaching out to Rihanna to make her pop dreams come true. And RiRi, it was said, was keen that she was the ONLY singer Cara worked with. 'Rihanna loves her friendship with Cara, and is even helping her with her budding music career,' a source told the *Daily Star*. 'But she has now told Cara she can't record with her right now if she's recording with her music rivals. So RiRi's message is, it's me or her.'

Rita would always make time for Cara but that performance at the DKNY event – when she'd grabbed the mic – had left a sour taste in her mouth. And she didn't take being played off against Rihanna well, either.

But just when she thought Cara was the only problem to deal with, a wayward relative threatened to bring shame on her family's proud reputation.

Ilir Tolaj was an uncle of Rita's, married to Jasmina, Vera's sister, and also the father of her best friend in Kosovo, Amantina.

But on 18 June 2013 Ilir was sentenced to eighteen months in prison for his involvement in a corruption case. He had been accused of demanding bribes from pharmaceutical companies in return for official contracts while permanent secretary at the Kosovo Health Ministry. He was also fined 1,000 Euros.

The situation became more severe when he was also accused of obstructing justice after sensational evidence emerged that an attempt was made to bribe prosecutors to drop his previous charges.

A special branch of Eulex, a European Union foreign mission

tasked with strengthening the rule of law in Kosovo, where corruption was rife, had brought the case against Ilir.

But when a British prosecutor unearthed evidence that suggested the prosecuting body itself was corrupt his case became international news.

The whole investigation blew up, embarrassing the European Union and in later years would be branded the 'EU's worst policy crisis in years', according to British news reports.

With such a big case, Rita would certainly have heard what was going on. Her uncle was first arrested in May 2012 and was immediately put in jail pending the results of the investigation. Such a high-profile scandal would have heaped enormous strain on her aunt Jasmina and her cousins Amantina and her brother Arianit, who lives in London. Rita is extremely close to that side of her family. Jasmina is the aunt her relatives say she takes after most and Amantina is a constant presence by her side when she goes back to Kosovo, also joining Rita and her family when they head to the holiday home in Ulcinj. Rita, Elena and Amantina have posted photos of themselves in bikinis and on boat rides on Instagram during their time there. Amantina often visits Rita in London and flies around the world to support her at shows.

With Amantina's father going through a personal crisis, it must have had a huge bearing on his daughter and the wider family, particularly when he was in jail.

The family might have drawn some comfort that, at first, it was a domestic matter that they may have hoped he had a good chance of emerging from with his reputation intact.

However, when it looked like the case would blow up into a wider international scandal, Rita's family must have been worried what implications, if any, it could have for the nation's most famous singing sensation. The story became big news in Kosovo but no one made the connection between Ilir and Rita or her family. It was a worrying time, particularly when at one stage it looked as if her aunt Jasmina might also be charged as a number of associates were investigated to see if they were part of a wider conspiracy to free him. Blerim Krasniqi, Eulex spokesperson, while not commenting on the specific names, confirmed they were looking at other people.

'Individuals who obstruct the investigation will be investigated, and if you gather enough evidence and proof, certainly against [them] there will [be] indictments,' he said. 'Interference and obstruction of evidence is a stain on the judicial system and those who commit such acts must be prepared for the consequences.'

Although she was spared the same ordeal as her husband, it was a devastating time for Jasmina and their children. Ilir and Jasmina were respected doctors in gynaecology and infectious diseases. They had been working together for twenty years and while they admitted their marriage was 'not ideal or perfect' it was a happy one. It seemed hard to believe that someone with such a background would corrupt a system, especially when the system seemed corrupt already.

Yet ordinary Kosovans would be shocked to think that a convicted criminal was related to Rita and her family given in what high regard her grandfather Besim was held, not to mention the love for Rita herself.

Hopefully, before they cast judgement, they would remember the words spoken by Besim before his death, fondly restated by Rita's dad Besnik: 'To love one another, you are brothers. As brothers treat all Albanians, that we all have the same mother and father, Albanian and country.'

And for people in other countries and cultures, it is easy to judge when convictions are laid down but it pays to remember just how Rita and her family have had to work and scrape and sacrifice to survive and forge lives for their children and relatives. Rita has never felt the need to explain or apologise for her desire to bend rules to get ahead. This is the girl who fibbed about her age to sing in clubs, just so she could inch one step closer to achieving her dream.

Her relatives have always strived for new opportunities and ways to better themselves and Rita was no exception. She gave an indication of how savvy she was when it emerged she'd lodged for one of the most extensive trademark patents of all time to cover the name 'Rita Ora'. Not only did it mean her image rights were protected but also, should she desire, she could lend her name to all sorts of products, everything from moisturisers and nail varnish to pets' clothing and video games.

Merchandising had become big business in the pop world with boy band One Direction appearing on products like toothbrushes and perfume. She may well have picked up the idea from the Kardashians who were the masters at turning their family into a brand.

Festival season kicked off once again with Glastonbury and Rita returned to the Pyramid Stage in a red-fringed outfit. But although she dazzled in the sunshine all anyone was interested in was why she wasn't caning it afterwards with Cara, who was at the festival but uncharacteristically wifey-less.

Could the 'womance' actually be over? It seemed hard to believe but Rita spent more time with Stella McCartney and referred to the designer as her 'new wife'. Although she and Cara were staying just metres away from each other in VIP Winnebagos they partied separately all weekend.

The cooling of their friendship could be traced back to the DKNY fashion party when Cara gatecrashed Rita's performance. They hadn't been seen together publicly since that night. But an even clearer sign that all was not well with the wifeys was that they had stopped messaging each other on social media, where they used to declare their love for each other every day.

Cara failed to show for Rita's appearance at the Wireless Festival at the Olympic Park in East London when she sang with Snoop Dogg and supported Jay Z. Instead Cara flew to Monte Carlo where she hung out with Rihanna.

'There's a lot of hurt on both sides but Rita's been working towards her singing career and carefully crafting her image for four years and it was all in danger of being a joke after that shabby performance,' one source said.

Rita's blossoming relationship with Calvin was a major factor, of course. Since the start of the year Rita might have flirted with guys for a brief spell but no one had seriously threatened to come between them, until he came on to the scene. 'It's early,' Rita said of Calvin. 'I'm not in love. But I'm definitely falling.'

But Cara knew how to push Rita's buttons. She seemed to be saying that she wanted her pop career and if Rita wasn't prepared to help her she'd go to someone who would – Rihanna.

In a telling interview with *GQ* magazine alongside her celebrity sister, Elena revealed Rita would not be feeling sorry for herself about the situation – they had not been raised that way.

'Mum told us, never play the victim,' Elena affirmed. 'And Rita never does.' If she is on the wrong end of a piece of gossip, Elena says her sister's response is always the same: 'She goes, "F*** it. We're going to be wrong and strong on this one."'

Events of the past few months made it clear to Rita who the important people in her life were. 'To me, I have my friends who I've known my whole life, and I can count them on one hand,' said Rita, who posed topless for the feature, but with her arms protecting her vulnerability. 'They're people I went to school with, my mum's friends' daughters. You know? Everyone else I meet from that point on, if they happen to become a friend, that's incredible – come and join the family – but if not ...'

You're on your own, she seemed to be saying. Nice knowing ya.

Things had gone well for her over the past year but some events were out of her control – and she had to stay focused on why she was doing this. Asked if it was all worth it, she said: 'Every minute. You always have to sacrifice something when you want to achieve something. Of course, I get lonely and I get sad, but I made a decision to do this... I'm in an amazing position to change my life, and change my family's life.'

And what if this time next year, it were all over? Would there be any regrets then?

'That's never ever f***ing going to happen,' she said, an icy smile on her face. 'Never.'

It might have sounded cold and calculated but Rita was determined. She had worked and fought so hard to get to this position. She wasn't about to sacrifice it for anyone.

16

A Fully-Fledged Player

AS she emerged from the waves, water running off her sun-kissed body, flicking her hair back and stepping through the surf in a hypnotising white bikini, her watching lover had only one thought going through his mind …

'Phwaor!'

Well, maybe two things.

Calvin and Rita were soaking up the sun during a rare break in Barcelona and he thought he had his very own Bond girl as she emanated sheer Ursula Andress from *Dr No* in that white bikini. He snapped the image and posted it on Twitter. 'Pure Ursula vibes happening right now, by the way.'

Rita retweeted the reference to Ursula and the picture, saying, 'HA #bllllaaaahhhhhh' to her followers, who by the summer of 2013 numbered an amazing 3,184,425.

She would have been delighted with the association – as she always wanted to be a Bond girl. 'That would be my dream role,' she said. 'It would have to be a bad Bond girl, that would be cool. Or I wouldn't mind being a good one, as long as I get to kick ass. I would want to be massively involved in all the action.'

Rita and Calvin looked like the perfect couple in love and she couldn't contain her joy. 'It's amazing. Everything is amazing. There's nothing better than when a girl feels great.'

Although they both had a busy few weeks, with a number of festival obligations to fulfill, they were able to carve out a few days for each other. As well as Barcelona, they managed to chill out in Ibiza as guests of Kate Moss and her husband Jamie Hince, Rita shared photos of herself looking amazing aboard a private yacht.

Spending quality time together gave them a chance to bounce ideas off each other. Calvin had gifted chart success to a number of other female singers and he had some ideas for tracks that would work for his other half. Rita's gain would be Rihanna's loss. After the incredible success of 'We Found Love' she asked Calvin for more tracks but only gave him forty-eight hours to come up with the goods. Never one to turn down a challenge he did try but decided against submitting something below his usual standards of perfection.

Certainly DJ Fresh was convinced Calvin and Rita would produce something together. 'She's his f*****g girlfriend, 'course they will,' he said. 'If you're going out together you've got to record at least one track.'

Other opportunities were presenting themselves. After her management stable mate Jessie J quit BBC's *The Voice* after two series, Rita was 8–1 to take over her mentor slot but turned it down because 'it takes up too much of the year'.

She also had her current commitments. First, photos appeared for her debut campaign for Madonna's Material Girl. There was a very British feel as she posed with a bearskin and Union Flag.

Rita joined Calvin on the bill at T in the Park (where she dyed the ends of her hair to match her trousers) and Oxegen in Ireland but a combination of performing and getting on and off flights to New York and back again played havoc with her throat and she was forced to cancel gigs at Haydock Park in Merseyside and Switzerland, on doctor's orders. 'I am so sorry for cancelling my shows this weekend,' Rita said. 'I've never and will never not perform unless I physically can't put on a good show for you. I am so sorry and, as soon as I get better, I will make it up to you. I promise.'

Rita recovered sufficiently enough to perform at V Festival, taking place at two venues in Staffordshire over the last weekend in August, but then came down with a bout of food poisoning. It was so bad poor Rita was vomiting offstage just minutes before she was due to perform on Saturday. And on Sunday, she was still unable to eat or drink. 'At least I've lost half a stone,' she joked.

Rita chose not to hang out with Cara, who was also at the festival.

Although the model had described one gossip columnist's take on their falling out as 'science fiction', she chose the company of model pals Clara Paget and Suki Waterhouse.

One 'spy' detected some awkwardness when there was a chance of Rita and Cara bumping into each other in the VIP area.

'Cara would walk into the VIP backstage area and Rita would walk out. Then when Cara came back, Rita was gone,' the source said.

In the days leading up to the festival Cara had tweeted: 'If someone wants to be part of your life they'll make an effort to be in it. So don't bother reserving a space in your heart for someone who doesn't make the effort to stay.' And she wrote on Instagram: 'Don't waste words on people who deserve your silence. Sometimes the most powerful thing you can say is nothing at all.'

It didn't take a genius to work out to whom she was referring. At V, Rita had been hanging out instead with Ellie Goulding, another Turn First artist, and someone who had snogged and bedded Calvin in the video for their song 'I Need Your Love'. Rita had no reason to feel threatened, however. 'We just laughed about it,' Ellie said. It might not only have been Calvin that linked the two women. Ellie's ex was Radio 1 DJ Greg James, and comedian Russell Kane hinted on Greg's show that Rita might have spent some time with him. 'You think I don't know that you took a pop star back to your house and she didn't leave until the morning, and all I can say is "R.I.P."'

Even if true, that was all before Calvin's time, of course, and Rita did have to accept her fella would be in even more demand. Calvin had just been named the world's highest-earning DJ by respected American magazine *Forbes*, which estimated his annual earnings at £30 million.

After years when he struggled to find artists to collaborate with now the biggest names in music were lining up for a shot at working with him.

Festival season gave way to awards season, and as pop and rock royalty prepared for the MTV Video Music Awards it seemed the industry was going the way of the film world, with increasing emphasis on stars and their frocks.

Rita's dramatic Alexandre Vauthier gown with a twenty-foot feathered train was so elaborate she needed the assistance of some helpers at the bash at New York's Barclays Center. She later changed into a slinky red dress for the after-show party.

Rita also added a touch of glamour to the GQ Men of the Year Awards and ended the night sharing a 3.30 a.m. McDonald's with Cara. The two friends ended their feud and like old times went partying at China Tang and the Groucho Club.

Not only had they seemingly patched things up but it was an emotional night for another reason. Now that her last gig of the year was over, Rita was going to be 'hibernating' to work on her album.

'It was a bit emotional because it was the last time me and my band are going to play until next year,' Rita said. 'I am just getting focused now on getting an album done without having to do shows.'

Rita headed to New York for some studio time – but still managed to make room in her schedule to not only take in a catwalk appearance during the city's Fashion Week, but steal the show!

Rita had just signed a deal to become the face of DKNY and she danced down the runway, waving her hands in the air, to the sounds of the Beastie Boys' '(You Gotta) Fight For Your Right (To Party!)' as she closed the label's show in a cropped T shirt and pleated A-line skirt.

Designer Donna Karan's youthful offering won widespread acclaim and Rita's infectious enthusiasm played a huge part.

Listing Rita as one of the most influential people in fashion, The Guardian newspaper called her 'a fully fledged player' in the industry. Not only did it take 'serious guts' for her to follow experienced model Karlie Kloss on to the runway but it said 'the Rita Crop', i.e. the waistlength, loose top which shows just a couple of inches of flesh when paired with a skirt or a cute pair of shorts, was everywhere throughout the week. 'The girl has influence,' it gushed.

What a time Rita was having – and she illustrated perfectly in just a matter of days the two extremes in her life.

After the buzz of her Fashion Week success she celebrated by getting another tattoo with Cara. Rita put a woman she calls 'Rosetta' on her ribcage, while Cara got her mum's name 'Pandora' on her arm.

Then Rita was over to the west coast for a more relaxing vibe, detoxing with Calvin. They hung out at an eco café where he introduced her to a healthy wheatgrass shot. They went for drives in his new McLaren MP4-12C supercar worth £168,000 and she got to walk a ten-week-old Husky pup called Bowie – due to his different-coloured eyes.

So much for hibernating!

Always thinking business, she also fitted in time for a meeting with Simon Cowell. That led to speculation that Rita would soon be joining the panel of *The X Factor* but she would keep people guessing for a while.

'I just went to see his place,' she said, 'but never say never.'

Rita had said she wasn't going to be performing again that year but she made an exception for a worthwhile cause. Unity: A Concert for Stephen Lawrence, held twenty years after the black teenager's death at the hands of racist thugs on the streets of London, saw a host of artists come together to champion youth and social empowerment. Rita, looking sophisticated and stunning in a figure-hugging red dress dedicated 'R.I.P.' to the teenager's memory before performing with Tinie Tempah.

The concert was all about music's social conscience, and Rita had cause to think again about the messages conveyed in her songs when 'How We Do' was among several tracks deemed to be glamorising alcohol. Calvin's 'Drinking From The Bottle' was another.

A study showed one in five songs in modern top ten charts contained some reference to booze, twice as many as ten years ago and three times as many as thirty years previously. Researchers at Liverpool John Moores University also found modern tunes were more likely to glorify alcohol than before. And when they broke it down by geography and genre they found mentions to booze were most common in songs from the US and in particular in R'n'B, rap and hip hop. The worry was that it was encouraging teenagers to drink. 'Health and other professionals should recognise increased alcohol promotion in popular music and ensure this does not reinforce the binge drinking culture,' the report concluded.

Rita and Calvin did not comment on these particular findings but there was acknowledgement in 2012 about the link between dance music and alcohol and drugs. 'I think it exists,' Calvin said. 'I never mention anything to do with drugs ever in any of my songs or anything. I don't do drugs.

'I drink, frequently to excess. I don't mention that either,' added the man who wrote 'Drinking From The Bottle' and 'Merrymaking At My Place'. 'It's just one of those things that goes with dance music. It always has done and it goes with a lot of other forms of music as well.' Coincidentally, the video for his latest single, 'Under Control', featured him cavorting with girls in the back of a limo while the drink flowed and at one stage drenching a girl in champagne. Clearly the video was conceived before the report was published but the images would do little to quell the researchers' angst.

One song was hardly enough ammunition to have a pop at Rita and she would surely argue that 'How We Do (Party)' merely reflected the culture of the times. She was a positive role model for kids, a fact that an increasing number of mega brands were waking up to. She attended Paris Fashion Week and was snapped stepping out in an outfit covered in dollar bills. It could have been knitted with spare greenbacks lying around her pad as two new endorsement deals meant she was now officially rolling in it.

Rimmel announced she would be the face of a new campaign and she marked the news by joining the makeup brand's long standing model Kate Moss and fellow recruit Georgia May Jagger at the London Film Museum for Rimmel's 180th anniversary celebration.

Ensuring headlines around the world, Rita and Kate locked lips, with Rita posting on Instagram: 'Love you ladies – tonight was a blast ... you can't compete with two gorgeous supermodels.'

To evolve from a girl who always packed red lippy to jazz up her school uniform to become the face of a makeup brand was another indication of how far she had come.

But if lipstick was her signature, fashion was her dream, and Rita needed to be pinching herself yet again when Adidas offered her an astonishing £1.5 million to design her own sportswear range. 'Rita has been talking about designing for the last couple of years,' a source told *The Sun*. 'She's really developed her own sense of style in the past twelve months, and that's when she caught the eye of Adidas. She was with Jeremy [Scott, one of Adidas's long-term designers] just a couple of weeks ago talking about it – he's had an incredibly successful series of collections over the past few years, so will be a great help. She's joining a lot of big names who've worked with the business recently.'

Rita might still have been a relative newcomer to the industry but her triumph in New York and her ability to switch effortlessly between high fashion and the high street put her on a level with Kate Moss. And Rita once again showed her star quality in New York when, surrounded by models, she stole the show at the Gabrielle's Angel Foundation Angel Ball. Wearing a stunning gold fishtail frock, which featured a draped gold-beaded neckline from the Donna Karan Atelier range, Rita made sure all eyes were on her at the event in aid of cancer research.

At Halloween she cast up her recent lucrative deals by dressing up as a huge credit card from the 'Bank of Unlimited Shopping' as she partied in New York. She might have chosen fun over horror for the night of dressing up but that didn't mean she was able to escape the haunting theme of the season. A ghost from her past had returned.

James Arthur, who Rita had dated for five minutes at the start of the year, crawled out of the woodwork to have a nasty dig at his old flame. First, he ungraciously kissed and told on their time together claiming theirs was a 'brief fling'. Then he had a go because she had simply been spotted with Dave Gardner.

'I saw Rita Ora out with me one night and then coming out of a club with David Beckham's best friend the other night,' James bleated. 'I was like, "Oh, f*** you then." A lot of attractive women are d**kheads. When an attractive woman shows any interest in me I'm immediately alerted.'

Despite the fact that there was no suggestion Rita had acted inappropriately, he then unloaded on Rita – and her pal Iggy Azalea – in a foul-mouthed radio rap called 'Fire In The Booth'. On Charlie Sloth's hip hop show on BBC Radio 1Xtra, with the rude bits bleeped out, he spat: 'I'm giving ten million f**** less than Rita does and that's a lot of f******.'

Incredibly, Arthur then insisted his rant wasn't meant to be disrespectful to Rita.

'For the record it wasn't a Rita diss!' he tweeted. 'She's a mate and I meant that I'd like to live my life to the full and give less of a f*** about everything just like she does! It's something I really respect.'

A nice try but Rita's fans weren't buying it and reacted angrily to the outburst. Public opinion was most definitely on her side, with

The Sun branding Arthur 'The Biggest Bell-end in Pop', after further rants at a rapper and fellow *X Factor* stars.

Rita was out of the firing line, in Miami shooting her Material Girl campaign. Though she still felt the heat, sweltering in 30°C temperatures. Working in such punishing conditions got too much and she collapsed with heatstroke and was rushed to hospital. She was carried on a stretcher from her trailer to an ambulance but later made a full recovery. 'Rita Ora was treated for heat exhaustion and dehydration. She was discharged and is fine,' said a spokesman for Mount Sinai Medical Center.

Rita had managed to wish her brother a happy birthday on Twitter hours before her ordeal and bounced back but, coming in a year where she had to cancel gigs for health reasons, there were concerns she was overdoing it.

Mercifully, she recovered in time to celebrate her own birthday, turning The Box nightclub in London into Studio 54, the legendary New York celebrity hangout of the Seventies, for one evening.

'Today, I'm allowed to be a f****** star,' she tweeted as she turned twenty-three.

It looked like Calvin might struggle to join her, however. He was in LA but had a gig in Sydney to play Australia's Stereosonic festival just three days after her party. His easiest option would be to fly the 7,500 miles to Sydney from LA. But the smitten Scot pulled out the stops and first flew 5,000 miles to London to be with her. He partied until 5 a.m. and then flew another 10,000 miles to Australia to be there in time to get set up for his gig. In all, he was airborne for thirty-two hours.

'Calvin was desperate to see Rita on her birthday, even though their schedules saw them on opposite sides of the globe,' a source close to the couple told the *Daily Mirror*. 'Rita was delighted that he made such a special effort for her.'

Among Rita's presents, from other guests, were a PlayStation 4 and a pair of Christian Louboutin heels. Rita donned a red, hooded frock slashed to her thigh for her big night, which started at Hakkasan restaurant with bestie-turned-stylist Kyle De'volle before they joined friends at The Box. Cara couldn't be there as she was working in Siena, Italy.

Calvin's epic journey was the talk of the party but when the couple at last had a private moment he presented her with the best gift of all – a song.

'Rita was in tears,' a friend told *The Sun*.

The track was one he'd written especially for her, called 'I Will Never Let You Down'.

Rita loved it.

By his actions Calvin's intentions were clear. But were Rita's?

It seemed hard to fathom at the time – but would *she* be the one to let him down?

17

Rita Laid Bare

RITA sighed and turned away from the camera.

'It is child abuse, really, isn't it?'

It was a staggering admission, particularly with cameras rolling, crewmembers watching, hanging on her every word.

This was Rita Ora laid bare, opening her heart, exploring her demons and laying her soul out for others to judge.

Discussing her first experiences of sex at just fourteen – under the legal age of consent – and being objectified by older men she displayed an honesty not normally associated with interviews recorded for television.

She opened up like never before – on the true nature of her family's ordeal when they first came to the UK, on the hopelessness of her life as a teenager when the only option seemed to be joining friends selling drugs, and on sex and being taken advantage of.

It was October 2013 – a time when to the outside world Rita had everything: a successful pop career, lucrative endorsements, a massive and fanatical fan base and the love of a good and successful man.

Why then did she choose that moment for some startling self-analysis?

To put things into context it helps at first to explain the circumstances.

Amanda de Cadenet, pop star wife, mother and celebrity photographer, had launched a series of thought-provoking interviews with successful women in what was a return to how she first made her name as a presenter on the zany but iconic late night Channel 4 series *The Word*.

With actress Demi Moore as an executive producer, *The Conversation with Amanda de Cadenet* was billed as 'an alternative interview series with women who have a story or experience to share ... talking about the universal language of women'.

Amanda's access was unparalleled and the format allowed celebrities like Lady Gaga, Gwyneth Paltrow and Eva Longoria to open up like never before. But no one at the show could have expected the bombshell Rita was about to drop. The strength of *The Conversation* was that Amanda conducted her chats like she was having a natter with a close girlfriend. Unguarded and away from brand messages or a film company's publicity machine, famous women talked about sex, relationships, their fears and their experiences.

Amanda wanted to launch the series in the UK but struggled to find celebrities willing to talk because they were worried the tabloid press would twist their words. But she was delighted to secure the chat with Rita. 'What she's done with her life is incredible,' she said.

And so in October it was into this arena that Rita found herself. She immediately warmed to the setting and seemed to appreciate the chance to talk at length on some of the remarkable things that had happened to her and her family.

She revealed detail she'd never before spoken about on her family's first days and weeks in Britain after fleeing Kosovo. She spoke about her guilt at being a wayward kid when her mum was diagnosed with breast cancer for a second time. She made the startling admission that before her career took off she had a moment where 'it was I either do something with my life or I just sit on this block and just sell weed with the rest of my friends'.

But most revealingly, she spoke about that time in her life when she started exploring her sexuality and found that older men found her attractive.

Fourteen was when she signed a production deal and started working on music. She was moving in an adult world and, although she looked and acted older than she was, she was still a child.

Before she got into the nitty gritty of that time, Rita said: 'Let's get deep. It's good for me to remember what I actually went through.'

'Where were you emotionally?' Amanda asked. 'You said you were young, you were having sex with older men. You were getting validated through them.'

'I can't begin to tell you how confident I felt when a man was interested in me,' Rita revealed. 'I felt like I was sexy, I felt like I had a form of respect, I felt like he listened to me. Now I know he listened to me because he obviously wanted to have sex with me. I felt good … that men fancied me. I would wear low tops. I would put red lipstick on, I would make my hair blonder. My mum would just completely be like, "What are you doing?" I think that's what got me dressing crazy, why I love crazy clothes. Because my mum always let me freely express myself. But she didn't know that I was expressing myself because I was seeing men.'

'Were they much older than you?' Amanda asked.

'Yeah, they were,' Rita admitted. 'I mean, I was fourteen when I started, when I got my first relationship with a guy.'

'How old was he?' Amanda wanted to know.

'I would say about twenty-six, and you have to remember I hadn't had a relationship before then at all,' Rita said. 'I didn't have sex. I was very new to the whole world of a man and a female.'

Amanda empathised with Rita's situation and disclosed that she had sex for the first time when she was just fifteen.

'It's really strange how once it starts you kind of feel like you can take over the world,' Rita said.

'It's an empowering feeling,' Amanda suggested.

'It so is,' Rita agreed. 'And don't get me wrong, even to this day if someone fancied me I'd feel so great. It was very different when I was fourteen. I was almost like obsessed with having a man feel like he wants me. It made me feel great – and I didn't care what he did or how old he was. It's crazy.'

Amanda understood where Rita was coming from but she had a stark observation to make.

'It's called child abuse now,' she said. She was right. Any sex with a person below the age of consent, particularly if it is an older man, grooming a child, as Rita had described, is abuse.

That is when Rita turned away from the cameras that were still rolling.

'It is child abuse, really, isn't it?' she said. For a moment it seemed like the enormity of what she was saying dawned on her. But then she remembered how she'd felt as a teenager – and perhaps wanted to protect the man who had abused her in the eyes of the law.

'I don't want to say that I suffered it because I wanted it,' she said, with brutal honesty. 'I don't want to say that I was forced to do it. I don't want people to think I was abused as a kid but I was definitely more mature than I should have been at the age of fourteen.'

'Me too,' Amanda said, before she offered an interesting insight. 'Here's the thing. I was a willing participant. What I would say is that my emotional capacity at age fourteen, in hindsight, wasn't really able to understand and to process what I was putting myself through. The truth is that that experience that you went through, that experience that I went through, this many years later I'm able to have that experience actually be a blessing for me.'

Rita seemed to agree. 'It is,' she said. 'You are one of the happiest people I know. You're happy.'

Rita's honesty throughout the remarkable conversation, and her unique take on what had happened to her, would have made anyone watching understand just how much she'd endured in her early life.

'You don't seem like you have been on the planet for twenty-two years,' Amanda said. 'You have an old soul.'

'I think that's why I was attracted to older men my whole life. 'Cause I connected with them,' Rita ventured.

The mood of the conversation shattered as Amanda laughed and said: 'You think that's what it was? Alright, Rita.'

For a moment Rita seemed sheepish, as if it struck her that she had revealed too much. She went on to discuss the difficulties of finding the right man when you were as successful an artist as she was.

'It is very intimidating,' she said, of the effect her status had on potential suitors. 'It's money. Money can be intimidating, money can be scary, money can be powerful. Once you find a set stone for you as a woman and living a life and you have a career and you kind of are, like, independent, you don't rely on your partner or your family or whoever – that's because you are financially and mentally stable.

'When you're looking for somebody you already have that bit covered so you're looking for a companionship. You're looking for a cuddle. Everybody loves a spoon. So when you're looking for a relationship, you're looking for that. A man's instinct is to be everything I've just said that I've covered. And when they find that the man has to be so secure with himself to be able to accept the fact that the woman only needs him for his comfort, his cuddles and his amazing penis.

'At the end of the day, that's all a woman wants, really. All a woman wants is a companion and a best friend and amazing sex,' she added.

It was sensational stuff that would have stunned viewers of the Lifetime Channel – if they'd been able to watch it. However, the programme – which also contained chats with journalist Caitlin Moran, who had previously defended Rita against Rob Kardashian's vile tweets, and model Rosie Huntington-Whiteley – was edited to remove many of the revelations regarding her family's treatment on their arrival into the UK and her underage sex.

Maybe it was decided that Rita's comments were too explosive, or that her words would be taken out of context. Amanda's own admission suggested she might have questions to answer over her attitude to underage sex. Whatever the reason, the most controversial segments of the interview were not aired on Lifetime.

However, four months after the interview took place, a different edit was conducted and the results of which were posted online. The full interview was finally available for fans to uncover.

Given the relationship Rita enjoys with her fans it is clear they would have appreciated her openness and been amazed at what she'd had to endure.

When the interview was picked over by the media, a different element was highlighted.

Not once had Calvin Harris been mentioned and some papers said Rita went further and said she was single. Rita was flippant about her relationship status: 'I'm not seeing anybody because I'm constantly eating raw onions. It's like my thing. Put some salt on that and bite it like an apple. I think that's why I tend to always be single. But I'm gonna stop. I think that when I find my companion ... it's going to stop.'

The interview was filmed weeks before her twenty-third birthday and Calvin's grand gesture. Was something going on behind the scenes?

Rita rubbished talk of a split. 'It's great. It's going well – I'm happy,' she said. 'When something is worth having, you make time for it. When you want something, you make it work.

'He's only the sexiest guy I've ever seen.'

Calvin was down to perform at a huge New Year's Eve party in Las Vegas and Rita was determined to be there. 'It's an incredible night and I am trying to reel in all my friends to come to Vegas.'

She might have been saying the right things but were her actions speaking louder than words?

She was spotted again with Dave Gardner, following the *Harper's Bazaar* Women of the Year awards at Claridge's hotel in Mayfair, where she picked up an award for Musician of the Year. It could have been that Rita was simply catching up with a good friend of course but it sparked gossip column speculation once more.

As the year drew to a close Rita revealed some of the work she'd been doing on her new album, which had been earmarked for release in 2014.

'It's so good, it's literally done,' she said. 'I've got a few things I want to tweak and then I'm done.'

She let slip that she had been working with Eighties pop legend Prince.

'I have met him and I have had the honour of being in the same studio as him,' she said. 'We messed around with some music and, you know, I can't believe he can play so many instruments. All I can say is that we've definitely done some music together.'

Not only did she have a new album to look forward to but she had also bagged a part in one of the biggest movies of recent years. She had beaten off stiff competition to be cast as Christian Grey's sister Mia in the movie adaptation of EL James' phenomenally successful kinky novel *Fifty Shades of Grey*. Fortune favours the brave and Rita was successful after approaching the British director. 'I heard about the audition and I approached Sam Taylor-Johnson with ideas for the soundtrack and said I'd love to be involved as I was such a fan of the book,' she said. 'And then Sam said, "Well, why don't you audition?" and I said, "Sure, I've got a few song ideas, I could send them over." I've done a bit of acting but I didn't expect to be put into that role. I thought, "What have I got to lose?"

There were a lot of people in the frame to get any special treatment.'

To land the part Rita had to hone an American accent and although she hadn't started filming yet she hoped the role might lead to bigger things.

'I love the look and base my style on style sirens of the golden age,' she said.

Filming was to take place in Vancouver early in January 2014, and it meant Rita would be tied up almost immediately after spending the New Year with Calvin.

That was to come, but in the short term Rita swapped S&M for M&S as she travelled to Camber Sands, in East Sussex, to shoot a new ad campaign for the high street store Marks and Spencer. It was a chilly winter's day to be posing on the beach but the fact that renowned photographer Annie Leibovitz was behind the camera made the experience much more appealing.

Rita was fronting yet another campaign, but this time the message was a serious one. Six million children's lives had been affected by the war in Syria and Rita joined actors Ewan McGregor and Michael Sheen, Tinie Tempah and Emma Bunton in raising awareness to their plight for children's charity Unicef.

In the midst of such a hectic schedule Calvin probably had a right to wonder where he fitted in. Cracks had been showing in their relationship and often when they spoke it was more cross words than kind. He was rounding off a triumphant UK tour but had commitments to appear in Las Vegas and Puerto Rico. Rita, in an attempt to make up for how busy she had been, flew out to the Caribbean to surprise him before their planned stay in Vegas for New Year.

Her surprise backfired.

'The rows escalated over New Year and Rita ended up sharing a room with a friend,' a source told *The Sun*. 'Things changed between them, and after New Year's Eve in Vegas, Rita was telling friends that she was single again. She is pretty cut up about everything but is throwing herself into work.'

Nothing official came from either star's spokespeople but in a digital age of social media there was a modern, and no surer, way of telling that Rita was erasing Calvin from her life – she unfollowed his Instagram account.

As Rita flew out to Vancouver to start filming *Fifty Shades of Grey*, Calvin was left to rue the rotten timing. He would be single as he prepared to celebrate his thirtieth birthday. However, before the end of the month, it appeared all was not lost.

Rita again used social media to relay her thoughts, posting cryptically on Twitter that she might have been harbouring some regrets.

'Have you ever wondered which hurts the most: Saying something & not wishing you had not, or saying nothing and wishing you had?' she wrote. Then they were spotted kissing during a date in West Hollywood ahead of the Grammy Awards. Calvin was also believed to have flown to Vancouver to join Rita on the set of her movie.

After their slight hiccup, things were back on track – literally – for Rita revealed more details about the song that would be her next single. It would be 'I Will Never Let You Down', the song Calvin gifted to her on her birthday.

'It's one of the coolest songs I've ever heard,' said Rita, who had overcome the fears she had about working with the greatest hit maker of his generation. 'You know what's funny, I never really intended on working with him, I honestly didn't. We were sitting at home, he started humming, then I started humming, then we hummed together!' she said.

Calvin's version of events was slightly different.

'I wrote the song with her in mind. I didn't write the song for anyone else,' he told Capital FM.

And it wasn't just songs Calvin gifted. He splashed out on a Mercedes motor for her, even though she was yet to pass her driving test.

On 14 February she responded by posting a photo of herself online posing in her underwear with the message: 'Happy Valentine's Day, baby.'

Clearly, a stipulation of them working out their differences was that they would try to make more time for each other. He joined her in Italy for Milan Fashion Week, where she tweeted a snap of a white gown, saying, 'My future wedding dress #1day #Gorgeous #SEX'.

They attended the Brits together, but was Calvin aware hours before Rita had once more been seen with Dave Gardner? The Sun reported she met up with the agent after catching Prince's secret gig at Ronnie Scott's jazz club in Soho, London.

Publicly, the couple behaved as if it was business as usual.

Calvin announced plans of his own. His latest single 'Summer' would be released in April, and the accompanying video showed a new beefed-up DJ, for whom the gym sessions and LA lifestyle were clearly paying dividends. His transformation was such that it prompted the *Sunday Times Style* magazine to gush he'd reaped the benefits of a 'sexover'.

Rita seemed to agree for she too needed little encouragement to highlight Calvin's sex appeal.

'I do like it when he calls me "darlin'" in his Scottish accent. That has to be my favourite word,' she said. 'Scottish accents just do something to me. I really love them. I know all the lingo now too. I say "aye" a lot. Even my friends ask, "What are you talking about?"'

Funny quips aside, Rita did start to acknowledge that Calvin had achieved what no other man had. 'There are so many things,' she said. 'The fact that he got something out of me that I never thought I had. Yes, like falling in love. I just didn't think I had it. I'd never experienced it before. And I was just like in the wilderness, thinking, "Will it ever happen?"'

And she said that her experience would come out on her new album.

"I didn't know what I was doing on my first album,' she said. 'I was a kid having the time of my life and I made a party album, party and bull****. This time, I'm still having a great time, but I'm in a great, loving place. Now I want people to see you can have fun and be in love at the same time.'

Fast-forward a month, however, and that love that Rita had spoken of so sweetly was withering.

At the MTV Movie Awards in Los Angeles, Rita was seen ripping actor Zac Efron's shirt from his back, while Calvin was one hundred miles away playing the Coachella Festival. This might have been insignificant and staged showbiz high jinx but two things Calvin would say later about this period cast the episode in a vastly different perspective.

When the time came for Rita to promote her single there was little sign of any rift. 'Adam was a massive inspiration on this record,' she said, continuing to refer to him by his real name. 'It really helps when you find someone who balances you out and really puts things into perspective. You don't want to mess it up.'

Referring to 'I Will Never Let You Down' she said: 'When I heard it I really fell in love with it and it really changed me. I thought, "If it's that easy for me to fall in love with it, I need to let the world do that too."

'The song is inspired by when my life turned for the better. It's a love song basically celebrating passion and being happy.'

She added: 'He wrote it in about an hour. And he writes as he takes a shower. What a genius.'

She explained that Calvin eventually contributed four songs to her new album, which then was slated for release in the autumn of 2014.

'There was no stress. It worked out great,' she said. 'He gets me, so he brought out the very best in me like nobody else could.'

Rita certainly sounded like someone in a loving relationship. She talked about how much she wanted to go on holiday with him. 'We need to go away together, we haven't done that for a long time,' she said.

When asked about *Fifty Shades of Grey* she told how Calvin, her father and her brother had all held a meeting to discuss whether it was the right project for her, given the explicit nature of the material.

Rita recalled their animosity towards each other when they first had their Twitter spat but when they finally met she ended up being intrigued by him.

'I was fascinated by how his brain works, what he was going to do next, what his thoughts were,' she said.

Calvin's single 'Summer' shot straight to number one. It stayed there for one week but shifted over 100,000 copies. In the US its performance was even more impressive. It reached number seven in the Billboard chart but would go on to sell more than a million copies.

'I Will Never Let You Down' followed 'Summer' by two weeks.

The couple would be sharing the bill at Radio 1's Big Weekend at Glasgow Green at the end of May but Calvin ruled out the prospect of them appearing together.

'We have our own things to do. She wouldn't like me getting in the way on stage,' he said.

Speaking ahead of the event he gave no hint there was anything up with their relationship, referring to Rita as 'the missus'.

'I'm lucky I can get to do music and do well and still do normal stuff unless I'm out with the missus – then I get a lot of attention,' he said.

But, in talking about how much time they managed to spend together, he didn't exactly sound like someone pining for more contact. In fact he seemed to suggest now the problem was when she was around, rather than when she wasn't.

'We see each other like four days every two weeks, so it's like an issue when she's around,' he said. 'We'd probably get sick of each other if we had a whole month (together).'

Rita also talked about the issues with a long-distance relationship.

'We're on different sides of the world all the time,' she said. 'But I've been taught that if you really want something, you make it work. So regardless of what happens, you make sure that when you are together it's incredible.'

However, she painted a picture of domesticity when they did manage to hook up.

Hoping her latest song would be her fourth UK number one, edging her closer to Calvin's tally, she said: 'Fingers are crossed, but you know Calvin is great. He's a good lad. Maybe we'll start putting our tallies on the kitchen fridge and keeping score.'

Two weeks after 'Summer' had hit the top spot, 'I Will Never Let You Down' matched it, continuing Calvin's remarkable run of chart-toppers.

He didn't appear to be with her for her celebrations. He remained in Las Vegas, where the singer Kesha – his ex – joined him for some games of pool.

That didn't mean he didn't care. He did tweet his girlfriend saying: '@RitaOra "Congratulations I told you!"'

And he admitted he'd been checking the charts constantly – as he did with all his singles – to see how it was doing.

'Don't think on the week of release I'm not refreshing iTunes every five minutes,' he said. 'Even Rita's single, which I wrote and produced, I was refreshing iTunes all week.'

Rita said she wasn't the jealous type – but that didn't dampen her levels of keen curiosity on occasion.

'I don't get jealous, I get suspicious,' she said. 'Any girl would, though. It's only because you miss that person, that's really the reason.'

'I'm not a fan of long-distance relationships. If you had a choice, you want that person with you. It makes me pretty sad. But you work with what you've got.'

They were reunited for the Big Weekend, where Calvin's set rocked so loud he set off car alarms in the streets surrounding Glasgow Green.

Afterwards he said he could 'relax and watch a bit of Coldplay with the missus'.

That was the last time either of them referred to themselves as a couple. A week amid rumours they were no longer together, Calvin confirmed that after a year they were splitting up, where else, but on Twitter.

'To address speculation,' he wrote, 'myself and Rita ended our relationship some time ago. She is a beautiful, talented woman and I wish her all the best.'

'Some time ago' didn't suggest a week or so. Could it be that he was waiting on Rita to score her number one before announcing their break-up? It sounds cynical to suggest that they led people to believe they were still together throughout Rita's promotional schedule so she wouldn't have to deal with any awkward questions – but another thing Calvin said added weight to this theory.

Speaking on Capital FM in November, five months after the split, Calvin gave his most candid comments.

'I don't like celebrities, celebrity women. Nah,' he said. 'I haven't seen her since March. It's brilliant, it's just stress free. It's beautiful.'

His claim that they weren't together properly since March suggests they had gone their separate ways before their promotional commitments began. Or maybe only he had.

Rita bided her time before she commented, posting on Twitter: 'I don't usually address speculation but I've had an incredible time w [sic] Calvin & i will treasure the memories. I've moved on from this topic so i hope people will respect that and do the same. Life can only be understood backwards but it must be lived forwards.'

It didn't stop the speculation about what caused the split of one of pop's power couples.

The Sun reported that Rita had been acting suspiciously, being vague about her whereabouts after they flew to LA for separate visits but were there at the same time. Things came to a head when Calvin coincidentally used the same driver, and he seemed to land Rita in it.

There was a claim that Justin Bieber had played a part. The Canadian chart sensation, whose star had waned in recent years amid increasingly erratic behaviour, was said to have pursued Rita to Cabo San Lucas, a holiday resort popular among celebrities in Mexico. 'He followed her down there and is totally besotted by her,' one source told the *Daily Star*. 'It has been getting hotter between them for weeks.'

Then came the claim that it wasn't Justin Rita was interested in but his rapper friend Khalil Amir Sharieff, with whom he had been arrested after going drag racing in January. Rita posted photographs on Instagram showing her partying and cosying up to guys, including both singers. Another photo she posted showed her standing topless, arms outstretched, as if embracing her future in Los Angeles. The message was clear. She would be OK. Whatever the speculation about what lay behind the split, the truth might have been that their differences were just too numerous to overcome.

'Calvin was obsessed, but she's a free spirit and he didn't like the fact that she would be out enjoying herself when he wasn't around,' another source told *The Sun*.

Calvin had an unexpected opportunity to contemplate the events of the last few months when he arrived back in London and turned up at his studio to find the locks had been changed. He posted a video of his plight on Instagram telling his 1.1 million followers: 'I haven't been in this London studio in so long they changed the f***ing locks. I'm just sitting outside on these f***ing stairs thinking about life.'

Some of that thinking he must have done resulted in devastating consequences for Rita. Although her album was as good as done, he dramatically pulled the songs he'd written for her. One or two songs she might have recovered from but Calvin had supplied four.

It caused terminal damage to plans for the project she was provisionally calling 'O'.

'Calvin wants a clean break personally and professionally,' a source told *The Sun*. 'He's already given her one massive hit so doesn't feel he owes her.'

Rita spoke publicly for the first time in August about the break-up and revealed she was still hurting.

'I'm gonna tell you the truth ... I'm not doing too great,' she said. 'But, I'm doing better than I thought. I adore him and he's an amazing human being. It was more about the situation, it was inconvenient, it was s***, it sucks.'

She then opened up further: 'I'm pretty much just worrying about me at the moment. I was, very much, definitely openly in a relationship. I was riding. You just never know what happens tomorrow or in an hour. I'm honestly still thinking how crazy it was. It is what it is and not to get too in detail or speak for anyone else, but I love hard. I'm just a girl that really loves. And I think when I am in the relationship and I spend time with myself I'm one of these people ... like, I can't be by myself.'

If Rita was fuming at Calvin over the album tracks she didn't say but when she was forced to pull out of the Teen Choice Awards in Los Angeles in August at the eleventh hour because he had refused to grant permission, she was less guarded.

Rita, who was in the US to promote the single's release there, told DJ Ryan Seacrest: 'I was supposed to perform, but for anybody who doesn't understand how it works he wrote and produced the song. He's an incredible songwriter – I'm never going to disregard his talents – so he has to approve anything TV wise. He owns the rights to it and he didn't approve the Teen Choice Awards.'

When he asked why he had said she couldn't do it, she replied: 'Ask Calvin.'

Rita insisted she wasn't surprised by his decision but then said: 'I was scheduled to perform and all my fans were texting me. We put a lot of effort and work into the show. Every time I do a show I rehearse for a month in advance. I could have got told a few weeks earlier, you know. That would have been nice. It was a last-minute change but you know it happens, we move on, we move forward.'

'Why is there this bitterness?' Seacrest asked her.

Rita replied: 'I don't know. I feel if you speak to Calvin you should ask him. I can't speak for him but I'm not like that.'

When Seacrest asks: 'But you were pissed?'

'Yeah,' she said, 'I'm not going to lie. I put my own money into the performance, like I always do.'

Calvin seemed to respond to those comments on Twitter, writing: 'You'll only know one side of the story because I choose not to talk to the papers about every aspect of my personal life. Just know I had a damn good reason.'

When Calvin appeared on the same show two weeks later, Seacrest showed him a clip of Rita singing. Instead of the words to the chorus, she changed them to: 'I might have let you down.'

Looking visibly taken aback, Calvin said: 'Yikes. That's crazy. I think that's unnecessary.

'This girl – she's going to be around for a lifetime. She works insanely hard. She makes some crazy decisions but she works insanely hard,' he said, refusing to be drawn on which decisions were crazy. 'She is focused on her career and that is the most important thing and I respect that so much.

'Looking in from the outside,' Seacrest said, of Rita's improvised lyric, 'you've said things that would make one look in and think she did something to hurt you.' But Calvin refused to shed any more light. 'She's funny,' was all he would say.

Calvin Harris was part of Rita's history. She made some crazy decisions he said. Would her next choice of man fall into that category?

18

On the Rebound

MOST dads probably have a checklist for the traits they least want in a boy who dates their daughter. Taking drugs, being heavily tattooed, having strange hair and a dubious track record with women would all be up there.

So when Rita rebounded from Calvin Harris into the arms of someone who ticked all of the above boxes one wonders what her parents must have thought. And, given what Rita said about Besnik and Vera hoping their girls married nice young Albanian men, it's fair to say they might not have been thrilled when Rita told them she was dating Ricky Hilfiger.

The son of fashion designer Tommy Hilfiger, Ricky, who styles himself as Rich, or Ricky Hil, was also probably a person as far removed from Calvin as she could possibly find.

Where Calvin was independently wealthy, successful, dependable and the type of bloke who'd open a car door for his date, green-haired Ricky liked to talk about his love of weed, lived off his dad's wealth and once bragged that he'd got three women pregnant in the space of a few months. He claimed to be a rapper but again his success was inversely proportional to Calvin's. While nearly every release of Calvin's went top ten, Ricky boasted he wrote five songs a day, just not ones that troubled the charts.

He did manage to secure a record deal with Warner Brothers, albeit thanks to his mate Abel Tesfaye, the singer who performs under the name The Weeknd. For a rapper who even speaks out of tune, Ricky released eighteen mixtapes, the most successful being

SYLDD (Support Your Local Drug Dealer), which bizarrely featured, among others, former *X Factor* winner Leona Lewis.

Ricky, the second of four children from his dad's first marriage to ex-wife Susie, had three sisters and a brother – Sebastian Thomas – from his father's second marriage to Dee Ocleppo. Before his musical career got going he seemed destined to play the role of the chubby son of a famous dad, best known for run-ins with the law – he was arrested for selling drugs in 2010 – and attending rehab. The experience taught him only one thing: 'I learned that alcohol and coke? Is kind of for faggots. You know, like, in my eyes. I'll drink alcohol to get a lean, don't get me wrong, but, like, something about the people who are addicted to alcohol and cocaine, they seemed like fags to me,' he said.

Such language might have been deemed offensive by Rita's friends, many of whom are gay, but Ricky qualified his terminology by saying: 'Not "fags" as in "gay". I have nothing against gay people. Mad people in my family are gay.'

One thing Ricky did have in common with Calvin was an appreciation for eighteenth-century Scottish poet Robert Burns. Calvin's first public performance was nervously reciting a Burns poem to his classmates in primary school and one of his favourite local pubs in his hometown of Dumfries in Scotland was a popular hangout for Burns. Ricky, while in rehab, read a lot of Burns, who he claims is his father's great uncle. 'He talks about the same shit that I talk about,' Ricky said of his alleged ancestor. 'Girls, love, loss, being high, and that's about it.'

Before Rita, Ricky was engaged to model Krystal Martos. 'I used to look at her in ads when she was modelling for ads,' he said. 'She used to be in those ads! Those ads I used to jerk off to as a kid! That's my wife! It's crazy, you know?'

Their engagement didn't last but Ricky appeared to be philosophical about love and loss. 'I have relationships and I get bitches, I have some ho's, I have some girlfriends, I have a couple wives,' he said, joking. Of the break-up with Krystal he said: 'I used to have a fiancée. She's tatted on my arm. We broke up. She was half Black, half Asian. We just ... people grow apart. But she's gone. She don't love me no more and I don't love her.'

Giving some insight into what sort of boyfriend he would have been for Rita he said of his ex-love: 'I mean, we love each other in a nice kind of way but not in an, "Oh, I need to see you tonight" kind of way. But we got respect for each other. I did it [proposed to her] because I love hard. Sometimes you search for your mother in a relationship and I think I was doing a little bit of that. Shit happens, you know.'

Expanding on the time he got three girls pregnant he explained: 'I've had a lot of girls pregnant this year. Like, more than three. I don't have any babies ... I'm against killing babies and all that, praise the Lord. I got a lot of girls pregnant, over three girls, just from being reckless. That's a secret I've never told nobody. I don't really give a fuck, man, it's the truth.'

Ricky's 'secret' was revealed in a video posted online for anyone to see. And he seemed unfazed about sharing all aspects of his life, admitting in one clip that he and his mate The Weeknd 'fuck girls together'.

If Ricky played fast and loose with women, he reserved his real love for dope. Saying he smoked weed 'all day every day', he added: 'If I can't get it I'm like a crack head.'

Ricky said he drew the line at snorting cocaine or injecting heroin but in one online video he revealed he was admitted to a psychiatric ward for losing his mind. He was handcuffed to a bed for five days, while he suffered withdrawal from Xanax anti-depressants. Coming off the medication had him blacking out and urinating on the floor, he said. He intended to write about his experience in a new song on his album *Candy Painted Coffins*, released this year, called 'Psych Ward Blues'.

Home for Ricky at one stage was a suite in the luxury Plaza Hotel in Manhattan, paid for by his father. With seemingly unlimited funds behind him it's little surprise he acted like the archetypal spoilt rich kid. He was banned from all but one recording studio in New York for running amok. 'He peed in workers' coffee cups, pushed over bookshelves, "drew dicks everywhere" and drizzled honey on keyboards, all of it captured on a security tape that he wants to obtain for a music video,' *The New York Observer* reported.

'Dark. Rich likes everything dark,' his producer Avery Chambliss said.

'It's like if you have a girlfriend, and she gets raped and then she tells you about it? That kind of shit,' his creative partner 'Uncle Panther' added.

Quite.

So what was it that Rita saw in this devil-may-care-lives-by-his-own-rules dude?!

If she was wanting to show how quickly she'd moved on from Calvin, he responded by hooking up with stunning younger model Aarika Wolf, who he met after she made an appearance in his 'Blame' video.

Rita didn't comment much about Ricky, who at just seven months older was closer to her in age than Calvin, who is six years her senior. She was happy to leave others to speculate. But what she did say cast a slightly different light on what was going on.

Despite appearing like a rough diamond, Rita said he was a good friend – and someone she could rely on to support her through a difficult time.

'He's the best friend that I've ever found,' she said. 'And I've known him for a very long time. So, it's not that. It's about friends supporting each other and he's been supporting me from the beginning. So, that's all it is.'

She appeared to deny there was anything more to it than that. 'At the moment I can't even talk about [dating],' she said. 'I've just separated myself from all that mentally because it was pretty difficult. I kind of just haven't even thought about it.'

Despite that, no sooner was it said that Rita was seeing Ricky than a woman claiming to be his ex spoke out to warn the singer what she might be getting into. Celia Kay, who said she had been seeing Ricky since February 2014, told *The Sun*: 'Ricky is a player and bad news for Rita or any girl.

'He was so full on and told me he loved me after just a few days and I really thought he was a nice guy. But he quickly forgot about me and moved on to Rita. He joked that he wanted a rich girlfriend so he could fly around in her private jet and not have to worry about working.'

Although Celia said she had been 'essentially living' with Ricky before they split, she went on: 'Ricky is an odd character – quite reclusive and loves smoking weed and drinking beer. He's also sex-obsessed. He's bad news. If anything, Rita is welcome to him – although I would warn her to be careful. He's no angel and I think he's more than capable of breaking her heart.'

Rita did seem to be going out a lot with her new friend and she was to discover early how different life would be with Ricky when he got embroiled in a punch-up at a party to celebrate world-famous photographer Mario Testino. The location was the super-trendy Chiltern Firehouse, where Rita hung out before it even officially opened.

One onlooker told the *Daily Mirror*: 'Rita and Ricky were both invited and welcomed by Mario to his birthday bash. But someone inside Chiltern started squaring up to Ricky and giving him a hard time. The guy was hurling abuse at him so Ricky punched him.

'Rita wasn't with him when it happened and had nothing to do with it. Ricky then briefly left the venue so it didn't turn into a full-blown fight and returned when the man left. It was all a bit embarrassing.'

At least Ricky's presence wasn't affecting Rita's music. Just a month after they started seeing each other she was back in the charts, featuring on her friend Iggy Azalea's hit 'Black Widow'.

A year earlier, Iggy had been playing second fiddle to Rita but what a difference twelve months makes. Iggy was now arguably the bigger star, having broken America with 'Fancy' hitting number one there in February, and her album *The New Classic* reaching number three in the spring.

As the name suggested, 'Black Widow' was a dark love song about turning the tables on a partner, and for anyone who knew the girls' shared history, notably regarding A$AP Rocky, it was an interesting subject matter. Iggy with Rita was a partnership made in heaven, her spiky rap blending perfectly with Rita's catchy chorus. Iggy had to fight to even hear the song. The track had been co-written by Katy Perry for her fourth album *Prism* but when it failed to make the cut Katy suggested it would be great for the blonde rapper.

Once Iggy got her hands on it she knew she needed someone with as big a voice as Katy's to sing on it. 'Rita is a great fit,' Iggy said. 'Her voice can blow people away.'

Rita was delighted to be joining up with Iggy again and was

thrilled to see her get so big. 'I've always loved her vibe and her energy,' Rita said. 'I knew [her new album] was going to be a shock and it was a good shock, and I'm really happy for her. What we've done together is so cool and "Black Widow" has an amazing message. We've always wanted to work together and we found the perfect song. It's all about women empowerment.'

In discussing the single, both Rita and Iggy talked about how they had dealt with being messed around by an ex.

'I don't think I do anything,' Iggy said. 'I'm more passive-aggressive. I just like to be, "You have to see my face everywhere now … you wake up and I'm there."'

Rita, perhaps tellingly, revealed she was much more direct: 'I'm more like, "He's just pissed me off so it's going down." I would, like, go there, harass his whole thing, mess his whole house up, completely scratch his car. I'm like the worst ex-girlfriend ever. I'm learning. My friends are teaching me – "Rita, tone it down, stop being so mental." But, you know, in the moment, when you're in love it's fine, but just don't cross with me.'

Iggy revealed the pair had tried to find a song to collaborate on before but it hadn't worked. 'We had a few near hits and misses. It was never right. We didn't get in the studio together, but we didn't really have to because we know each other so well. Katy was really happy with it. She texted me and she told me she loved it.'

'I was really happy about it,' Rita added. 'It's good when two girls support each other, especially two blondes, they're stronger than one.'

The video was based on Quentin Tarantino's martial arts flick *Kill Bill* and features the girls kicking seven shades out of a bunch of chauvinistic men with bare hands, feet, swords and just about anything else they can muster.

'We did two days of straight martial arts training,' Rita said. 'It was us learning how to hold a sword and it was so difficult. It's like a dance choreography ... we put a lot of time into this video because we wanted it to be right. We didn't want to be two badasses that weren't really badasses. We wanted to know what we were doing so we both trained together and it was funny. Iggy's just got a puppy and it was weeing all over the place. When we were trying to train I was, like, stepping in wee. But it was all love and I'm happy now I know a few things. Be careful ...'

'We're always around each other but we are genuinely friends,' Iggy said. 'Our mothers are friends now too, actually.'

Iggy gave Rita what she hadn't been able to achieve so far – a top ten hit in America. The single reached number three on the Billboard Hot 100 and was only denied the top spot by two monster sellers – Meghan Trainor's 'All About That Bass' and Taylor Swift's 'Shake It Off', which held the top two positions for eleven weeks. The song would end the year selling more than two million copies in the States alone.

In the UK, it peaked at number four, at the time Iggy's highest chart placing in Britain.

The summer smash showed Rita had fully recovered from her setback with Calvin. However, the dispute over his tracks meant that her album would be delayed indefinitely. Memories of the struggle she'd faced to release her debut resurfaced.

At least she was able to channel some of that frustration into her music. Details leaked of one song that would definitely be making the final cut.

Rita was planning a scathing song about an ex. Called 'Poison', she compared a former lover to a serpent coming from the Garden of Eden.

Rita was following in the footsteps of singers like Adele and Taylor Swift who famously settled scores through music.

What Ritabots would want to know was who she was thinking about?

Rob Kardashian, Calvin, Dave Gardner, James Arthur? Or was it someone from further back in her life?

Clash magazine described the track as 'powerful and exposing'. Rita said: 'This is about my bad luck with love.'

Would it be different with Ricky?

There was a calmness about their activities, as if Rita had realised the grand statements on Twitter and gestures only come back to haunt you if things go wrong. They were spending a lot of quality time together and it was even said he was helping her house hunt in Notting Hill and Marylebone. She had long dreamt of owning a house in the place she grew up. The area has such special signifi-cance for her and her family.

As they viewed several traditional stucco-fronted homes, it seemed she might finally get her wish. Her parents had advised her to invest her money, to have something to show for it should her pop career flounder. It was said she had £4 million to spend and was looking for at least three bedrooms and some outside space.

Rita's album might have been delayed but other projects were progressing apace. In the autumn Rita was launching her sports-wear collection for Adidas. And as she trailed her new line she said: 'It's going to be a load of tracksuits with big, floral prints and things like that,' she said ahead of the launch. 'I just want to put clothes on girls and I really want them to be happy and comfortable and sexy.

'I made tracksuits and sports bras and things like that. Sorry, men, I haven't got to you yet, but women's fashion is what matters right now.'

Her film career also looked set to take off. After her role in *Fifty Shades*, Rita landed another juicy role, this time alongside Jake Gyllenhaal in the boxing movie *Southpaw*, directed by Antoine Fuqua, famous for *Training Day*. She had studio giant Harvey Weinstein to thank for getting her the part but she didn't let him down.

'Her scene is just breathtaking,' he gushed. 'She's a very glam-orous, beautiful woman but we made her up to look like a tough junkie who's got a kid to protect. She is heartbreakingly real and wonderful – my biggest discovery as an actress this year.'

It was quite a claim, given the number of actors and actresses whose careers Weinstein had boosted through movies like *Reservoir Dogs*, *Pulp Fiction* and *Good Will Hunting*.

One thing was undeniable, however. Rita was in demand.

The President of the United States of America wanted her to per-form at the annual Christmas in Washington party.

Yet, more importantly, the most powerful man in television, Simon Cowell, once again wanted her to join the judging panel on *X Factor*. She'd turned him down a second time because her schedule wouldn't have allowed it.

When Simon's ITV rival the BBC came calling to sound her out about replacing Kylie Minogue as a mentor on *The Voice* she was initially going to give them the same reply.

Heading into its fourth season, *The Voice*, which aired in the New Year, was a reality show aimed at identifying talent based purely on hopefuls' singing ability. Four judges/mentors famously sat with their backs to the performers so they could judge them purely on what they heard. The series had launched with Turn First's Jessie J in one of the hot seats alongside will.i.am, Tom Jones and The Script's Danny O'Donoghue but after two series she left to be replaced by Kylie, while Danny made way for Kaiser Chiefs' frontman Ricky Wilson. Now the Australian was stepping down after one series and producers were desperate for the hottest name in pop to fill her shoes.

Rita wasn't convinced it was right for her.

'When *The Voice* approached me, my initial thought was: 'No, I'm working on my second album,' said Rita. 'But then will.i.am called and said: "Why aren't you doing it?" and I said: "Because I just don't feel I can give anything to anybody." He said: "You need to wake the f*** up because what you can give is that you're current and you've had four number ones on your first album – embrace that and give it to somebody else and stop being selfish for a second."'

So she was turning down Simon for the BBC?

'I'll tell you the truth: timing was all it was,' Rita said. 'Schedule-wise, I wouldn't have been able to record *The X Factor* when they were filming. *The Voice* was perfect for my schedule.'

Rita was less concerned about replacing a national treasure like Kylie than she was at the prospect of being the token female.

'Kylie has a different perspective on the music industry,' she said. 'But I was nervous being the only female – *The Voice* Girl – and I wanted to be prepared so I watched the last series to see how Kylie did it. She has been in music for so long that she can tell you all the history, but what I can tell you is the now. I have the same aspirations as the acts, which the other coaches don't have.'

Some people weren't happy. Twitter trolls, the type of people who rarely see the positive in anything, took to their keyboards to spit some nasty comments about her. And Louis Walsh, a near permanent fixture on *X Factor* said she was making a big mistake. 'She was on *X Factor* as a guest judge and was good,' Louis said. '*X Factor* is much better than *The Voice*. I think she will live to regret that decision. *The*

Voice haven't had a One Direction, Leona Lewis, Olly Murs, or Ella Henderson yet. I think it will probably get axed soon and it should be axed because it's not working.'

Louis was right about something – one of them would soon be out of a job. Would it be Rita?

19

Silencing the Critics

IT was hugs, jubilation and tears of joy all around … until the camera panned to Rita.

Her luscious red lips were rounded to a pout and her gaze was permanently fixed downwards. Her eyes began to glaze over but Rita dug deep and held it together just long enough for the cameras to stop rolling.

A week earlier, the nation's new sweetheart had been credited with adding an astonishing four million viewers to *The Voice*. Now, on semi-final night, she had become the first judge in the programme's short history not to have a single act performing in the final.

If she looked dejected on stage as her protégées – teen mum Karis Thomas and P.E. teacher Joel Woolford – were voted off the show, off air she approached inconsolable as the tears she'd been holding back broke through her guard.

'What have I done wrong?' she sobbed to fellow judge Tom Jones, the legendary crooner who at seventy-four was fifty years Rita's senior.

A seasoned veteran of the entertainment industry, Tom knew Rita had in fact done everything right – charming viewers with her friendly and occasionally cheeky banter and dazzling in a variety of flashy outfits. She had swiftly and efficiently silenced critics who said she didn't have enough experience to justify her position alongside Tom, will.i.am and Ricky Wilson. And she'd pulled it off while juggling the type of exhausting schedule that was now her trademark.

'It is a big thing, especially for someone new like that,' Tom explained. 'The two young singers she had were gutted, too. As soon as it happened I thought, "My God, I hope this doesn't put her off." I'm hoping it hasn't made her want to go.'

She could have been forgiven in that moment for taking the blow personally and letting all the old doubts come flooding back. Anyone on the lookout would have seen the omens in plain sight.

During the audition stage of the hit TV show where each judge tries to assemble their team of wannabe stars, Rita found many reluctant at first to choose the newbie judge as their mentor.

As contestant after contestant opted for Rita's male counterparts, she began to worry no one would ever pick her. Maybe she had made a mistake after all.

Simon Cowell, clearly bitter over her rejection of his *X Factor* offer, joined the chorus of people who, before the show even started, said she'd made a wrong move. 'I was surprised Rita chose *The Voice* not *X Factor*,' he said. 'She made the wrong decision. As things happen, things have worked out fine. Mel B [the former Spice Girl Simon hired instead] has been better than she would have been anyway.' Could those damning words have been circling around her mind?

If that wasn't bad enough, pressure mounted even further when Rita was then the subject of four hundred complaints from BBC viewers. They took offence in their droves when she went on the prime-time TV programme *The One Show* with her fellow judges to promote *The Voice* wearing trousers and a jacket with nothing underneath, revealing some serious cleavage. One wondered if her father was among the outraged considering the lecture he'd given her previously about wearing a bra.

The BBC escaped punishment after the government watchdog Ofcom were called to rule on her choice of clothing. But the flak resulted in Rita getting more negative comments.

'I do not want to see her boobs hanging out on a family programme,' one angry viewer wrote on the BBC's *Points of View* message board.

Although, with proper perspective, it was clear Rita's small steps back were just hiccups when compared to the bounds cleared going forward.

Rewind just a few weeks to December and the outfit of choice was nothing short of dazzling. Radiating vintage Hollywood in a glamorous off-shoulder black gown paired with her favourite long black leather gloves, Rita found herself performing for a room of dignitaries, millions of television viewers – and the leader of the free world.

She had jetted into Washington DC to lead an emotional, rousing version of Band Aid's 'Do They Know It's Christmas?' for none other than President Barack Obama and his family at their annual festive concert.

Her platinum hair hung in sumptuous waves and her lips bore her signature red.

If only Rita's ten-year-old self could have seen her then! Not even Rita's adoring grandfather Besnik, who spotted her extraordinary talent when she was just a baby, nor Hana Hajaj, who had seen something brave in the little girl stealing the limelight at her brother's school show, would have dreamt Rita would one day be singing for the American president.

It was a unique performance. Usually the song is sung by a host of pop stars but here Rita was on her own, save for a backing by the Washington Youth Choir. She looked a picture of confidence.

But before her performance Rita asked fans to wish her luck and afterwards she took to social media to reveal she'd been a bundle of nerves. Posting a picture of herself, she wrote: 'Ok I can't help it little sneak peak of my face before walking on the Obama stage. My legs were like jelly!! Thank you Audrey Hepburn for the inspiration!! #breakfastattiffs'

Back in England the song, which made history when it raised millions for starving Africans in 1984, had been reworked for a special thirtieth anniversary release. Rita joined the likes of One Direction, Ed Sheeran and Emeli Sandé for the updated version. She managed to arrange time off from filming *The Voice* so she could dash from Manchester to London to record her contribution.

Perhaps Rita drew upon her monumental experience at the White House to rally and pull herself through the semi-final upset on *The Voice* a few months later. No doubt, there was certainly a touch more defiance in her response to critics during the entire process.

'I get negativity all the time,' she said. 'I have it on Twitter constantly and I get it walking down the street.

'When I was first in the public eye I had so much random s**t and so many crazy things happened. It was with everything – from how I dress to what I say and how I sing. So I really had to commit to the way I am.'

Rita, who had filmed the auditions in the lead-up to Christmas, might have been able to brush off the haters but she did admit jitters before the series aired in the New Year were at times too hard to suppress.

'I've been getting so nervous about what people will think of me. People have a different perception of me compared to what I'm actually like. I guess people see pictures and my music videos and don't know the kind of person I am.

'So being on the show is intimidating. It's like I'm giving myself to people. But I'm going to watch and I will be looking at Twitter.'

Rita hoped her sincere approach on the show would win her new fans.

'I think I'm really honest. I like to make the acts feel like they can talk to me and be really open,' she said. 'I try to be as approachable as possible.'

She did admit, however, that she found the blind auditions gruelling. 'You don't know what's going to happen next. I expected it to be a lot more controlled. I'd almost rather be on stage for three hours straight singing and sweating than be in that chair for longer than seven hours.'

Apologising for the earlier fashion faux pas, Rita said: 'I thought to myself, "Well, I have to be a bit appropriate if I'm going to be on TV every Saturday."'

She kept her promise – but still pushed the style boundaries to their limits. When the programme aired, Rita was seen taking her place in the red chair for the start of the blind auditions in a sheer black lace dress with her hair tied up in three knots – her punky undercut visible. It was a clear homage to her idol Gwen Stefani.

From that first night dissenters, the Twitter trolls and complainers were forced to eat their words. *The Voice* – thanks in huge part to Rita's presence – pulled in 8.05 million viewers, more than double the ratings for *Stars in Their Eyes*, the rival on ITV1. The BBC was delighted. The figures were twenty-five per cent up on the previous year.

The second show was even better. It was the BBC's second most popular programme of the month, beaten only by period drama *Call the Midwife*.

And finally Rita's team started to take shape – many of the younger contestants opting for her. Her confidence soared. Viewers started to fall in love with her antics: playfully dancing in her seat, rushing to the stage to comfort dejected singers and swooning over hunky male performers.

Rita wasn't just winning over new fans at home. Those working on the show couldn't help warming to her infectious personality. Presenter Marvin Humes, who first found fame with JLS on *X Factor*, said: 'The highlight is Rita. She's done so well. You forget she's only twenty-four and she's sitting there next to Tom Jones, who is seventy-four, and she can hold her own and stand her ground.'

Backstage, crew workers marvelled at her very un-diva-like demands. They revealed her only requests were a full breakfast in the morning and some Yorkshire tea.

There were rumours Rita was also getting friendly with fellow judge Ricky, as reports of flirty massages between the pair surfaced. The *Daily Mirror* interviewed a fan who claimed they'd heard Ricky boast: 'You should have seen me before I came out, Rita was putting oil on me backstage.'

Luckily, Rita found her own fears about how she would handle the demands of television were unfounded. 'It's actually the best decision I've made,' she said. 'It's so fun. I love it. I'm learning a lot about myself, being a coach. I'm starting to trust my instincts. When you're sitting in that chair, you can't ask what anyone thinks, you just have to do it.'

In the wake of the positive reaction to *The Voice* Rita received yet more sensational news. Incredibly, she was in the running for an Oscar – not for her cameo in *Fifty Shades of Grey* but for her song 'Grateful', which she had recorded for the soundtrack to the movie *Beyond the Lights*. Not only that but Rita was asked to perform at the fifty-seventh Academy Awards in Los Angeles in February. She faced stiff competition to win the iconic gold statuette, up against 'Glory' from the acclaimed film *Selma* and the insanely catchy 'Everything Is Awesome' from *The Lego Movie*.

And she'd scored another top ten hit – this time featuring on 'Doing It', the third single from Charli XCX's album *Sucker*. The song, which reached number six, was notable for the video – a Thelma and Louise-style desert chase where they nearly crashed their car and a bucking bronco scene where they took 'close working relationship' to a whole new level.

'I had to hold Rita's boobs,' singer-songwriter Charli said. A fellow Brit, aka Charlotte Emma Aitchison, had been writing with Iggy Azalea and Gwen Stefani after her breakthrough smash 'I Love it', with Icona Pop. Now she had teamed up with Rita for another feel-good hit.

Appearing alongside Charli on *The Graham Norton Show* in January, Rita said: 'I heard this song when she wrote it and I really, really fell in love with it.'

As talk turned to Rita's other projects a stunned Graham told her: 'I feel like more fanfare should be wrote about this, that you are Oscar-nominated tomorrow, why don't we know this?! I feel like we should all know this.'

In response, a smiling Rita explained: 'I don't know. I just like to think that I'm a bit humble, I don't walk around saying I'm Oscar nominated.'

'Well, somebody should,' Graham declared. 'That's a big deal!'

Fellow guests, actress Julie Walters and Rita's *Fifty Shades* co-star Jamie Dornan concurred. 'It's huge!' Julie said.

The BBC must have been delighted to bask in some reflected glory from Rita's wave of successes but already there were fears she was simply becoming too big to remain on *The Voice* for more than one series.

'Rita is blowing up across the world right now,' presenter Marvin said. 'I wouldn't be surprised if she was too busy to come back next year. She was nominated for an Oscar, she is constantly releasing number one singles and she has another album coming. You don't get more current than that. Recording the show is a huge commitment. Jessie and Kylie both quit so they could tour, so it wouldn't be a huge shock if Rita did the same. But if that's the case it shows she was a great booking in the first place.'

She certainly was – and she continued to confirm it. As the series entered its quarter-final stage eleven million viewers were tuning in to watch the drama unfold. And when asked what she brought to the talent show it was clear she had, temporarily at least, put her earlier insecurities well behind her as she stated: 'Four million viewers.'

Even she was amazed by the impact she was having. 'I go to Tesco's to pick up flowers for my mum every week, when I'm in town,' she said. 'I see grandmothers and they say, "You're doing really good on *The Voice*." And I'm like, "You know who I am!" So thanks to *The Voice* for expanding my fanbase.'

Tom Jones said Rita had fitted into the judge's panel perfectly. 'She hasn't been in the business that long but she has learnt a lot and the public loves her,' he said.

That's why the timing of her acts failing to progress to the show's finale could not have been worse for Rita. It was a management disaster for the BBC. Rita was the first coach not to have an act in the final. Previously the judges were guaranteed one singer would make it but the rules had been changed for this series.

Rita was devastated but her fellow judges had her back.

will.i.am slammed the decision. 'It's not fair,' he said. 'I don't like the new rule. I wouldn't allow a coach not to have someone from her team in the final.'

He questioned whether Rita should even be there for the final, when her role would be redundant. 'In theory she shouldn't have to be there,' he said. 'She was saying, "Why do I have to show up?"'

He too feared it might make her decide not to return for a second series. 'I hope she comes back,' he said. 'She is the best for multiple reasons.'

Rita's despair might have had something to do with the poor viewing figures for the last episode. Only 7.9 million people tuned in to watch Scot Stevie McCrorie – one of the handsome male contestants Rita had flirted with – be crowned champion.

But by now Rita had become a different animal. After all she had achieved she wasn't going to let this damage all the hard work she had done so far on the show.

After taking stock Rita came back all guns blazing. She covered up in a demure white suit after yet more complaints about her revealing tops, proving to be a consummate professional for the last night.

She became the highlight of an otherwise disappointing final with a striking live performance of 'New York Raining', rapper Charles Hamilton's song co-written by The Invisible Men. The single, which Rita had a featuring credit on, was from the ground-breaking Fox TV series *Empire* – about African Americans being exploited by whites – in which she was also scheduled to make a guest appearance.

Fans hoped her presence would be more than the cameo in *Fifty Shades of Grey*. When the movie hit the screens on Valentine's Day one of the most commented things about it was how small Rita's role was. She might only have had four lines but, as Rita was quick to point out, her character developed throughout the trilogy. And many actresses would have killed for any part in such a huge film.

'This was such a great cameo to be involved in, and even though I'm only in it for a little bit, it's opened the door to a lot of movie things that I haven't announced yet,' she said. 'If you read the novel you see that my character is literally only in it for one scene which is that scene in the movie.'

Rita revealed she did pester author EL James, who had retained creative control over the film, about whether her character could be developed. 'I said to her why don't you write a bigger part so I can get a bigger moment in the role. She's like, "Have patience, there's a second and third book." In the second and third book I get kidnapped and there's a whole palaver.'

The promise of an enhanced part seemed to counter a suggestion made in leaked emails that appeared on the Wikileaks website that Sony movie executives didn't know who Rita was. She had been the subject of an email discussion which all seemed extremely positive. One executive praised Rita for being an 'incredible spark'. When the other exec in question asked if she knew her it seemed to suggest she had never heard of her, not an outlandish situation given Rita's profile in the States was nothing like it was in the UK.

However, given the panning the movie received in general from critics Rita might have been relieved her part was minor and that some important people didn't know her. But when the film opened it was clear movie fans were following the same trend as book buyers. While critics hated it, cinemagoers loved it and *Fifty Shades* was one of the biggest movies of the year at the box office. EL James' original books about the kinky sex games that go on between business magnate Christian Grey and his college graduate lover Anastasia Steele were equally slated, but went on to smash sales records, shifting an incredible 125 million copies worldwide.

During filming there were rumours of tensions on set. But Rita said: 'I didn't have any problems with anybody. I loved the movie and I think Sam Taylor-Wood is an amazing storyteller and a female in this industry who is really powerful so I think she did a great job.'

Rita used the release of the film to talk about her sexual preferences. She was quoted as saying 'I always use a little whip', and then she qualified it slightly. 'It depends on who I am in bed with. There's nothing wrong with it,' she said. Asked if, like Christian Grey, she had ever pushed a partner beyond their comfort limits, she said: 'Yes, many times. I still do. There's nothing wrong with it. I just think that if you get someone a little bit uncomfortable, it's never a bad thing. You have to trust your instincts, be at one with your body. I have been very lucky to say I have not felt uncomfortable. Sex is a language that everyone speaks and the mind is a dirty place, thank God. Why wouldn't you use it to your advantage? I honestly don't think it's a bad thing.'

Not only was her part shorter than she might have liked in the film, but Rita had a double disappointment when songs she had been working on for the soundtrack never made the final cut. She had spoken about running through some tracks to be considered for the movie. 'There is such a different vision for the movie to my own music, so there is a specific kind of vision for that soundtrack,' she said.

Fans were puzzled why, when she intended to put in so much effort, her songs didn't make the cut. But sources close to her shed some light on what happened. It was yet another repercussion of her split from Calvin.

'Rita is disappointed not to be involved because it's something she really wanted to do,' a source told the *Daily Mirror*. 'She had been really excited about recording something dark that would fit the tone. She was due to release her second album at the end of last year. So when that was pushed back she had to give it her full attention. As the spot on the soundtrack was never confirmed, when something had to give, that was what gave.'

Instead, Rita's fellow Turn First artist Ellie Goulding was granted a slot on the soundtrack for her song 'Love Me Like You Do' which became the fastest-selling single of the year when it was released just before the film. The track went to number one, knocking Mark Ronson hit 'Uptown Funk' from the top spot.

When asked when fans might get to hear her long-awaited and now much delayed second album, Rita could only say: 'It will be ready when I say it's ready.'

The seemingly endless delay was deeply frustrating but at least Rita didn't need the album from a financial point of view. Figures released showed she was in extremely rude health cash-wise. Thanks to a fortune amassed from high-profile advertising campaigns with Donna Karan, Roberto Cavalli, Marks and Spencer and Calvin Klein, and her Adidas range, her company Ora Multi Services Ltd was now said to boast assets in excess of £2.5million. The outfit also had a healthy cash reserve of £1,853,055 – more than three times the £612,000 it had in 2013. As a testament to Rita's commitment to her family, both her parents, as well as Elena and little brother Doni, are company shareholders.

A second business covering her music career had yet to file accounts, meaning her wealth would be even greater still.

'The past year has been sensational,' a source told the *Sunday People*. 'This has gone beyond anybody's expectations, she has literally not stopped working.'

Awards season in the US kicked off with the Golden Globes, where the gongs are dished out by the Hollywood Foreign Press Association. Rita attended the bash, traditionally more laid back and raucous than the Academy Awards, as the guest of Harvey Weinstein. The sixty-two-year-old studio boss had clearly taken a shine to Rita and was keen to champion her talents in Hollywood.

At his private party Rita was delighted to hook up with Cara Delevingne once again. Relationships and punishing work schedules had limited their time together so they relished the chance to let their hair down like old times.

But at the Grammys – the American music industry awards – that followed swiftly afterwards it wasn't Cara she was kissing but Miley Cyrus, the former Disney star whose reputation still hadn't recovered from her 'twerking' controversy of August 2013 at the MTV Video Music Awards. At the pre-awards gala in Beverly Hills, Rita and Miley kissed and cuddled, according to onlookers.

Rita's passion for smooching with girlfriends fed into a wider accusation that female popstars were spicing up shows with 'fake lesbian kisses'. Among those criticising the trend was Iggy Azalea, perhaps unsurprisingly, given her attitude previously. Rita was unfazed. 'Madonna has been doing it for years and there is nothing wrong with it — you will not go to jail, unless you are playing a show in Uganda,' she said.

At the after party a potentially awkward situation arose when Rita arrived on her own to find Calvin there with new flame Aarika Wolf. She performed a quick body swerve and collared producer Mark Ronson for a chat instead.

Rita was still seeing Ricky Hilfiger but while he decided not to accompany her to the music parties, he was by her side in New York for Fashion Week, particularly at an event at the Park Avenue Armory to celebrate his dad Tommy's thirty years in the business.

You had to take your hat off to Rita. Who else could juggle a high-profile stint on the nation's leading reality TV show with the preparations needed for the American awards season? It was one thing to secure the right dress for a red-carpet event like the Golden Globes but, as the Academy Awards approached, Rita knew she had to be at the top of her game. She would be performing in front of a world TV audience of one billion.

For an event on that scale Rita needed three knock-out dresses, one for the red carpet, which for the Oscars is a show in itself, one for her performance of 'Grateful' and a third for the after show.

Tasked with the job of making the right first impression was London designer Georgina Chapman, co-founder of the Marchesa label and, not coincidentally, the wife of Harvey Weinstein. She had a double challenge. Not only did she want Rita to showcase her own label but she would have wanted the singer to shine to justify her husband's faith in her. Georgina's choice was a stunning midnight-blue fishtail creation.

'Rita is such a nice girl and so talented,' Georgina gushed. 'I've worked with her for a few years now, but this was obviously a very important dress and we went over several ideas and spent about a month making it. The morning of the Oscars is always fraught and I was very nervous. I was doing last-minute tweaks before the dress was sent over to Rita's hotel. When it arrived, Rita's stylist sent me pictures so that I could make sure that it had been fitted perfectly.

'Rita took a chance on me, and that's a tremendous responsibility,' she added. 'She looked amazing, and thank goodness there were no wardrobe malfunctions. She sent me flowers the next day to say thank you.'

For her performance, Rita would not only have to change into another stunning strapless dress but she would have her own bodyguard to protect the jewels around her neck. 'As soon as it's done, it's like, "Take my soul away,"' she joked.

Rita, as fans now expect, was sensational with no hint of the nerves she said she had beforehand.

And then it was time for the outfit change that would command column inches in magazines around the world – the sheer Donna Karan number that showed off her shapely derrière. What a moment for the woman who as a teenager so disliked her own body shape. Now she was proudly showing it off for the world to see.

At an Oscars party Oprah Winfrey, the doyenne of American television, took her aside and whispered some words of wisdom. It was as if she was floating on air.

Back in Blighty and it was back to earth with a slight bump. Not only was there the disappointment of *The Voice* finale awaiting her but at the Brit Awards it must have felt like she was returning to an arena where she didn't seem to get the recognition she deserved.

The year just gone hadn't been prolific for her, admittedly, but fans must have wondered what went through her mind when she saw Paloma Faith pick up the British Female Solo Artist gong with three top ten hits and a solitary number one and Sam Smith crowned British Breakthrough Act, with just two number ones. Rita had achieved far more the year before and had left empty-handed.

If she was thinking such thoughts she certainly wasn't airing them. She had bigger dreams to fulfill.

In May 2015 she was off to Cannes. Her film career to date might have extended to an outing when she was fourteen and four lines in a flop thereafter, but she was heading to the film festival with the intention of doing her damnedest to change that.

By her side she'd have Elena and her Kosovan cousin and best friend Amantina Tolaj who, despite the controversy with her father, remained close to Rita and by now regularly travelled to visit her the world over.

The next few months would be a turning point for Rita. She'd be closing one chapter on her life and about to embark on something even bigger and more exciting.

She'd be getting rid of one bad boy … but an alliance with another meant controversy was lurking just around the corner.

20

Queen of Prime Time

IT was an unconventional business meeting. But when the most powerful man in television needs to speak urgently to the most in-demand woman in pop music then convention goes out of the window.

Rita was jetting to Los Angeles in just a few hours to finish her album. Simon Cowell was slap bang in the middle of another series of *Britain's Got Talent*. But he had to see Rita before she left the country. And so he sent a car to collect her and at midnight she was making her way through streets teeming with late night revellers to his West London mansion. It was the first time Rita had been to the mogul's home and she was immediately impressed. 'It was incredible,' she said.

Simon welcomed her in but this was no late night soirée. They had business to discuss. 'We didn't drink,' Rita said. 'It was very professional and straight to the point.'

Simon had an offer to make her. Even though he was up to his eyes with one talent show he was already thinking about the next. *The X Factor* would be returning on ITV1 in the autumn. But after a lacklustre run that had seen it slip behind its BBC rival *Strictly Come Dancing* in the ratings and a fall in viewers from 14 million in 2010 to a series average of 8.6 million in 2014, it needed a drastic revamp. He needed to appeal to a younger audience. There was only one woman who could give him that.

A year earlier Rita had turned him down but twelve months on she was in a different place. The album she'd been toiling over for two years was nearing completion. She had enjoyed her time on *The Voice* – despite the final – but crucially her schedule had changed. She could commit the time now but not in the New Year when the BBC series would be airing again.

When Rita had signed for *The Voice* Simon had brushed off what he'd seen almost as a defection by claiming he had the right judges in place. But he was kidding no one. He knew he had to try again to land the woman who could transform his show. Despite what was at stake, Simon kept the mood light. 'It was actually a very no-pressure vibe, it felt very natural,' Rita said.

Simon explained his vision to overhaul the show. Ever-present judge Louis Walsh was going, so was ex-Spice Girl Mel B. Long-standing host Dermot O'Leary would also be seeking a new challenge. Simon wanted two new judges – Rita and her good friend and Radio 1 breakfast show DJ Nick Grimshaw. Former *X Factor* runner-up Olly Murs and his *Xtra Factor* co-presenter Caroline Flack, the 2014 *Strictly Come Dancing* champion, would be hosting the main show.

The offer was a lucrative one. If reports were to be believed Rita's £1.5 million deal would make her the highest paid judge, above former golden girl Cheryl Fernandez-Versini, making her the queen of prime-time TV. Simon was also said to be chucking in the use of his private jet and a 'whole new wardrobe'. While he clearly didn't mean the type that comes in flatpacks from Ikea, it was hard to imagine Rita being swayed by the promise of a few new bits of clobber, and she already flew by private plane.

For Rita it wasn't about the money – it never had been with her – it was about it being the right move. It also wasn't about Simon telling her how it would be. She had impressed him on *The Voice* and he was keen to hear her input. In the end though it was an easy decision to make.

'I had a lot of questions and he did too,' Rita said. 'But it just fit into place perfectly. And the time commitment worked perfectly for me. What made it special was when Simon asked me about *X Factor*, he told me about his plans for the show and how he was going to change it up.

'And Simon is the one who first put me on TV a few years ago as a guest judge so going to *X Factor* is like going home.'

Rita was keen to stress that she wasn't ditching *The Voice* for a rival. She wasn't intending to return anyway. 'I loved my time on the show but I'm going to be out of the country when *The Voice* is shooting so I wasn't going to be able to do it anyway,' she said. 'For me, the second album is so important because I've spent two years on it. Everything else always has to work around that. It was a very simple decision.'

Rita was delighted to be joining her close friend Nick on the new-look judging panel, but she denied he was a deciding factor. 'He's my friend. I value his opinion so I obviously asked,' she said. 'It didn't make me go one way or another, it just gave me more information. That was all. I make my own decisions. I'm determined to stay in control of what I have because I've worked very hard. I wanted to make sure that the decision came from me.'

Rita also moved quickly to dispel any talk that a rivalry might develop between her and Cheryl. 'That's not something I'm focused on,' she said. 'Anyway, I think that will be looked at differently now. You see female pop stars supporting each other more. Plus, I had only met Cheryl once before. But she is very hot and pretty.'

The X Factor would be holding auditions in the summer, with the series launching on television at the end of August. Before then Rita had a new single and a movie to promote.

But the sisterhood of support among female pop stars to which she alluded when discussing Cheryl was going to be crucial for Rita. Out of the woodwork came crawling an old acquaintance – to deliver a stinging, shocking and unprovoked attack.

A$AP Rocky, the Harlem rapper with whom Rita had hung out back in 2012, chose a time when she was garnering headlines around the world to reveal they had a fling together.

Fondly reminiscing about a special time they shared together might have been excusable but A$AP kissed and told in typically colourful fashion – by dissing her disgustingly in a track. Rocky's song 'Better Things' contained lyrics where he name checked Rita, claiming she had a big mouth and the next time he saw her he might 'curse' her out. There were also crude references to sex acts and what he made her do.

What was initially bizarre about the track was that no one until that point had linked the two of them, so it appeared it was in fact Rocky, ironically, who had the big mouth. He wouldn't have too long to wait to 'curse' her out – as they were both on the bill for the Wireless Festival in Finsbury Park, London, albeit on different days.

It was hard to know what Rocky was trying to achieve but publication of the lyric backfired on him spectacularly. Rita fans took to Twitter to defend their idol and Rocky was widely criticised. Amid the general furore, the true background to the incendiary lyric wasn't explored – until now.

Rocky claimed the song wasn't current and that he was merely expressing his emotions from a time when he was angry. What he was exactly angry about wasn't completely clear, but he gave some clues.

'First off, this song is old. It's one of the older songs on the album,' Rocky said. 'What I will say is ... I got into a lot of trouble over her at times when I didn't need to. She caused a lot of grief ... Maybe I should have muted her name but at the time that's how I felt. I got in trouble,' he told American DJ and rapper Sway Calloway.

'When you get in trouble with women, I'm sure everybody can put two and two together. I wasn't supposed to be doing things with her ... I got in trouble. And she got me on purpose, you know. It's girly stuff. But at the end of the day I don't have nothing against her ...'

The key lines were Rocky admitting that he was doing things with Rita that he wasn't supposed to and that she 'got' him 'on purpose'. People didn't have to read between the lines to get that he was admitting cheating on a girlfriend with Rita and that she told the other woman. Given Rita was getting to know Rocky at the same time Iggy Azalea was seeing him and she was getting close to her too, could one assume that this was the 'trouble' she caused? By accusing Rita of getting him 'on purpose' was he saying that Rita set him up to show Iggy that he was cheating on her?'

When asked by Sway why he had brought it up when no one had any inkling he and Rita had history, he said: 'People who shouldn't have known in the beginning shouldn't have known either.'

Realising his words were going to be picked over, Rocky did try to issue a disclaimer: 'I just want to clarify, this isn't me saying: People don't go listen to Rita Ora, or she's an ugly person, or nothing. I'm not saying she's a terrible person, I'm just saying that when I was in a relationship and I did things with her that I wasn't supposed to do, she had a big mouth.'

Rocky also tried to insist his lyrics didn't mean he was generally disrespectful towards women: 'I'm starting to feel bad about it … I don't want to make it seem that I'm out here degrading women and shit. Like I'm a pig. That's not the case at all. I just wanted to tell you what was going on in my life.'

He might have a tough job convincing people of that. It wasn't just Rita that Rocky name checked in his lyrics. In 'Jukebox Joints' he also made a crude reference to Iggy and suggested he had history with Rihanna too, claiming he liked nothing better than a 'big forehead bitch' and rapped about 'Cinderella's under my umbrella … ella ella ay', a clear reference to RiRi's monster hit 'Umbrella'. While his relationship with Iggy was well known he was more coy about Rihanna. 'I like bitches with big foreheads, what's wrong with that? That's the beauty of music and art, you make up your own interpretation. I wouldn't say that [it's about Rihanna].'

After Iggy, Rocky was engaged to the model Chanel Iman but it was less likely that theirs was the relationship where Rita caused trouble as they continued until October 2014 – long after Rocky wrote the song.

As the flak flew and Rocky continued to address claims he was being degrading to women, he bleated: 'I thought it was going to be like the Nineties and people would let art be art. You know, when you had Eminem saying all types of shit he didn't have to explain that shit in interviews or on the radio or on camera or shit. People just said what they said and you had to listen to the next song to hear how they felt.'

Rita didn't respond for several weeks. But when she did she appeared to care less about the impact it was having on her personally and more about what it meant for women in general.

'I'm not looking at it like, "you're upsetting me" because I don't actually give a s***,' she said in a radio interview. 'I think about it and I don't want people to think it's okay to speak about women like that. That's it.' She added: 'I don't care what you say about me. I don't give a flying f***. That's just how it is, but you know got to keep it moving. I'm very happy with what I do and I'm proud of who I am and what I represent.'

Sadly, this wasn't the first time Rita had been named and shamed as a sexual conquest in a song. In October 2013 the rapper Chip, formerly Chipmunk, remixed Drake's tune 'Pound Cake'. He changed the lyrics to say: 'I've had Rita cake, I want Rihanna cake. I got you thinking what kinda cake.'

The lyric seemed to suggest something had gone on between them. What was strange though was why he chose to air it in a remix of someone else's song – Drake no less, who had his own close connection with Rita. Drake's original had featured Jay Z and to single out Rita and Rihanna – both the Roc Nation boss's protégées – seemed a curious thing to do.

Chip's rap came after a time when he and Rita had grown close. The pair had discovered they had something in common when they first met – their birth dates. Chip, real name Jahmaal Fyffe from Tottenham, North London, and Rita immediately hit it off. 'The first time I met him I was like sixteen-seventeen,' Rita told Capital FM's Max during a joint interview with Chip in 2012. 'We just talked and he was like, "When's your birthday?" and I was like, "the twenty-sixth" and I was like "when's yours?" and he was like "twenty-sixth" and I was like "what!" And then we've just been friends ever since.'

Chip had experienced mainstream success before Rita and their paths crossed repeatedly over the years. Chip had won two awards at the 2008 MOBOs – the year Rita performed there with Craig David.

And years later her success came as no surprise to Chip. 'I think it was inevitable that it was going to happen,' he said. 'It's good to see it. It's good to see it and live it and breath it.'

Chip, who had been signed by Sony, then joined American rapper T.I.'s label Grand Hustle Records in 2012. Before he decided to immortalise Rita in song, Chip and she regularly partied together and were snapped together at Mahiki in February of that year. Why he decided to brag about her has never been explained and his lyrics have not been picked over like Rocky's were.

If he and Rita did indeed take things further what was the timescale? Did it pre-date the period when she was seeing Rob Kardashian or after?

Certainly, when it came to ex-lovers Rita had plenty of ammunition of her own.

And it was the theme of 'poisonous relationships' that she chose to explore for her comeback single. After several collaborations, Rita treated fans to her first solo single in more than a year since 'I Will Never Let You Down'.

'Poison', a song that had been in development since the start of her work on the second album was finally being released in May 2015. Rita was never going to stoop to the level of attention-seeking rappers but she was now older and wiser and had her share of bitter experiences. Confirming the song was about being backstabbed, she said: 'But I'm not going to blurt it out. I have my own therapist that I talk to. I've stopped pretending that I'm this constantly happy person. I never tell people how I feel, my friends literally have to force it out of me. So "Poison" is about having that mentality and it really poisoning you.'

She added: '"Poison" was a long time coming for me. It's about how I envision love and a time in my life when it was poisonous. It's a really honest song for me as I do love a beer in the morning when I'm hungover or a Bloody Mary. I wanted to say things that actually happened to me.'

Given the gap between releases she knew a lot was riding on this song. 'It was really important for me to come back with the right song. It's been a while and I wanted to come back with a bang,' she said.

'Poison' was a thumping chunk of power pop and if the song showcased a new, more mature, Rita, the accompanying video was equally sophisticated. Rita played the role of the street-smart kid we'd grown to know and love but she became a muse for an enigmatic photographer who wanted to take her away from her boyfriend and the life she knew. The storytelling promo had Rita transform into a glamorous model, feted by the art world before she realised it was all an illusion. Fans were quick to notice the echoes of pop art pioneer Andy Warhol, represented by the white-haired snapper, with Rita playing his muse, an Edie Sedgwick-style model.

Rita threw herself into promotion, singing live on *The Graham Norton Show* and *The John Bishop Show* and performing a raunchy routine at London's G.A.Y. club ahead of the single's release. It looked like her efforts had done the trick. On the first days of 'Poison' going on sale it was heading for number one. However, despite racking up opening week sales of nearly 56,000 copies it failed to reach the top spot, entering the charts at number three.

It chalked up 200,000 sales in a month but despite its strong showing in the UK, Roc Nation did not release the song in America – a move that had her fans wondering once again what sort of song her label wanted before giving her a huge promotional push in the US.

'Poison' did, however, give fans a taste of what the new album would sound like. They'd had to wait so long that even Rita said *Ora* seemed 'like a lifetime ago'. 'The new music is still pop but has a lot more depth to it. It's real,' she said. As she spoke about the new album she set the record straight on why it had been delayed, confirming that rather than Calvin blocking her, it had been a case of Rita needing time to work things out.

'I wasn't actually ever stopped, let's be clear on that,' she said. 'That was not the case. I could have released anything at any point, but I was in a different headspace.'

She did reveal though that the album – which by early autumn 2015 was still untitled – would draw on the turmoil she'd endured going through such a public split. 'Two years ago, I was living in the States due to personal reasons,' she said of her time with Calvin in LA. 'I was happy for a moment. So I thought this album was going to be about happiness and la la la. And then I started to recognise things that I'd never seen before about the people around me. Maybe it was the lack of sleep that made me open my eyes to things. When my friendships get destroyed I really take it personally. And a few of those relationships got mishandled.' She added: 'There are more emotional parts in the record. There's a lot of things lyrically I wouldn't usually say as I don't really open up.'

Rita revealed she had teamed up with Ed Sheeran for one song for her album. 'I did this incredibly beautiful song with Ed about our friendship – he's one of my best friends.'

And another song that would definitely make the final cut was 'Pink Champagne' a track she recorded from her sessions with Prince. The 'Purple Rain' star had penned the track in tribute to Rita's youthful exuberance and had invited her to record it among the doves he keeps in his Paisley Park studio near Minneapolis. 'We just wrote a bunch of music, laughed and danced,' Rita said. 'He is sexy in so many ways.'

The important thing was these were her choices – a far cry from before.

'When I started I was only seventeen,' she said. 'I was over-whelmed with the power of men in the industry and the thinking that you have to fulfill somebody's image. Obviously I love my record label. [My first album] was an amazing success but I wasn't completely satisfied because I'd listened to a lot of men. I accepted tracks [they wanted] because, you know, it was a "legendary writer" or something. This time, I feel more comfortable in my skin. I've experienced a bit more, I've been in and out of relationships ... and so in some respects this feels like my first record. I've actually had fights about tracks that were not being approved by the label. Now I'm like, "I don't care who wrote it." And when someone says, "No, this isn't right", I say, "No, this is f***ing right because it's my album." That's me being brutally honest.'

Some things were still beyond her control however. The question of whether 'I Will Never Let You Down' would appear still had to be resolved. Calvin had relaxed his stance on the song, explaining that in hindsight perhaps he shouldn't have stopped Rita performing it at the Teen Choice Awards. Rita was performing it live again and still loved the song but when asked if it would feature she said: 'I really don't know yet. I'm not a lawyer.'

Calvin's softer stance might have had something to do with his new loved-up status with Taylor Swift. After the Brits, he'd swiftly dis-patched his model girlfriend to make way for America's sweetheart Taylor, who'd effortlessly made the transition from country darling to fully-fledged pop princess with her impressive *1989* album.

Rita had endured the awkwardness of seeing them at award ceremonies together but she only had good wishes for her ex and quashed any chat of a rivalry with Taylor. 'I think she's one of the most incredible songwriters of our generation,' Rita said. 'I'm not even just saying it. I absolutely adore her music and love what she stands for.'

Rita extended her sisterly love to Madonna too, who had been receiving flak for kissing Drake at the Coachella festival earlier in the year, and, bizarrely, for still releasing music at the age of fifty-seven.

'You pay respect to people who deserve it – Beyoncé and Madonna,' Rita said. 'When Madonna was going through it on this last record, I was one of the first people to post my support on Instagram. Don't battle her because of her age.'

Madonna appreciated the support. After Rita had defended her in the wake of the Drake incident, Madonna said: 'Thanks, Rita! Good to know you appreciate the beating I'm taking so all you ladies don't have to endure this kind of discrimination!'

The Material Girl then enlisted Rita to appear in the video for her single 'Bitch, I'm Madonna', which also featured Beyoncé, Katy Perry, Kanye West, Chris Rock and Miley Cyrus.

The association wouldn't have done Rita any harm in America but the video drew comparisons with Taylor Swift's 'Bad Blood', which also had a host of celebrity cameos, including Ellie Goulding and Cara Delevingne, whose personal life had taken an interesting turn. Cara had been filmed kissing sultry actress Michelle Rodriguez, Rita's co-star in *Fast and Furious 6*, while topless in the waves off Mexico a year earlier and in June 2015 she confirmed she was in a relationship with the musician Annie Clark, better known as St Vincent. In coming out as a lesbian Cara explained that a past heart-break made her confront her feelings. 'It took me a long time to accept the idea,' she said, 'until I first fell in love with a girl at twenty and recognised that I had to accept it.'

The period to which Cara was referring was when she and Rita were inseparable. Could that be the love she was talking about?

Michelle Rodriguez congratulated Cara on speaking about her sexuality but said she knew for others it was hard. 'I have tons of friends who are in the closet, and you know what? Respect,' Michelle said. 'Because you can't control how people are. You've got haters out there.'

Cara wasn't the only one re-evaluating relationships.

As Rita embarked on a new chapter on *The X Factor* she decided to call time on her relationship with Ricky. After just over a year together she realised that with a TV series, album and tour to commit to she couldn't devote the time a relationship needed to work.

Ricky had been a regular fixture with her, particularly in London, where he joined her at festivals and on several occasions was spotted hanging out with her and invariably her new Maltipoo puppy Cher.

In the weeks before they parted speculation mounted that they might take their relationship to the next level by getting engaged or moving in together.

'Rita and Ricky found it difficult to continue their relationship due to their ongoing work commitments,' a source told *The Sun*. 'They both tried to make it work but their schedules made it difficult. They are on two different sides of the Atlantic and Rita is going to be based in the UK for the next five months. It has been an amicable split and they remain friends. Rita has been very upset that things didn't work out with Ricky but has been throwing herself into her work to keep her mind off it.'

Rita did indeed throw herself into *X Factor*, once the auditions got underway. They were temporarily cancelled because of the tragic death of Simon Cowell's mother Julie. Then, when the dates were re-arranged it clashed with a prior engagement she had at Paris Fashion Week and she was forced to miss a day's filming. In Paris, Rita was appearing at the Chanel show at the request of the fashion house's head designer Karl Lagerfeld, who she jokingly refers to as her 'uncle'.

Back in the UK and in her judge's chair for the resumption of the auditions, Rita was surprised by how upsetting she found the hopeful's moving stories. 'It's already been emotional,' she said. 'I had my first cry.' Rita was also shocked when someone she remembered from Sylvia Young appeared in front of the judges for a shot at stardom. Cory Spedding hoped her history with Rita might stand in her favour but she was left gutted when the judges decided not to put her through.

Rita became the butt of Nick Grimshaw's jokes when she mistook Scousers for Scots and thought someone from Kingston-upon-Thames, in Surrey, had come from Jamaica. The banter looked set to make good TV and Rita was someone everyone was warming too. Simon was impressed. 'She's a bit of a ditz, but that's just part of her personality,' he said. 'What I like about her is that she's not afraid to admit that. She doesn't say something and then scream at the producers to edit it out. She can poke fun at herself.'

Cheryl and Rita were also relieved that, as they had predicted, there was no hint of rivalry. 'I'm so happy I became a judge,' Rita said. 'They're not cultivating a rivalry between me and Cheryl. I think when you watch it you'll be like: "This might be the first time I've seen *The X Factor* where it doesn't feel like there's anything dodgy going on."'

If Rita was concentrating on her work, Ricky Hil had people guessing whether he too had composed an anti-serenade for Rita. In a song called 'Superman', released online, he rapped about a girl who performed better in bed than 'all them other girls'. He did not comment whether it was about Rita, however. As songs go, while crude, it wasn't the worst way to be referenced and he was possibly just trying to be noticed. If the song didn't do that, stepping out with a former Hooters girl and model would certainly ensure he still made the gossip columns.

Rita wasn't responding, however. She was heading to Italy after signing another fashion deal. This time she was showcasing an autumn/winter collection for Italian lingerie brand Tezenis. The brand was a perfect fit for Rita. She liked how Tezenis catered for curvaceous women. 'I'm not, like, the skinniest in the world,' she said. She also didn't mind that the brand had edge. A year earlier it had to withdraw a pair of ladies' briefs after complaints over a 'crime scene' logo emblazoned across them.

Such controversy wasn't enough to put Rita off but she did have a view about the treatment of women in general. Giving a talk to students at the ELAM (East London Arts and Music) College in Stratford, East London, she expressed frustration that at times she felt like people were more interested in who she was going out with than in her music. 'It's unfortunate that people are blinded by who you're going out with. If anything, it's about remembering what I've done as an artist.'

She wouldn't have been happy then when it was reported she had been hanging out with rapper Wiz Khalifa two nights in a row in Hollywood. Rita had taken advantage of a break in filming for *The X Factor* and flown out to Los Angeles for the Teen Choice Awards. At the event it was said she and Wiz had their arms around each other. On the second night they'd gone to a recording studio together after a night out at The Nice Guy hotspot.

Although there was nothing else yet to suggest they were anything more than friends, Wiz (real name Cameron Jibril Thomaz) ticked many of her boxes, going by some of her past loves. He was a rapper, he loved smoking weed and he had a complicated love life and a controversial track record with women. He had one son from his marriage to model Amber Rose but she had filed for divorce in 2014 citing 'irreconcilable differences'. Later that year he was at the centre of a sex-tape storm after it was claimed a romp he had with *Playboy* model Carla Howe was filmed and being touted around Hollywood.

Rita wanted people to concentrate more on her music but she must have known she would be courting yet more controversy with her next collaboration. After a year's drought, a second single from her new album was released in August. 'Body On Me' was a slick, sexy R'n'B number – and the first to feature Rita on the writing credits – but by joining forces with Chris Brown she invited criticism that she wasn't as committed to the sisterhood as she'd like to make out.

Chris was Rihanna's violent ex, and given how much the media liked to stir up the rivalry between the Roc Nation superstars, this was playing right into their hands. Rita defended the union, saying: 'If you have a great song, then no one cares.' And when asked about his criminal past, she added: 'What was the controversy with that? I'm a positive person, I don't dwell on negatives, I don't believe in regrets and looking back. I think music speaks for itself, and that's all I'm going to say on that.'

She sounded like she was on the defensive and she needed to be.

Some fans took to Twitter to register their dismay and disgust that she felt the need to be associated with such a singer. One fan said she was 'heartbroken', while another branded her a 'traitor to women', a slur sure to sting. Still she was unrepentant. 'Chris Brown is strong, powerful and someone that is important to me personally and professionally,' she said.

The move to work with Chris might not have pleased everyone but it showed Rita was not going to drift off into TV land quietly.

Anyone who thought she didn't possess the power to shock should think again.

And her video, directed by R'n'B veteran Colin Tilley, the brains behind Nicki Minaj's 'Anaconda', did nothing to dampen the disquiet. It was Rita's steamiest yet, a sultry, sensual mini-movie dripping with sexual tension. Showing Rita and Chris as neighbours whose apartments overlooked, their desire was sparked when they bumped into each other by chance in an elevator. As their fantasies consumed them Rita was seen writhing sexily draped in a Union Jack before, in thigh-length blood red boots and denim hot pants, she joined Chris on the roof for a passion-laden climax.

'It's probably one of the most intimate videos I've ever done, but it's really exciting,' Rita said.

She wasn't wrong. Not only did it show she wouldn't shrink away from controversy it demonstrated how much she smouldered on screen. The message to any Hollywood director watching was clear. Put Rita Ora in a movie and watch the screen sizzle. Gone was the girl from her earliest videos and online diaries. Here was a woman confident in her talent and ready for her next big challenge.

Whether on TV, on film or with her music, Rita Ora was on fire. She was sexy, she was sparkling, but most of all … she was *Hot Right Now*.

Epilogue

WHEN that one-year-old baby was hurried onto the last flight out of Pristina, few people would have imagined she carried the hopes of her fledgling nation with her.

Yet, twenty-three years on, as Rita Ora stepped into the Kosovan embassy in London, her service to her country was recognised in the highest manner possible. In July 2015 Kosovan president Mrs Atifete Jahjaga made Rita an honorary ambassador for her contribution to raising awareness for her homeland.

It was an incredible moment in a journey that began with her parents fleeing with little more than the hope of a better life in the UK. All of the hardships, the fight to have their children released from a care home, their struggle to find work and reclaim the lifestyle they'd sacrificed, had all been worth it.

Besim Sahatçiu was right – his granddaughter was a star. Not only that though, she was a true ambassador for her nation. Never shy about talking up her country's virtues, shining a light on its culture when she could, Rita had been flying the flag for Kosovo ever since she realised she could sing.

'Rita embodies all what we are about as a nation,' President Jahjaga said. 'What we have been through and what we can achieve when given the chance. Beyond her talent and success that makes us all proud we are most thankful that she's a Kosovo girl that is proud of her roots, the best bridge between Kosovo, the country she was born in and Britain, the country she now calls home.'

'I will wear the title of honorary ambassador with great pride and responsibility,' Rita said, beaming. 'I grew up in Britain, a country which has given me so much for which I'm grateful. But I will always have a special place in my heart for Kosovo, my country of birth. I'm lucky I'm in a position to travel the world and bring more awareness to my country of birth and let the rest of the world know what a beautiful country it is and how friendly the people are.'

For the ceremony she was a model of sophistication. In a way life imitated art as she looked every inch the feted model in the video for 'Poison'. Only this time it wasn't an illusion. With even her trademark red lipstick toned down Rita showed once more how effortlessly she could slip between styles.

She vowed to do what she could to further raise awareness of issues in her homeland. 'My generation just doesn't know enough about politics, we don't know what we can do and what we can't do,' she said. 'I think people care more about voting for the VMAs than voting for a politician or a prime minister.'

Sadly she was right. In an age of celebrity culture it often seemed more importance was given to the lives of pop and movie stars than those of ordinary people. Yet, if anyone could help start to redress that balance it was Rita. Always mindful of her roots and of the trials of her family, she repeatedly states she is working so hard not for her own glory, but for her 'movement' – her people and her family.

'The kids, the people in the streets, everyone is so grateful that [I'm] doing something to represent them,' she says. 'They don't have the opportunities we have.'

In many ways she is an unlikely role model – a feminist who keeps making wrong choices with men, an honorary ambassador who dropped out of school twice. Yet in the modern world she is perfect for the part.

Her five million fans on Twitter bombard her with questions like 'I've just started school, what classes shall I take?' or they ask her advice about boyfriends.

'I'm like, "Pah! I'm not the best person to give advice on boyfriends. Clearly. You might not want to listen to me."'

But listen to her they do. They love her because of her flaws, her mistakes, her 'nip slips' and her fashion faux pas, rare as they may be. They love her because, while she might have her vices, she's not a hypocrite.

Yes, she follows trends and does juice cleanses every month but, rather than fad diets, she credits her dance training for giving her muscle memory.

She loves things like Jaffa Cakes and banoffee pie and shops in Tesco. She speaks out about eating disorders but doesn't just pay lip service to causes – she meets victims in special units and urges fans not to starve themselves for beauty. She donated one of 5,000 dresses pinned to washing lines in Pristina Stadium for the striking *Thinking of You* art exhibition to highlight the suffering of victims of sexual violence during the Kosovo war.

With a mother who epitomises the term 'survivor', who arrived in the UK with cancer, beat it twice and retrained to be a psychiatrist (now practising in a London hospital) and a father who arrived with nothing to build his own chain of pubs, she doesn't have to look far for inspiration. Add to that a sister looking out for her at every turn and a brother forging his own path, and it would appear her 'movement' is unbeatable.

One day Rita would love to settle down, own a home with her own garden for her children to play in. But for now she is still intent on paying back her parents for the life they gave her. When they arrived in Britain they had nothing, nowhere to live. Could Besnik and Vera ever have dreamed their youngest daughter – little Rita Pita – would one day give them a home?

Yet that is what happened, as recently she gave them the keys to a £1.3 million house. 'They need it more than me. I'm never really in one place,' she said. 'I'm back to square one but at least my parents have a place.'

Singer, actress, TV star, fashion icon, ambassador. Not bad for a girl whose first experience of the UK was inside a children's home, separated from her family.

She is growing all the time but inside that little girl remains.

'I've definitely grown up a bit but I'm not a completely different person,' she said. 'I've just experienced more. I've been in a relationship, I've seen what happens to people. I've even seen the drug life around me. Being around them is a scary place. You see how it really changes people, so I've experienced a lot of things. Being around it all just kinda woke me up.'

And the secret to her success?

'I've always put out the truth. I'm a very honest person. The way I dress is really who I am. The way I say things is how I am, my videos, my interviews... I'm real honest. I don't sugarcoat anything,' she says.

'I surprise myself because it's always been a dream, and I never forget that I used to be in my council flat in West London, sharing a room with my sister, in my single bed dreaming about doing this.

'I never take it for granted, that's why I focus on it so hard because I really want it to be great.

'I can only do the best that I can do.'

Selected Source Material

Prologue:
'Singing For a Billion People ...', *Sunday People*, 22 February 2015
'From Kosovo to Coutts', *Daily Record*, 4 April 2015
'Hot Right Now', *Evening Standard*, 25 June 2015

Chapter 1
'Hot Right Now', *The Scotsman*, 26 June 2013
'Vera Ora How to Raise a Superstar' www.globalwoman.com,
25 April 2015
'How "Rita Pita" Escaped Brutal Persecution ...', *The Sun*, 11 January
2015
'The Golden Ora', *GQ*, 1 August 2013
'She's the Real Thing', *Sunday Times*, 2 September 2012
'The Conversation with Amanda de Cadenet ...', www.vimeo.com,
24 March 2014
'Q&A: Rita Ora', *The Guardian*, 22 August 2015

Chapter 2
'Hot Right Now', *The Scotsman*, 26 June 2013
'Cometh the Ora', *The Sun*, 1 February 2015
'Introducing Rita', *Evening Standard*, 1 February 2013
'Rita is Hoping to Put on a Model Performance', *Irish Daily Mirror*,
2 August 2013
'Interview with Rita Ora', www.amarudontv.com, 22 February 2012
'Some Like it Hot', *Daily Mirror*, 24 August 2012

'My Choral Manifesto: Suzi Digby', www.sinfinimusic.com, 26 September 2013

'Rita Ora…' *Evening Standard*, 5 September 2014

'Hot Right Now', *Evening Standard*, 25 June 2015

'There's an Aura about Rita', *Nottingham Post*, 25 January 2013

Chapter 3

'Rita Ora: The Hot Desk', www.youtube.com, 10 January 2014

'Blonde Ambition', *The Guardian*, 19 May 1999

'It's Rita Ora's Older Sister Elena', www.popcrush.com, 7 November 2012

'Hot Right Now', *The Scotsman*, 26 January 2013

'Introducing Rita', *Evening Standard*, 1 February 2013

'Some Like it Hot', *Daily Mirror*, 24 August 2012

'When I Said I Wanted to Sing, Mum Went "Huh?"', *The Sun*, 10 August 2012

'Educating Rita', *Sunday Times*, 8 April 2012

'Rita Ora: Video Diary 1', www.youtube.com, 28 September 2011

'3 a.m.', *Sunday Mirror*, 27 January 2013

'She's the Real Thing', *Sunday Times*, 2 September 2012

'My Time has Come', *Daily Record*, 27 May 2012

'An Aura of Success for Singer Who's Hot …', *Yorkshire Post*, 25 January 2013

'Rita's Not Petiter', *Daily Star*, 6 July 2013

'Cometh the Ora', *Sunday Times*, 1 February 2015

'Rita Ora – Post Codes Part 2: My Area', www.youtube.com, 14 May 2012

Chapter 4

'My Time has Come', *Daily Record*, 27 May 2012

'Hot Right Now', *Evening Standard*, 26 May 2015

'How "Rita Pita" Escaped Brutal Persecution …', *The Sun*, 11 January 2015

'Introducing Rita', *Evening Standard*, 1 February 2013

'Rita Ora: The Hot Desk, www.youtube.com, 10 January 2014

'Interview with The Breakfast Club', www.youtube.com, 23 April 2014

'Educating Rita', *Sunday Times*, 8 April 2012

'There's an Aura about Rita', *Nottingham Post*, 25 January 2013
'Rita Ora: Incredible Ora', www.bluesandsoul.com, April 2012
'The Conversation with Amanda de Cadanet', www.youtube.com, 23 June 2015

Chapter 5
'The Interview: Kyle De'volle', www.hungertv.com, 2 April 2013
'Cometh the Ora', *Sunday Times*, 1 February 2015
'Interview with The Breakfast Club', www.youtube.com, 23 April 2014
'Rita Ora: The Hot Desk', www.youtube.com, 10 January 2014
'There's an Aura about Rita', *Nottingham Post*, 25 January 2013
'1Xtra – Craig David and Tinchy Stryder ...', www.youtube.com, 16 October 2008

Chapter 6
'Introducing Rita', *Evening Standard*, 1 February 2013
'There's an Aura about Rita', *Nottingham Post*, 25 January 2013
'Ora the Explorer Knows Exactly ...', *Irish Mail on Sunday*, 19 May 2013
'Some Like it Hot', *Daily Mirror*, 24 August 2012
'She's the Real Thing', *Sunday Times*, 2 September 2012
'My Time has Come', *Daily Record*, 27 May 2012
'It's a Very Scary Business for Solo Artists', *The Guardian*, 2 December 2013

Chapter 7
'Introducing Rita', *Evening Standard*, 1 February 2013
'Educating Rita', *Sunday Times*, 8 April 2012
'She's the Real Thing', *Sunday Times*, 2 September 2012
'Rita Ora: Interview with Power 106FM', www.youtube.com, 25 October 2012
'Rita Ora talks ethnicity ...', www.youtube.com, 26 April 2012
'There's an Aura About Miss Ora', *Evening Standard*, 30 January 2013
'I Used to Deal Drugs With Jay Z ...', *The Sun*, 14 October 2013
'Rita Ora on celeb fragrances, bleached brows ...', *Cosmopolitan*, 4 July 2014

'Why Life's Now Suite for Rita', *The Sun*, 4 October 2012
'Rita is Hoping to Put on a Model Performance', *Irish Daily Mirror*, 2 August 2013
'Hot Right Now', *The Scotsman*, 26 January 2013
'My Parents Fled Conflict Kosovo to the UK ...', *The Sun*, 9 May 2012
'When I Said I Wanted to Sing, Mum Went "Huh?"', *The Sun*, 10 August 2012
'Rita's Mum a Jay Z Lady', *Sunday Mirror*, 26 August 2012
'Educating Rita', *Daily Record*, 24 August 2012
'Hot Right Now', *Evening Standard*, 25 June 2015
'Rita + Bruno', *The Sun*, 17 August 2012
'Why Everyone is in Awe of Ora', *The Sun*, 17 January 2015
'My Time has Come', *Daily Record*, 27 May 2012
'Some Like it Hot', *Daily Mirror*, 24 August 2012
'Rita Ora ka realizuar ...', www.lajme.org, 19 January 2010
'Dafina Zaqiri ne lidhje ...', www.flashlajme.info, 21/9/12

Chapter 8
'Rita Ora – Interview: KiddKraddick', www.youtube.com, 27 June 2012
'Rita Ora: Video Diary 1', www.youtube.com, 28 September 2011
'"Hot Right Now" Was Originally ...', www.capitalfm.com, 14 February 2012
'K-Club is Coming to Town', *Evening Standard*, 2 November 2012

Chapter 9
'Rita Ora Interview With Amaru Don', www.youtube.com, 20 February 2012
'Rita Ora Interview With Amaru Don', www.youtube.com, 4 March 2012
'Rita Ora Interview with Max', www.youtube.com, 19 February 2012
'Vevo Lift', www.youtube.com, 18 May 2012
'Rita Ora talks ethnicity ...', www.youtube.com, 26 April 2012
'Rita Ora discusses upcoming collaborations ...', www.youtube.com 9 April 2012
'Jay Z Thinks I Could be as Big as Rihanna', *The Guardian*, 12 April 2012

'Interview with The Breakfast Club', www.youtube.com, 23 April 2014

'Non-stop Rita has no Time to Put Feet Up', *Metro*, 18 June 2012

'Keynote: Vevo & Rita Ora', www.youtube.com, 3 February 2014

'Cheryl's Got my Cast-off', *The Sun*, 25 April 2012

'Drake's Progress', *The Sun*, 28 April 2012

'Educating Rita', *Sunday Times*, 8 April 2012

'Rita's a Real Gem a Pop Do', *Daily Star*, 9 May 2012

'No.1 and All is Rita', *Daily Star on Sunday*, 13 May 2012

'Rita's in a Doze', *Daily Star*, 16 May 2012

'Rita, Crew and Rob Too', *The Sun*, 15 May 2012

Chapter 10
'Drake Interview with Max', www.youtube.com, 16 June 2010

'Rita Ora Talks Giving Drake a Ring', www.wordonroad.net, 8 July 2012

'Rita Ora UK Tour Diary Part 1, www.youtube.com, 25 April 2012

'Drake Says He's Not Married', www.popcrush.com, 29 March 2012

'No.1 and All is Rita', *Daily Star on Sunday*, 13 May 2012

'Wild 107.5: Kristina Interviews ... Rita Ora', www.youtube.com, 29 July 2012

'Rita Ora – What If I Kissed You Right Now', www.youtube.com, 6 April 2013

'Bizarre column', *The Sun*, 19 May 2012

'Rita's Looking Ir-RiRi-sistible', *Daily Mirror*, 21 May 2012

'Rita Has Aura For X Factor', *Daily Mirror*, 29 May 2012

'Rita's Off to a Flier', *Daily Mirror*, 30 May 2012

'Educating Rita', *Daily Record*, 24 August 2012

'Rita Ora vs Rihanna', *Evening Standard*, 29 May 2012

'It's N-Ora Big Secret', *Daily Record*, 19 June 2012

'Some Like it Hot', *Daily Mirror*, 24 August 2012

'Interview with Max', www.youtube.com, 20 July 2012

'I'm More Than Just a Party Girl!', *Daily Star*, 21 August 2012

'Rita Ora Got the Party', *Metro*, 24 August 2012

'Rita's £10K Bar Bill', *Daily Star*, 24 August 2012

'She's the Real Thing', *Sunday Times*, 2 September 2012

'Bizarre column', *The Sun*, 3 September 2012

Chapter 11
'How Iggy Azalea, from Country NSW ...', *The Australian*, 12 July 2014
'Iggy Azalea Confirms Romantic Relationship ...' www.vibe.com, 13 January 2012
'A$AP Talks Iggy Azalea ...', *XXL*, 9 July 2012

Chapter 12
'Hot Right Now', *The Scotsman*, 26 January 2013
'The Golden Ora', *GQ*, 1 August 2013
'Bright New Things to Returning Heroes', *The Observer*, 25 November 2012
'Rita is Hoping to Put on a Model Performance', *Irish Daily Mirror*, 2 August 2013
'Getting to Know: Rita Ora', www.youtube.com, 18 January 2013
'Kos You're Worth It', *The Sun*, 14 September 2012
'Big Gig for Rita', *Daily Star*, 2 November 2012
'It's Shock and Ora', *The Sun*, 9 November 2012
'Rita Pops Out to Give Us Ora Best', *The Sun*, 12 November 2012
'Rita Ora was Enjoying the Chance ...', *The Sun*, 12 November 2012
'Saucy! Spice Ban for Rita', *Daily Star*, 9 November 2012
'It's Riha vs Rita', *The Sun*, 25 November 2012
'Lotsa Dosh for Model Who's Posh', *The Sun*, 29 November 2012
'Fast and Furihous', *The Sun*, 26 November 2012
'It's C-Ora Blimey', *The Sun*, 30 November 2012
'Girl Ora Boy', *Daily Mirror*, 1 December 2012
'"Scared" Rita Still Looking for First Love', *Metro*, 3 December 2012
'Rita and Rob: It's all Ora Now', *The Sun*, 3 December 2012
'3 Up Rita', *Sunday Times*, 7 December 2012
'Rob's Giving Off a Really Bad Ora', *The Sun*, 5 December 2012
'You Let Me Get You Pregnant ...', www.dailymail.co.uk, 4 December 2012
'Riri & I are Very Different', *Daily Mirror*, 10 December 2012
'Night of the Big Bucks', *Sunday Express*, 30 December 2012
'Rita Ora's Holiday Snaps ...', *The Sun*, 31 December 2012
'There's an Aura About Rita', *Nottingham Post*, 25 January 2013

Chapter 13

'How Did Rita Ora & Calvin Harris ...', www.youtube.com, 20 February 2014

'Armend Milla ne Shoqerine ...', www.visit-ulcinj.com, 16 August 2013

'Rita Ora Next Message ...', www.alvigossip.blogspot.co.uk, December 2013

'Photo News: Rita and Ledri ...', www.shqiptarja.com, 20 June 2015

'Rita Ora invites Ledri ...', www.alvigossip.blogspot.co.uk, December 2013

'Rita Ora e pëlqen Ledri ...', www.10minuta.com, 5 December 2013

'Ledri Vula Biography', www.lyrics.al

'Angry Rita Twits Back', *Daily Mirror*, 4 January 2013

'Rita Rants at Geordie Girl Over Sex Claims', *Metro*, 4 January 2013

'Ora: I Don't Take Notice ...', *Evening Standard*, 31 January 2013

'Bizarre column', *The Sun*, 9 January 2013

'It's in His Kiss', *Daily Mirror*, 9 January 2013

'Bizarre column', *The Sun*, 11 January 2013

'I'll Ask Wifey If She's Up ...', *The Sun*, 19 February 2013

'Rita: I was Stranded on Desert Island ...', *The Sun*, 7 February 2013

'Rita Ora and Snoop Dogg Pose With Roll-ups ...', www.mirror. co.uk, 28 July 2015

'Bizarre column', *The Sun*, 19 January 2013

'Unlikely Duo of the Day', *Daily Mirror*, 22 December 2012

'3 a.m. column', *Daily Mirror*, 2 February 2013

'3 a.m. column', *Sunday Mirror*, 3 February 2013

'Guilty Pleasures column', *Metro*, 7 February 2013

'Bizarre column', *The Sun*, 15 February 2013

'Tease for Two', *The Sun*, 14 February 2013

'The Eyes Have It', *The Observer*, 10 February 2013

'Is the Oh-so Posh Face of Fashion ...', *Daily Mail*, 25 February 2013

'Rita has Revenge on Rob', *The Sun*, 5 March 2013

'Interview: Rita Ora', www.youtube.com, 25 March 2013

'Ora Throat Won't Stop Partying', *Daily Mirror*, 5 March 2013

'Banks' Gob', *The Sun*, 12 March 2013

'Azealia Snaps at Rita's Secret Pix', *Metro*, 12 March 2013

'Azealia Banks, a Young Rapper ...', *New York Times*, 1 February 2012

'Rita Ora Move Over, Alexa …', *Metro*, 14 March 2013
'Azealia A Failure in Bid …' *The Sun*, 17 March 2013
'Guilty Pleasures column', *Metro*, 20 February 2013
'Party-loving Cara's …' *Daily Mail*, 18 February 2013
'Boring Brits was the Pits', *Daily Star*, 22 February 2013
'No Eater Ora', *Daily Mirror*, 22 April 2013

Chapter 14
'Me and My Cal', *The Sun*, 8 May 2013
'Calvin Takes Rita Up the Shard', *The Sun*, 15 May 2013
'Madge Love Rita', *The Sun*, 16 May 2013
'Cara's £1m Clothing Deal Under Threat …', *Daily Mail*, 6 May 2013
'The Goss column', *Daily Star*, 8 May 2013
'Reets is So Sweet on Calvin', *Daily Mirror*, 25 May 2013
'Bizarre column', *The Sun*, 2 June 2013
'3 a.m. column', *Daily Mirror*, 2 June 2013
'The Red Carpet column', *Irish Daily Mail*, 7 May 2013
'The Goss column', *Daily Star*, 1 June 2013
'Winner Ora Swaps all the Glamour …', *Metro Herald*, 6 June 2013
'Good Night? Cara Delevingne Arrives Home …', www.dailymail.co.uk, 5 June 2013
'Ora the Explorer Knows Exactly …', *Irish Mail on Sunday*, 19 May 2013
'I Have Designs on Rihanna's Body', *Daily Star*, 13 June 2013
'Vin Diesel: Rita Ora Kicked Butt …', www.contactmusic.com, 8 May 2013
'"You Go Girl": Michelle Rodriguez Reacts …', www.dailymail.co.uk, 25 June 2015

Chapter 15
'The Goss column', *Daily Star*, 14 June 2013
'The Goss column', *Daily Star*, 17 June 2013
'Tolaj Shpallet per Shmangie …', www.kosovolive360.com, 18 June 2013
'EU's Biggest Foreign Mission in Turmoil …', *The Guardian*, 5 November 2014
'Penguesit e drejtësisë …', www.rajonipress.com, 13 July 2012

'Ilir Tolaj Sentenced to 18 Months ...', www.drejtesianekosove.com, June 2013

'Tolaj Found Guilty of Tax Evasion ...', www.eulex-kosovo.eu, 18 June 2013

'British Fraud Hunter Exposes EU ...', www.dailymail.co.uk, 22 November 2014

'3 a.m. column', *Daily Mirror*, 22 June 2013

'Get Yer Rita Ora Nose Hair Trimmer Here', *The Sun*, 23 June 2013

'It's All Over for Rita and Cara ...', *Mail on Sunday*, 21 July 2013

'3 a.m. column', *Daily Mirror*, 3 July 2013

'The Golden Ora', *GQ*, 1 August 2013

Chapter 16

'Rita My Bond Girl ...', *Scottish Daily Mail*, 25 July 2013

'Jay Z Made Me Feel Sick', *The Sun*, 6 July 2013

'Guilty Pleasures column', *Metro*, 8 July 2013

'Brit of Ora Right', *Daily Record*, 12 July 2013

'The Green Room column', *Metro*, 12 July 2013

'Hot Right Now', *The Sun*, 10 August 2013

'Feel All Reet, Now?', *Daily Mirror*, 20 August 2013

'Cara Cold Shoulders Rita', *Mail on Sunday*, 25 August 2013

'Ellie: Rita Didn't Mind Me Kissing Calvin', *Metro*, 19 August 2013

'Rehab column', *Daily Star on Sunday*, 6 October 2013

'Battle of the Divas', *Daily Star*, 27 August 2013

'The Red Carpet column', *Irish Daily Mail*, 27 August 2013

'Retiring Rita Too Shy to Get Lucky', *Metro*, 5 September 2013

'Rita Steals Show', *Evening Standard*, 9 September 2013

'The Talk of New York', *The Guardian*, 11 September 2013

'3 a.m. column', *Daily Mirror*, 26 September 2013

'Ink About It Rita', *The Sun*, 16 September 2013

'Rita 'n' Cal are Clickin', *Daily Star*, 23 September 2013

'Stars United for Stephen', *The Sun*, 30 September 2013

'Warning Over Chart Hits that Glorify Alcohol', *Daily Mail*, 2 October 2013

'The Green Room column', *Metro*, 3 October 2013

'Rita: Kiss Me, Kate', *The Sun*, 12 October 2013

'Rita's £1m Adidas Pay Day', *The Sun*, 28 October 2013

'I Love Women But I'm Not Like Some ...', *The Sun*, 12 October 2013
'A Reet Strop From James', *Sunday Mirror*, 27 October 2013
'James X-Rated Rita Rap', *Daily Mirror*, 12 November 2013
'James Arthur's Gay Rant', *The Sun*, 16 November 2013
'Ora Back on Track After Her Collapse', *Metro*, 20 November 2013
'Bizarre column', *The Sun*, 28 November 2013
'DJ Calvin is Rita's Soarer', *Daily Mirror*, 28 November 2013

Chapter 17
'The Conversation with Amanda de Cadenet', www.vimeo.com, 24 March 2014
'Amanda de Cadenet Launches ...', www.huffingtonpost.co.uk, 4 November 2013
'Rita's Single ... and it Stinks', *Sunday Mirror*, 3 November 2013
'Rita Ora Denies Rumours She's Split With Calvin ...', *The Sun*, 4 November 2013
'That's Not Who You'd Expect Rita', *The Sun*, 8 November 2013
'Rita's Cal For Help', *The Sun*, 7 December 2013
'Bizarre column', *The Sun*, 11 December 2013
'Singing For a Billion People ...', *Sunday People*, 22 February 2015
'The Green Room', *Metro*, 11 December 2013
'Rita's Had a Field Day', *The Sun*, 26 December 2013
'Rita's Online Clue to Her Rift With Calvin', *Daily Record*, 17 January 2014
'Love is on the Air', *Daily Record*, 31 January 2014
'Ora Over After the Shouting', *The Sun*, 17 January 2014
'Now Calvin's Not Alone Any More', *Daily Mail*, 27 January 2014
'Rita Song a Humdinger', *The Sun*, 31 January 2014
'Bizarre column', *The Sun*, 22 February 2014
'What's Ora This About?', *The Sun*, 23 February 2014
'Rita's So Hot Right Now for Calvin Lingo', *The Scottish Sun*, 31 March 2014
'Yes, This is My First Romance ...', *Daily Mail*, 2 April 2014
'Has Rita Given Cal the Zac?', *Daily Mirror*, 15 April 2014
'Rita Ora ...', *Daily Star*, 8 June 2014
'Who is Khalil Amir Sharieff ...', www.abcnews.go.com, 23 January 2014

'Rita Ora …', *The Sun*, 17 June 2014
'Rita Ora …', *Metro*, 14 August 2014
'Rita Ora …', *The Sun*, 18 July 2014
'On Air with Ryan Seacrest,' www.youtube.com, 12 August 2014

Chapter 18
'Rita Ora …', *Daily Record*, 7 August 2014
'On Air with Ryan Seacrest,' www.youtube.com, 12 August 2014
'It's So Sweet Calvin Wrote Me a Love Song', *Daily Record*, 17 May 2014
'Rita Ora …', *Sunday Times*, 26 October 2014
'Isn't He Rich? Rich Hilfiger's Rap Career …', *New York Observer*, 9 August 2011
'I Wanted to Make Out With Her', www.dailymail.co.uk, 27 August 2014

Chapter 19
'Rita Ora & Charles Hamilton Interview …', www.youtube.com, 21 April 2015
'Ora Bummed Out, Says Si', *Daily Star on Sunday*, 14 December 2014
'Work With Rita? That Just Would Not be Reet', *Daily Mirror*, 14 November 2014
'Cleave it Out', *The Sun*, 7 January 2015
'Rita No More', *The Sun*, 10 January 2015
'Rita Ora …', *The Sun*, 11 January 2015
'Rita's on Song as *The Voice* Attracts 8.05m', *Metro*, 12 January 2015
'Rita's Frock Bottom', *The Sun*, 13 January 2015
'All Reet Now!', *Daily Star*, 13 January 2015
'Rita is Voice Magic', *Sunday Express*, 1 February 2015
'Why Everyone is in Awe of Ora', *The Sun*, 17 January 2015
'Marvin: We Have to Find a Real Star', *The Scottish Sun*, 19 February 2015
'Ora Best for Staff', *Daily Record*, 19 February 2015
'Rejection? I Always Just Ign-Ora it, Says Rita', *Metro*, 20 February 2015
'Show Hit Rita "To Quit"', *Daily Star on Sunday*, 1 March 2015
'What do I Bring to *The Voice*? 4m Viewers!', *Sunday Express*, 22 March 2015

'Star Fears for Sick Will.I.Am', *Daily Star*, 4 April 2015

'Ora and Out', *Daily Star on Sunday*, 5 April 2015

'Rita's Fifty Shades of Grey Day', *Daily Mirror*, 10 January 2015

'Mogul Voices His Support for Rita the Movie Queen', *Metro*, 13 January 2015

'Singing For a Billion People ...', *Sunday People*, 22 February 2015

'Ghastly Grammys', *Daily Mail*, 10 February 2015

'Frock & Ora', *Daily Mirror*, 10 February 2015

'Three Looks For the Price of One', *The Times*, 17 February 2015

'How to Tame a Hollywood Dragon', *Mail on Sunday*, 29 March 2015

'Rita Has a Bodyguard But is He Only Here ...', *Metro*, 23 February 2015

'Rita Has WINfrey Formula', *Daily Mirror*, 23 February 2015

Chapter 20

'Simon Had Me in His House at Midnight', *The Sun*, 26 June 2015

'Cowell Offers Rita £2m, His Jet and a ...', *Daily Mail*, 10 June 2015

'Hot Right Now', *Evening Standard*, 25 June 2015

'House is Or-some Present For Mum', *The Sun*, 24 June 2015

'A$AP Rocky on Controversial Rita Ora Lyric ...', www.nme.com, 9 July 2015

'You Are Welcome to Cal, Pal!', *Daily Star*, 20 May 2015

'Rita Gets Ex-Rated', *Daily Star*, 25 May 2015

'Rita-ta Ricky', *The Sun*, 17 July 2015

'The Girl With the Golden Ora', *Metro*, 30 July 2015

'Rita: Remember Me For My Songs, Not Who I've Dated', *Daily Mirror*, 3 July 2015

'Rita, You Ora Know Better!', *Daily Star*, 10 August 2015

Epilogue

'Who's That Girl?', *Daily Star*, 1 April 2015

'Sophisticated Rita Ora Puts on a ...', www.dailymail.co.uk 10 July 2015

'Dresses Donated by Rita Ora Hang Among ...', www.dailymail.co.uk, 12 June 2015

Acknowledgements

A sincere thank you to everyone who shared their memories of Rita with us. It's clear she was – and continues to be – loved and respected by those who knew her well.

A particular thank you to Kosovan journalist Selvije Bajrami whose determination and skill helped us piece together the earlier years of Rita's family life. Thank you as well to Shaqir Foniqi for sharing his lovely memories of Rita's grandfather and her family's story before they left Kosovo.

A special mention to Rita's childhood friends Yemi Akintoye Dedier, Omar and Hana Hajaj, Martin Dykes, Kai Taylor and Antonio Fumarola for their heartfelt recollections. Much appreciation to her former teachers Ilona Buttinger and James Falconer, and to Rita's beloved school caretaker Jill Biggs.

A big thanks to Greg Gobere for your contributions and ideas. Thanks Leon Cherry for your design expertise.

Huge thanks also to all at Whitefox and to Kerr MacRae for your help in making this book possible, and to Alison Rae for your expert scrutiny.

And thanks especially to Rita Ora for inspiring this book. After learning so much about you it's even more clear you deserve to be a superstar.

Douglas Wight thanks:
To Jennifer Wiley, thanks for being the best co-writer anyone could hope for. You've been awesome!

Thanks also to Jane Atkinson for your constant support and help. And to Lorna Hill for, well, everything.

Jennifer Wiley thanks:

To Douglas Wight for always being kind and humble despite your ridiculous talent! I've learned so much through this process and will be forever grateful.

Thanks again to Greg Gobere for all your help with the book and your love and support behind the scenes.

Like Rita, I've had a team of inspirational women who've supported my writing career – my mom, Bev Wiley, grandmothers Lottie Wiley and Rita McCormick, who made it possible for me to follow my dreams to work as a journalist in London, Tracey McCormick (thanks for all the pens!) and Jeanette Barnes (thanks for all the hugs!), as well as all my other aunts, cousins and incredible friends. Thanks to Jahnique Gobere for your help on the book too.

And to the men who've always fought my corner – my dad George Wiley, brother Ben Wiley and all my uncles, cousins and amazing friends.